Critics of the 'Nineties

CRITICS

OF THE

'NINETIES

DEREK
STANFORD

5 ROYAL OPERA ARCADE
PALL MALL LONDON SW1

© 1970 DEREK STANFORD

First published in 1970 by
JOHN BAKER (PUBLISHERS) LTD
5 Royal Opera Arcade
Pall Mall, London SW1

SBN 212 98378 4

Printed in Great Britain by
CLARKE, DOBLE & BRENDON LTD
PLYMOUTH

CONTENTS

To my good friend
ELIZABETH THOMAS

PREFACE

Hitherto there has existed no representative collection of critical writing by authors of the 'nineties – a lack which, in a small way, I have sought to make good in this volume.

The revival of interest in this decade (with its roots in Pre-Raphaelitism and the Aesthetic Movement) which started some years back has been more than maintained; and in Beardsley – the greatest exotic of the period and its most representative type of mentality – I have found the two properties which seem to me to characterize the arts of the 'nineties : an increased sense of sex and style. I have, accordingly, in my Introduction, taken these Beardsley elements as clue-lines to the culture of the epoch; and I should like to offer the reader these brief notes by way of assistance. Section I of my Introduction deals with a little of the evidence concerning the heightened sense of style, while Section II presents certain facts pointing to an intensified sense of sex in the life and art of the period. The relationship between these two expanded senses is not finally established until Section XI which concludes the Introduction. As to the prefatory notices which serve to introduce the twelve critics chosen, I need only say that I am writing here as a literary historian very much *en pantouffles* and not as a critic armed *cap-à-pied*. Exposition not assessment is the book's first purpose.

Perhaps the best claim I can enter for this anthology is that the authors and critics of the 'nineties were, and remain, uncommonly *readable*. No one bothers to resurrect *writers who cannot write*. My hope, then, of justifying this book is based on the readability of those represented. To peruse their pages is to form an image of them – adapting an ironic description of one of their own number – as persons who have 'a few superficial agreeable qualities, such as wit, good breeding, and a love of art'. It is to encounter the work of men who, whatever their position or condition, sought to write as scholars and gentlemen.

In making my selection, I decided to stay within the boundary years of the decade, finding within the stretch of time between 1890 and 1900 enough memorable, good, or interesting writing as not to warrant my going outside. There will, therefore, be found in this volume no article or essay save those written or published in the 'nineties either in magazines or books. In my selection I have also been influenced by a decision to print the less known, or less accessible, piece of writing (if intrinsically valid) rather than the better known, more accessible passage. Names I could wish to have presented here – were requirements of space no objection – would include Francis Thompson, Alice Meynell, Henry Harland (in his role as 'Yellow Dwarf' of *The Yellow Book*), Edmund Gosse, Andrew Lang, Henry James, G. S. Street, Francis Adams, Vincent O'Sullivan, James Huneker, and Robert Ross.

Most of my debts, in the writing of this book, are to those recent scholars of the period whose texts I have studied. I should especially like to remark on the information or illumination I received from the following works: Professor Graham Hough's *The Last Romantics* (1947) and *Image and Experience* (1960); Dr Ian Fletcher's *The Complete Poems of Lionel Johnson* (1953), *Walter Pater* (1959) and his symposium *Romantic Mythologies* (1967); Miss Barbara Charlesworth's *Dark Passages: The Decadent Conscious-ness in American Literature* (1965, U.S.); Lord David Cecil's *Walter Pater: The Scholar-Artist* (1955) and *Max: A Biography* (1964); Mr Rupert Croft-Cooke's *Feasting with Panthers: A New Consideration of some Late Victorian Writers* (1967); Professor Quentin Bell's *Victorian Artists* (1967); Dr John Dixon Hunt's *The Pre-Raphaelite Imagination 1848–1900* (1968); Mr R. V. Johnson's *Aestheticism* (1969).

Once more, too, I should like to acknowledge a continuing debt of gratitude to Margaret, my wife, whose patience and care in the revision of my draft have enabled me to present my publishers with a typescript of this book without fear and trembling.

Preface

Again, I must also thank my friend John Clifford Bayliss who has helped me to lay my hands on original or early editions of the 'nineties, now harder and harder to come by.

Bedford Park,
London, W.4
30 September 1969.

INTRODUCTION

I

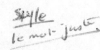

An extension of the sense of style and of sex – these, taking a ranging look at the art and literature of the 'nineties, and of their reflection in the writings of the critics, would appear unavoidable as clear characteristics of the period. Is this hazardous *ad hoc* judgment able to stand up to reasonable scrutiny? I believe it is.

Style – 'The one word for the one thing, the one thought amid the multitude of words' :[1] the devotion of the men of the 'nineties to this notion does not require fresh evidence. One need only think of the following masters and their emulous disciples engaged in common worship : Stevenson 'playing the sedulous ape' to a dozen dead authors to shape himself a style; Pater – 'a lover of words for their own sake . . . a constant observer of their physiognomy'[2] – looking to literature as 'a sort of cloistral refuge, from a certain vulgarity in the actual world',[3] regularly translating as an undergraduate at Oxford a page from Flaubert, whose first great book *Madame Bovary* had but recently appeared, or manipulating as a young secluded don the language-game he so patiently perfected. 'In his sitting-room,' William Gaunt tells us, 'he would settle down in the morning to wring a few reluctant, anxiously-weighed words from his pen. The table would be covered with small lozenges of white paper – each bearing a phrase or a word, with here and there a blue lozenge, this representing a key point. Such were his "notes".'[4]

His artistic successors, as Max Beerbohm noticed, refused to work in 'the ordinary official way, and "wrought", as they were wont to

[1] 'Style' (*Appreciations* by Walter Pater, 1889)
[2] *Ibid*
[3] *Ibid*
[4] *The Aesthetic Adventure* (1945)

asseverate, "for the pleasure and sake of all that is fair".[5] Neither did they stint themselves of the eager pains and arduous difficulties of the medium they sought to honour. We recall Wilde's jest about a hard day's labour : 'This morning I took out a comma, and this afternoon – I put it in again.'[6] We think of Yeats agonizing over his verse –

> There's something ails our cult
> That must, as if it had not holy blood
> Nor on Olympus leaped from cloud to cloud,
> Shiver under the lash, strain, sweat and jolt,
> As though it dragged road-metal.[7]

– content if his tally showed a dozen lines for so many hours, convinced of the author's stark alternative :

> The intellect of man is forced to choose
> Perfection of the life, or of the work,
> And if it takes the second must refuse
> A heavenly mansion, raging in the dark.[8]

We see Henry Harland, 'still in pyjamas and dressing-gown', his bath and breakfast waiting till 'the real business of the day, a page of "perfect prose", was accomplished. Not always a page, by any means – a perfect sentence or two was sometimes a good morning's work'.[9]

Mock as Max the incomparable might at Pater for his stringent over-writing – 'bored by that sedulous ritual wherewith he laid out every sentence as in a shroud – hanging, like a widower, long over its marmoreal beauty or ever he could lay it at length in its book, its sepulchre'[10] – or at that composite ghost Enoch Soames for the pseudo-Mallarmean errors of his syntax – style was his Penelope, his *première maîtresse*, as it was to all the élite of that era. Like them, in the manner of Hugh Selwyn Mauberley (Ezra Pound's own backward-turned *persona*) :

[5] '1880' (*Works*, 1896)
[6] *The Romantic '90s* by Richard Le Gallienne (1926)
[7] 'The Fascination of what's Difficult' (*The Green Helmet and other poems*, 1910)
[8] 'The Choice' (*The Winding Stair and other poems*, 1933)
[9] *The Romantic '90s*
[10] 'Diminuendo' (*Works*, 1896)

Introduction

> He fished by obstinate isles;
> Observed the elegances of Circe's hair
> Rather than the mottoes on sundials.[11]

Style, then, for these men of the 'nineties was a formal pursuit of beauty rather than an instrument of homiletics. It was this artistic discipline which redeemed the time, not the exactions of the moral will.

II

Mention of Circe serves to introduce the second notion canvassed by me as characterizing 'nineties culture : a ubiquitous extension of the sense of sex.

Again, employing an ideographic approach, what are the supporting pictures, the images, the phrases which come to mind?

Education for women, votes for women, the erotic rights of women . . . the cult of woman. Woman as an idol, a sacred object; a sinister, beautiful love-machine stylized by Beardsley, Mucha and Munch. The literature of the orgasmic moment, presented often symbolically : Wilde's Salome, at the end of the play, addressing the severed bleeding head of John the Baptist – 'I have kissed thy mouth, Jokanaan' – before the soldiers, who at Herod's word, rush forward to crush her beneath their shields (hints of the Theatre of Cruelty, re-inforced in book form by Beardsley's drawings). Ella D'Arcy's tale *The Pleasure Pilgrim* – initial sketch of a nymphomaniac to be made by a female British author.

Infatuation and obsession; the 'barren passions' of Dowson and Keats for Missie and Maud Gonne respectively; the dividend of these devotions in terms of verse includes the immortal 'Cynara' ('an experiment; the first three lines in Alexandrines, a favourite rhythm of Lionel's; but one in which at present my Muse is not quite at ease').[11a] The human counter-part of these exclusive dedications : Yeats staying virgin till thirty-three; Dowson seeking oblivion in drink and women of the street ('Dowson found harlots cheaper than hotels').[12] The literary cultivation of light love and carnal sex. Arthur Symons, the friend of Yeats – commemorating 'the Juliet of a night'[13] – a man 'whose curiosity and emotion was roused by every pretty girl'.[14]

[11] *Hugh Selwyn Mauberley* (1920)
[11a] *The Letters of Ernest Dowson* collected and edited Desmond Flower and Henry Maas (1967)
[12] *Hugh Selwyn Mauberley*   [13] 'Stella Maris' (*London Nights*, 1895)
[14] 'The Tragic Generation' (*Autobiographies* by W. B. Yeats, 1926)

13

Theodore Wratislaw, Symons' disciple, turned from his self-paraded orgies – 'Thy breasts, thy hands, their hair upcurled'[15] – to write about the joys of some 'divinest boy/And the dull ennui of a woman's kiss.'[16] The first tacit outlines of a literature of camp. 'I am the love that dare not speak its name.'[17] Wilde's prose-sonnet letter to Lord Alfred Douglas cited in Court during his case against his friend's father the Marquis of Queensberry : 'My own boy . . . it is a marvel that those rose-red lips of yours should be made no less for the madness of music and song than for the madness of kissing.'[18]

The imaginative literature of homosexuality was supplemented, almost for the first time in England, by a small body of critical and scientific writing. 'Unisexual love', as J. A. Symonds called it, is the key to an understanding of many of his essays and books : the title-composition to *In the Key of Blue* (1893) which contains an image of Angelo Fusato, a Venetian gondolier with whom Symonds was intimate –

> You rise, you clasp, a comrade, who
> Is clothed in triple blues like you:
> Sunk in some dream voluptuously
> Circle these azures richly blent,
> Swim through the dusk, the melody;
> Languidly breathing, you and he,
> Uplifting the environment;
> Ivory face and swart face laid
> Cheek unto cheek, like man, like maid.

– the study on 'The Dantesque and Platonic Ideals of Love' (contains in the same volume); the volume on Michelangelo (1892) and *Walt Whitman* (1893).

Symonds' theoretical writings on this theme – *A Problem in Greek Ethics* (1883), *A Problem in Modern Ethics* (1891) – culminated in *Sexual Inversion*, the first volume of Havelock Ellis' *Studies in the Psychology of Sex*, to which Symonds contributed. This seminal work never appeared under joint authorship in this country.

---

[15] Ερος δ'αντε... (*Caprices*, 1893)
[16] *Ibid*
[17] 'The Two Loves' (*Poems* by Lord Alfred Douglas, 1896)
[18] *Bosie: the Story of Lord Alfred Douglas, his Friends and Enemies* by Rupert Croft-Cooke, 1963

Symonds died in 1893; and, at the last minute, 'when the English edition was already bound and on the eve of publication, the Symonds family seem to have taken alarm and Horatio Brown [the author's executor] bought up the edition, though numerous copies nevertheless . . . succeeded in getting into circulation.'[19] Before its publication, in 1897, with all mention of Symonds' name and nearly all of his matter removed, it had, however, appeared in original form the year before in Germany. Havelock Ellis' *Sexual Inversion* was thus the first 'scientific' work by an English author on this subject to be published in English; since Raffalovich's *Uranisme et Unisexualité* – a book-length extension of his pamphlet *L'Affaire Oscar Wilde* (1895) – appeared in French in the *Bibliothèque Criminologie*. Despite the learned credentials of the editor of this series, Dr A. Lacassagne, Raffalovich's book had started in a fit of jealousy and not that fine impartiality from which, one is told, scientific knowledge stems. Raffalovich, friend and patron of the poet John Gray, had seen his protégé taken up by Wilde, who had paid for the publication of Gray's first volume of verse *Silverpoints* (1892).

All one may find in print, however, pales beside the revelations made by Phyllis Grosskurth in her biography *John Addington Symonds* (1964). Quoting or paraphrasing passages from his secret autobiography (causing us to think of the Roger Casement diaries), she exhumes the buried life of this ambiguous Victorian. Homosexual and humanist, Symonds felt himself to be a muffled man, unable to trumpet to the world the evangel of male love which was his own proud confession of faith. A minor but more energetic Pater, a premature and equivocating Gide, Symonds appears to us, through Mrs Grosskurth's pages, as a half-gagged *soi-disant* prophet engaged in an underground warfare with the culture of his time, trying just how far he may voice his ideas without their explicit message emerging.

Her book also demonstrates something else. One learns through Symonds' correspondence, just how fine, blurred, or non-existent was the line between the Platonic love of friends, the Socratic relationship of teacher and pupil, and often admitted and committed pederasty. A quick skim through Mr Rupert Croft-Cooke's uncritical but entertaining volume *Feasting with Panthers: A New*

---

[19] *My Life* by Havelock Ellis (1940)

Consideration of some Late Victorian Writers (1967) will show how sexual perversion pervaded the culture of the times.

One well understands how Ruskin, reared in a Puritan and matriarchal family, should have remarked of Swinburne's *Poems and Ballads* – a lyrical pot-pourri of perversions : 'rose graftings set in dung', as that critic called them – 'It sometimes seems to me the peculiar judgment-curse of modern days that all their greatest men should be plague-struck.'[20]

✦ Another aspect of the period was the increase in pornography – under-the-counter, as it then was, erotica. 'The view of human sexuality,' Professor Steven Marcus declares, 'as it was represented in the subculture of pornography and the view of sexuality held by the official culture were reversals, mirror images, negative analogies of one another. For every warning against masturbation issued by the official voice of culture, another work of pornography was published; for every cautionary statement against the harmful effects of sexual excess uttered by medical men, pornography represented copulation *in excelsis*, endless orgies, infinite daisy chains of inexhaustibility; for every assertion about the delicacy and frigidity of respectable women made by the official culture, pornography represented legions of maenads, universes of palpitating females; for every effort made by the official culture to minimize the importance of sexuality, pornography cried out – or whispered – that it was the only thing in the world of any importance at all.'[21]

➛ Such erotica might establish a distinct alliance with *literature as art*, a case in point being Beardsley's 'romantic novel' *Venus and Tannhauser* (1907). This fantasy of a 'polymorphous pervert', which his publisher sold in secret after his death, possessed enough of the qualities of 'fine writing' for it to appear in abbreviated, slightly changed and expurgated form, entitled *Under the Hill*, in numbers I and II[22] of *The Savoy* – the leading *avant-garde* periodical of the day – and for its rococo style to be acclaimed as 'surpassing the best rhythms of Wilde'.[23] Holbrook Jackson has commented how in *Venus and Tannhauser* 'there are passages which read like

---

[20] *The Swinburne Letters* ed. Cecil Y. Young, New Haven, 1959
[21] *The Other Victorians* (1966)
[22] April and July 1896
[23] *The Men of the 'Nineties* by Bernard Muddiman (1920)

romanticized excerpts from the *Psychopathia Sexualis* of Krafft-
Ebbing.'[24]

Even allowing for the fact that Beardsley's romantic rococo style
wears, so to speak, a mask or domino, over the features of the
erotic, the impact of the novel cannot be gainsaid. Haldane MacFall,
a Scots critic whose curiously ambivalent attitude to Beardsley is
'a compound of attraction and repugnance,'[25] describes the story
as that of one 'bent only on satisfying every lust in a dandified way
that casts but a handsome garment over the barest and most filthy
licence. It contains gloatings over acts so bestial that it staggers
one to think of so refined a taste as Beardsley's judged by the
exquisiteness of his line, not being nauseated by his own impulses.'[26]

In its limited fashion, *Venus and Tannhauser* is an erotic classic
(only some two thousand odd words out of the twelve-thousand
word unfinished text being of directly obscene order). Commercial
or 'hard-core pornography'[27] was an increasingly flourishing
business; but it was in the 'nineties or late 'eighties that England
was bequeathed a pornographic classic in the field of erotic autobiography – a work written with economy and power, and able to
stand up against Restiff de la Brettonne's *Monsieur Nicholas,* a
work whose first volume appeared in 1794, described admiringly
by Wilhelm von Humboldt as the truest book ever written, and
ironically by some anonymous French wit as the *'Liaisons
Dangereuses* of the lower classes'. Its English counterpart *My Secret
Life,* appeared anonymously, each of its eleven volumes bearing
the imprint *Amsterdam. Not for publication.* 'There is no date, but
we can be reasonably certain that it was printed over a period of
time in which 1890 can stand as a mid-point.' *My Secret Life*
constitutes a unique document. These eleven volumes, as Professor
Steven Marcus says, 'are the sexual memoirs of a Victorian gentleman who began to memorialize himself at a very early age and who
continued to do so for more than forty years. . . . At about the age
of thirty-five, he met a woman with whose aid, and the aid of those
to whom she introduced him, he "did, said, saw, and heard, well
nigh everything a man and woman could do with their genitals".

[24] *The Eighteen Nineties* (1913)
[25] *Under the Hill* completed by John Glassco (1959)
[26] *Aubrey Beardsley* (1928)
[27] *Private Case and Public Scandal* by Peter Fryer (1966)

Under the impact of this experience, he "began to narrate these events when quite fresh in my memory" and shortly thereafter "set to work to describe the events of the intervening years of my youth and early middle age".'[28]

But if Beardsley's tale could provoke so powerful a broadside of moral indignation, it could also be lightly dismissed as a mere curio of erotic escapism. This latter was not the reaction in reading the easy naturalistic prose, with its four-letter words, of *My Secret Life*, or the pithy unvarnished case-histories of the first two volumes of Havelock Ellis' Studies in the Psychology of Sex.[29] Here one encountered, in unambiguous terms, in clear precise details, *what people really did*. The relevance of this reading matter to the movement of Realism in the arts; the relevance, too, of its feeling-tone to the hot-house Romanticism of the 'nineties is unquestionably apparent. Not without cause and not without insight had the journalist and poet Robert Buchanan stigmatized the Pre-Raphaelites as 'the Fleshly School of Poetry'.[30]

It may, of course, be suggested that these features drawn from the social and cultural life of the time represent the largely fortuitous interchange between the erotic and the artistic which may be discovered at any time. It is my contention, however, that the connection is an intrinsic one, and that the erotic and the aesthetic, as Kirkegaard showed in *Either/Or* (1843), within the content of nineteenth-century Romantic thinking, are significantly counterpart ways of life.

In the last twenty odd years of Queen Victoria's reign aestheticism, hedonism, and feminism came electrically together. The new *entente* between art and fashion was recorded lightly, but not unjustly, by Max Beerbohm in his essay *1880*. After speaking of his bookish nostalgia for 'those bygone days when first society was inducted into the mystery of art, and . . . babbled of blue china and white lilies, of the painter Rossetti and the poet Swinburne,' he goes on to pay his homage to the impressario of this socio-aesthetic revolution. 'Beauty had existed long before 1880. It was Mr Oscar Wilde who managed her *début*. To study the period is to admit that to him

[28] *The Other Victorians*
[29] *Sexual Inversion* (1897), *The Evolution of Modesty: The Phenomena of Sexual Periodicity and Auto-eroticism* (1899)
[30] *Contemporary Review*, October 1871

Introduction

was due no small part of the social vogue that Beauty began to enjoy. Freed by his fervid words, men and women hurled their mahogany into the streets and ransacked the curio shops for the furniture of Annish days. Dados arose upon every wall, sunflowers and the feathers of peacocks curved in every corner, tea grew quite cold while the guests were praising the Willow Pattern of its cup. A few fashionable women even dressed themselves in sinuous draperies and unheard-of greens. Into whatever ballroom you went, you would surely find, among the women in tiaras and the fops and the distinguished foreigners, half a score of comely ragamuffins in velveteen, murmuring sonnets, posturing, waving their hands. . . . Aestheticism (for so they named the movement) did indeed permeate, in a manner, all classes. But it was to the *haute monde* that its primary appeal was made.'[31]

Another ten years or so, and the sense of sex in this society was to be indefinitely extended. The French novel, and all it implied for the average English reader, would become the cultivated person's contemporary fictional choice. Even to Arthur Symons – an almost professional anti-Puritan – the *physical obtrusiveness* of such an author as Zola would appear a conspicuous feature. He notes, for example, 'the worrying way in which *le derrière* and *le ventre* are constantly kept in view, without the slightest necessity.' 'I should not like to say,' he continues, 'how often the phrase "sa nudité de jolie fille" occurs in Zola. Zola's nudities always remind me of those which you can see in the *Foire au pain d'épice* at Vincennes by paying a penny and looking through a peep-hole.'[32]

Then there were the tales, long and short, of Maupassant; the devilish cleverness of their engineering failing to hide the writer's obsessions : sex and the fear of death. 'Blind and intoxicated with foolish pride must he be who believes himself more than an animal.'[33] The English short-storyists reproduce his themes, the English women authors focus on the sex-war.

On the same wave-length, though less tridently so, was that illustrated magazine *The Yellow Book*. The publisher's Announcement, complete with one of Beardsley's predatory females, appeared in the March of 1894. 'It will be charming, it will be daring,' the

[31] *Works*, 1896
[32] 'A Note on Zola's Method' 1893 (*Studies in Prose and Verse*, 1904)
[33] *Pierre et Jean* by G. de Maupassant, 1888

19

editor and publisher declared. 'And while THE YELLOW BOOK will seek always to preserve a delicate, decorous, and reticent mien and conduct, it will at the same time have the courage of its modernness, and not tremble at the frown of Mrs Grundy.' Apparently, 'the courage of its modernness' must have triumphed, for when the first number appeared in April, *The Times* reported that its dominant note 'was a combination of English rowdiness with French lubricity', while the *Westminster Gazette* simply called for an 'Act of Parliament to make this sort of thing illegal'. One more phase in the war between the aesthete and the philistine. The social stage was now all set for the trial and debacle of Oscar Wilde almost exactly a year later.

III

So far I have been seeking to present, by means of ideogrammatic examples, the sensibility or feeling-tone of the period. An intensified sense of style and sex are seen as the two determinant preoccupations and obsessions of the time. But these are interests located in the instructive or somatic consciousness of the writers. To uncover the intellectual attitudes at the command of these two interests we must institute a more academic approach and study a little the facts and theories leading up to the literature of this era.

The critical writings of the eighteen-nineties constitute a great clearing house of ideas. Among the movements, theories, and tendencies of the time are many notions and suggestions which have gone to shape much of twentieth-century culture. To think of the decade is to call up a formidable inventory of 'isms' : Realism, Impressionism, Aestheticism, Symbolism, Wagnerism, Ibsenism; together with a host of other influences such as occultism, Art Nouveau, Fabianism, Decadence, and the Celtic Twilight.

Out of Symbolism, as Mr Graham Hough has clearly shown in *Image and Experience: Notes on a Literary Revolution* (1960), there came the Imagist Movement; out of Aestheticism, the Art-for-Art's sake fiction of James Joyce – his two vast alembicated epics in prose. Alfred Jarry's drama *Ubu Roi* (1896), with its strident anti-symbolist overtones, leads on direct to the anti-art of Dada – a cultivated attitude of rejection which reached its apogee when a French existentialist author declared that the leading problem for philosophy today was the issue of suicide – to be, or not to be.

Introduction

From occultism, one understands that the Surrealists derived certain psychic procedures; for instance, their technique of automatic writing, as well as a commonly held 'magical' view of the universe, even though they sought to domesticate this by the dialectical materialism of Marx. (André Breton's novel *Nadja* (1928) would certainly have interested more followers of Madame Blavatsky than Lenin.)

From Impressionism, by way of reaction, was derived Post-Impressionism, whose great God-figure Cézanne provided Roger Fry and Clive Bell with their key-phrase to art – the sesame of 'significant form'.

And just as those twentieth-century creators, who held to an exclusively aesthetic approach, found a justification in the Art-for-Art's sake movement of the 'nineties, so too did those who looked beyond art for an extra-aesthetic vindication. The Socialist-Realist poets of the 'thirties – or 'pink triumvirate' as they were called, with their Arms-for-Spain and their belief in Revolution – could claim to be in line with such men of letters as Bernard Shaw and H. G. Wells who brought their creative and critical talents to the service of Fabian Socialism.

Faced with such diversity, such plurality of creative currents, can we in any way limit or stream-line their main, seminal, or parent-notions? I think that we can, and will therefore say that two main elements meet to produce the cultural theories of the 'nineties : one of these is French, and one English (or, more precisely, Anglo-Italian); in short, Baudelaire, and Pre-Raphaelitism. These two streams of ideas came together in Swinburne (Baudelaire plus Pre-Raphaelitism producing the Aesthetic Movement). From Swinburne onwards, they run side by side through Pater and Wilde to form the staple of the 'nineties.

Both of these streams had much in common. The man and the movement were both in revolt against the industrialized way of life : the creeping eczema of factories, mills and mines; the joyless gospels of labour and profit. Intuitively or logically, they stood in opposition to the naïve scientism of much progressive thought. The shallow optimism of free trade did not impress them, neither did they see in the rabid competition of an acquisitive society anything more than a degraded goal. The whole cash-and-comfort ethos of a mercantile philistine middle-class filled them with angry, ironic contempt.

In like manner also, both man and movement were part of the logical development of an earlier Romanticism. A modern translator and editor of Baudelaire has spoken of his 'purified and re-stated Romanticism',[34] while the poet himself remarked that 'to say the word Romanticism is to say modern art, that is intimacy, spirituality, colour, aspiration towards the infinite, expressed by every means available to the arts.'[35]

On the origins of the English painters and poets, Graham Hough observes that 'historically speaking, pre-Raphaelitism is a late flowering of the major Romantic movement, induced by the new excitement about visual art for which Ruskin was responsible.'[36] Nor does this 'excitement about visual art' make the movement irrelevant to the development of literary style and standards. 'Rossetti's literary inspiration,' as Graham Hough remarks, 'needs no underlining; but even Holman Hunt and Millais as *par excellence* the professional painters of the group, regard "the discipline of the formative arts to that of letters" as a "perennial law". In return, pre-Raphaelitism became far more than a school of painting : it became a movement of thought and feeling whose influence soaked deep into the late nineteenth century, and even spread to the next age.'[37]

A few dated incidents serve to establish the Romantic origins of the Pre-Raphaelite movement.

About 1845, Holman Hunt (aged eighteen) was lent a copy of Ruskin's *Modern Painters*, the first of whose five volumes appeared in 1843. He sat up all night enthralled by it. 'Of all readers,' he tells us, 'none could have felt more strongly than myself that it was written expressly for him.'[38] As a young student, in the 1840s, Hunt had picked up a copy of the works of Keats – 'this little known painter',[39] as he then was – in the fourpenny box of a bookshop. The poet, in those days, was still an 'unsure' taste. Even so, Millais –

[34] *Baudelaire: The Painter of Modern Life and other essays*, translated and edited by Jonathan Mayne, 1964
[35] *Ibid*
[36] *The Last Romantics*, 1947
[37] *Ibid*
[38] *Pre-Raphaelitism and the Pre-Raphaelite Brotherhood*, 1905
[39] *Ibid*

with all his instinct to play conventionally for safety – was converted by his friend to a like enthusiasm, and no more Keatsian a picture has ever been produced than his *Mariana* (1851) – even though its title and theme derive from Tennyson, not Keats. Beside it, his earlier *Isabella* (1849) – deriving direct from Keats' poem – is gauchely naturalistic and ineptly dramatic, and quite without the suavely worked detail caught up into a swoon of voluptuous colour which both *Mariana* and the narrative Keats afford.

In 1847, Rossetti had bought – for ten shillings, which he borrowed from his brother – 'the imperishable *MS Book of Blake*',[40] as Arthur Symons hyperbolically puts it.

The substance of two poets and the author of the greatest prose poetry in English were therefore fed initially into the Pre-Raphaelite blood-stream. Hunt, Millais, and Rossetti, as Graham Hough comments, 'regarded it as part of their mission to deliver painting from vulgarity of thought and triviality of subject by flooding it with ideas from the romantic literature of the earlier part of the century.'[41] Literature, one might add in digression, re-paid the compliment by establishing a fashion, through Wilde and Symons, for the short picture-poem. (We can think here of the former's 'Impressions', 'Symphony in Yellow', 'Le Réveillon' and 'Les Ballons';[42] and the latter's book of verse-etchings *Silhouettes*, 1892.) The visual bias of Pre-Raphaelite poetry culminates, of course, in Pound's 'Phanopoeia'[43] – image-poetry, or verse for the eye – and his adaptation of 'The Chinese Written Character as a Medium for Poetry' – 'a vivid shorthand picture of the operations of nature.'[44]

The literary bias and affiliations of the Pre-Raphaelite Brethren – a group of seven young artists who banded together in 1848, the year of revolutions – was the short-lived magazine, which, beginning in January 1850, ran to no more than four numbers. *The Germ*, as it was called, bore as a sub-title words meant to serve a manifesto-purpose : 'Thoughts towards Nature in Poetry, Literature and Art.' According to the editor William Michael Rossetti, 'they indicated

[40] 'The Rossettis' 1919 (*Dramatis Personae*, 1923)
[41] *The Last Romantics*
[42] First appearing together in Wilde's collected *Poems*, 1908
[43] *How to Read* 1928
[44] The title of Ernest Fenellosa's essay adapted and translated posthumously by Pound, the author's literary executor in the latter's volume of essays *Instigations*, 1920

accurately enough the predominant conception of the Pre-Raphaelite Brotherhood, that an artist, whether painter or writer, ought to be bent on defining and expressing his own personal thoughts, and that *they ought to be based upon a direct study of Nature.*' [My italics.]

But if Naturalism appeared as one of the Pre-Raphaelite platform notions, then there was equally an opposite one – an antithetical *pronunciamento* implicit in the work of the Movement such as is to be found more explicitly in Baudelaire. In the first number of *The Germ* there appeared a parable by D. G. Rossetti about a gay Italian artist Chiaro del Erma. The story is entitled *Hand and Soul*, suggesting a division of loyalties – craftmanship serving a civic end : imagination serving an inward vision. Equally well, one can see the 'Hand' as an image of these values maintained by Martha, while the 'Soul' stands for values which Mary cherished in contemplation. One day, as Chiaro stood at his window, he saw the large allegorical fresco of Peace which he had painted on a church wall spattered by the blood of townsmen fighting among themselves in the square. In despair he felt that religious belief and ambition and even morality had failed him. At that moment a beautiful woman appeared in the room. She called herself the image of his own soul and told him to distress himself no further over whether or not he was fulfilling God's will : 'What He hath set in thy heart to do, that do thou, and even though thou do it without thought of Him, it shall be well done.'

Two small matters here call for emphasis if we are to read the conclusion aright. First, that young Chiaro feels that all *the social and external props* which make life meaningful – *religious belief, morality, ambition* – had been removed from his existence when he saw his own townspeople defiling, with the blood of their conflicts, his large 'public' outward-turned painting of Peace. Secondly, when the beautiful woman appears in Chiaro's room she describes herself as *an image of his own soul.* The woman represents, it would seem, *the narcissism of the imagination* dedicated only to reflecting its likeness in the mirror of a pure subjective-minded art. As Barbara Charlesworth remarks of the conclusion, 'It is, in other words, God's will that the artist work for art's sake',[45] contracting out, with easy conscience, from these extra-aesthetical obligations which more

[45] *Dark Passages* (1965)

24

communally-minded or 'other-directed'[46] (to employ Daniel
Riesman's phrase) have observed. Writing from a not dissimilar
viewpoint, Arthur Symons said once of Rossetti that he painted 'like
a perfectly contented prisoner to whom the sense of imprisonment
is a joy'.[47]

Deriving principally from Rossetti, just as Ruskin's Naturalism
had been championed and practised chiefly by Hunt, this imaginative private-minded art links Pre-Raphaelitism with the Ivory Tower
attitude of earlier and later French and English authors.

IV

The essence of the Ivory Tower artist [is] his detachment from the
external world. This does not necessarily imply any dismissal of
the drama before one; only an avoidance of involvement or com-
mittment (engaged in by many of the old-style Romantics) and
the cultivation in its place of an attitude of observation. The art
of the Ivory Tower is an aspect of the contemplative life: the art
of Romanticism, a by-product of the life of action.

Partisan or spectator? The Ivory Tower author chooses the latter
role; and no better enunciation of it can be found than the poem-
preface which Gautier affixed to his *Emaus et Canéas* – miniatures,
enamellings, and cameos in verse – which appeared in 1852: 'In
the midst of the wars of the Empire, Goethe assembled, to the
cannon's sound, his *Oriental Divan*, a fresh oasis where art could
breathe in peace. . . . So I – like Goethe, on his couch at Weimar
shutting himself off from things to cultivate roses with Hafiz –
ignoring the storm which whips my closed windows, have created
these enamellings and cameos in verse.'

In passing one may note that by 1886 Austin Dobson of the
Board of Trade, in 'Ars Victrix' ('imitated from Théophile
Gautier') had translated into faultless quatrains the French poet's
Parnassian exhortation:

> Leave to the tiro's hand
> The limp and shapeless style.
> See that thy form demand
> The labour of the file.

[46] *The Lonely Crowd* (1952)
[47] 'Dante Gabriel Rossetti' (*Figures of Several Centuries*, 1917)

All passes. ART alone
 Enduring stays to us;
 The Bust out-lasts the throne –
 The Coin, Tiberius.

Baudelaire took Gautier – 'perfect magician of the art of letters in France' – to be his 'dear, deeply respected master and friend'. So he is styled in the poet's dedication to his *Fleurs du Mal*, 1857 – 'the brightest gem in Baudelaire's crown'.[48]

At a first reading, his works in verse and prose offer the same antitheses, the same co-existence of self-contradictions as we find in Pre-Raphaelitism. Already, before the latter artists had banded together in 1848, Baudelaire had published his first two studies in the criticism of art: his *Salon of 1845*, followed by his *Salon of 1846*. In the second of these 'we find,' as Mr Mayne puts it, 'the first of the great Baudelarian key-words themselves defining key-positions in his critical strategy . . . Individualism, Romanticism . . . the Ideal.'[49] If we did not know of his inexhaustible and continuing admiration for Delacroix (on whom he was to write in 1863 as the artist of 'the invisible, the impalpable . . . the soul'), we might find it difficult to square these concepts with a general view of his practice in verse. Glancing casually at *Les Fleurs du Mal*, one may wonder at the poet's diatribes in prose against 'that herd of vulgar artists and scribblers whose myopic intelligence takes shelter behind the vague and obscure word "realism",[50] for to the average British reader of French poetry that book may well have appeared outstanding as realism in verse – a Racinian realism, it is true; but for all that, realism none the less. As late, for example, as 1888 Eugene Lee-Hamilton eulogizes Baudelaire, in a poem by that title,[51] in the following fashion :

A Paris gutter of the good old times,
 Black and putrescent in its stagnant bed,
 Save where the shamble oozings fringe it red,
 Or scaffold trickles, or nocturnal crimes

[48] *The Life and Intimate Memoirs of Charles Baudelaire* by Théophile Gautier, 1868
[49] *Baudelaire: the Painter of Modern Life and other Essays*
[50] *The Life and Work of Eugène Delacroix*, 1863
[51] *Imaginary Sonnets*

It holds dropped gold; dead flowers from tropic climes;
　Gems true and false, by midnight maskers shed;
　Old pots of rouge; old broken phials that spread
Vague fumes of musk, with fumes from slums and slimes.

An everywhere, as glows the set of day,
　There floats upon the winding fetid mire
The gorgeous iridescence of decay:

A wavy film of colour, gold and fire,
　Trembles all through it as you pick your way,
And streaks of purple that are straight from Tyre.

On the face of it, Lee-Hamilton's poem appears as a gesture in
favour of a realistic interpretation of the poet. Read the sonnet
again, however, and one notes how the imagery of realism is off-set
by that of a more romantic order : gutter, shamble, scaffold/gold,
gems, maskers; 'vague fumes of musk, with fumes from slums and
slimes.' As the octave gives way to the tercet, the romantic note is
strengthened, till the sonnet concludes with the traditionally
evocative word 'Tyre'. Thin as this is beside a sonnet by the
Frenchman, it none the less incapsulates the essence of the poet :
his see-saw between 'Spleen and the Ideal' : [52]

There floats upon the winding fetid mire
The gorgeous iridescence of decay:

All of Baudelaire is in that : the 'fetid' volatilized . . . refined until
it becomes the 'gorgeous' as if it was actively aspiring towards it.
'Delacroix,' as Baudelaire remarked, 'is the most *suggestive* of all
painters.'[53] This praise may justly be adapted to its author, since
it would be true to say that 'Baudelaire is the most suggestive of
all poets'.

Baudelaire's objection of 'realism' belongs to his ideology as
theorist rather than to his performance as an artist. 'Realism,' as
Mr Mayne puts it, '(associated by him with Positivism) was for
Baudelaire a flat negation of the Imagination – it was little less than
a blasphemy.[54] Realism was in fact linked by him with the philosophy of 'philanthropists, progressionists, utilitarians, humanitarians,

[52] 'Spleen et Idéal' is the title of one section of poems in Baudelaire's
Fleurs du Mal
[53] *The Life and Work of Eugène Delacroix*
[54] *Baudelaire: the Painter of Modern Life and other Essays*

Utopians, and of all those who pretend to reform things', of whom
'Baudelaire had a perfect horror'.[55]

Even so, Realism plays a distinguishing role in Baudelaire's
poetry. I speak of it as a 'distinguishing role' because it is what
serves to distinguish his verse from the verse of earlier poets. The
poem *Les Petites Vieilles* affords a ready illustration of this:

LITTLE OLD WOMEN

. . . Under their tattered skirts and skimpy garments, they crawl along,
whipped by the malignant winds, trembling at the din of the buses
thundering past, clutching against their ribs, like holy relics, their little
handbags embroidered with flowers of puzzling patterns. They trot along
like puppets, or hobble like lame animals, or, though they don't intend
to, they do a kind of jig, like puny bells swung by a merciless demon.[56]

But the Realism playing this 'distinguishing role' is itself a Realism
readily distinguishable. One way, perhaps, would be to describe it
as a Romantic Realism – a realism of the spirit as well as of the
fact, a realism in which the details form a window giving on to a
landscape of meaning. Thus, in the poem *Spleen*, we find a factual
statement, followed by a long-sustained metaphor returning the
reader to another literal statement, before setting off on further
metaphorical comparisons:

I have more memories than if I had loved a thousand years.

Even a huge chest of drawers stuffed with accounts and verses, love-
letters and law-suits, drawing-room ballads, and heavy plaits of hair
rolled up in receipts, has less secrets to hide than my unhappy brain. It
is a pyramid, a vast burial vault, fuller of dead than a charnel house.[57]

This intensified sense of fact, of fact as animated as if it held a
soul, is something one discovers likewise in the work of certain early
Pre-Raphaelite painters. Ruskin, in a lecture delivered at Edinburgh
on 18 November 1853, praised the movement for its 'absolute,
uncompromising truth in all that it does, obtained by working everything, down to the most minute detail, from nature, and from
nature only. . . . Every Pre-Raphaelite landscape background is

[55] *The Life and Intimate Memoirs of Charles Baudelaire* by Théophile
Gautier
[56] *Baudelaire: Selected Verse* with an Introduction and Prose Translations
by Francis Scarfe (1961)
[57] *Ibid*

painted to the last touch, in the open air, from the thing itself.'[58]
This explains the working-method of many Pre-Raphaelite canvases,
good, bad, or indifferent, alike; but it does not explain, for example,
the apparitional unity of lilies, young woman and young man (is
he a phantom or only pale with longing?) in Arthur Hughes' small
picture *The Tryst*. Neither can it cover with its explanation Rossetti's
superb portrait-poem *Jenny*, written for the main part in a 'realistic'
style, but flashing out revealingly every so often into something
which the minute imitation of Nature cannot alone transmit.
When the poet speaks to the sleeping girl ('Poor handful of bright
spring water/Flung in the whirlpool's shrieking face') :

> Why, Jenny, as I watch you there –
> For all your wealth and loosened hair,
> Your silk ungirdled and unlaced
> And warm sweets open to the waist,
> All golden in the lamplight's gleam –
> *You know not what a book you see*
> *Half-read by lightning in a dream*   [my italics]

we realize that if art is an *imitation of Nature*, it is also *life seen
through a temperament*. The soul-dramas discoverable in many
good Pre-Raphaelite pictures and poems answer to a fusion of these
two formulae : something objective and mimetic; and something
subjective and creative.

The essence of Ruskin's teaching consisted of a sort of factual
perfectionism. His doctrine that the painter learns from Nature
by copying her creations quite literally, down to the smallest detail,
was translated, then, by the Pre-Raphaelites in their most inspired
and individual moments in a quite undogmatic fashion. Robin
Ironside, an ex-director of our National Gallery, has summarized
their happy vision, independently achieved, in the following words :
'It was, at first, as if the [P-R] Brotherhood looked at the world
without eyelids; for them, a livelier emerald twinkled in the grass,
a purer sapphire melted into the sea. On the illuminated page that
nature seemed to thrust before their dilated pupils, every floating
prismatic ray, each drifting filament of vegetation, was rendered,
in all its complexity, with heraldic brilliance and distinctness; the
floor of the forest was carpeted with not merely the general variega-

[58] *Lectures on Architecture and Painting* (1854)

tion of light and shade, but was seen to be plumed with ferns receiving each in a particular fashion the shafts of light that fell upon them; there were not simply birds in the branches above, but the mellow ouzel, fluting in the elm.'[59]

Between the lyrical particularity of this type of naturalism and Baudelaire's more loaded realism, there is some difference. Yet both the French and English artists could have claimed that their 'grand, unique and primitive passion' was to 'glorify the cult of images'.[60]

Realism, presumably, implies the reproduction of facts life-scale while Romanticism, engaged in looking at the world through a magnifying-glass, may well lead to distorted proportions. But in whatever degree Realism and Romanticism combine, in certain works of Baudelaire and the Pre-Raphaelites, they result in *a revival of intensity*. Whereas an earlier Romanticism was, according to Heinrich Heine, 'a passion-flower sprung from the wounds of Christ,'[61] that of Baudelaire and these later English artists depicted each blossom of field or garden as bright as if freshly stained with human blood.

V

The difference between the Realisms of Baudelaire and the Pre-Raphaelites, both as to theory and practice, is this : the first is urban, and the second pastoral. The prescribed forms to which the artist should resort for the purposes of study are chiefly, in the teachings of Ruskin, those of organic or inanimate nature, while in Baudelaire's critical and creative writings, it is the artificial manufactured forms of man's constructions which are mainly accented. The principal work in which Baudelaire develops the ideas of a *metropolitan aesthetic* is his study of Constantin Guys : *The Painter of Modern Life*, 1863.[62] This is how the author envisages the responses of a representative 'modern' artist to the urban *décor* :

He marvels at the eternal beauty and the amazing harmony of life in the capital cities, a harmony so providentially maintained amid the turmoil of human freedom. He gazes upon the landscapes of the great

[59]*Pre-Raphaelite Painters* by R. Ironside and J. Gere (1948)
[60] 'My Heart laid bare' (*Intimate Journals* of Charles Baudelaire translated by Christopher Isherwood, 1930)
[61] *The Romantic School* (1833)
[62] But written earlier, during the years 1859–60

city – landscapes of stone, caressed by the mist or buffeted by the sun.
He delights in fine carriages and proud horses, the dazzling smartness of
the grooms, the expertness of the footmen, the sinuous gait of the
women . . . in a word, he delights in universal life.[63]

Here, quite plainly, there begins a conscious concern with a *poetry
of the town* which the poets and critics of the 'nineties were largely
to elaborate after a surfeit of nature-verse throughout the century.
The following typical statement of this *poetry of brick-and-mortar*,
to be found in the preface to the second edition of Arthur Symons'
volume of poems *Silhouettes* (1896), clearly derives from Baudelaire.
'I am always charmed,' wrote Symons, with a touch of affectation
concealing real truth, 'to read beautiful poems about nature in the
country. Only, personally, I prefer town to country; and in the
town we have to find for ourselves as best we may, the *décor* which
is the town equivalent of the great natural *décor* of fields and hills.
Here it is that artificiality comes in; and if anyone can see no
beauty in the effect of artificial lights, in all the variable, most
human, and yet most factitious town landscapes, I can only pity
him and go on my own way.'
Arthur Symons was followed here by T. S. Eliot, Edgell Rickward,
and John Betjeman. After the poetry of the town (city or metropolis), there comes the poetry of the suburbs, and it is this last
terrain that John Betjeman has taken as his special field.
An amusing by-way opening out from the central premise of
Baudelaire's aesthetic was that represented by Oscar Wilde's
Intentions (1891). Baudelaire had posited the beauty of artificiality
(in the sense of art-facts – things *made by man*). Wilde, standing
this proposition on its head, maintained the artificiality of beauty
which becomes in his thought a mode of affectation. From the first
position is derived the stern dialectic between organic life and the
state of art in Yeats' two great 'Byzantium' poems :[64] from the
second, a modish denigration of nature, culminating perhaps in the
'trick' false thinking of that aesthete's credo : Wallace Stevens'
Anecdote of the Jar.
For a while, Wilde's paradoxes held the attention of drawing-
rooms captive. How relaxing and refreshing it was after the eye-

[63] *The Painter of Modern Life*
[64] 'Sailing to Byzantium' (*The Tower*, 1928), 'Byzantium' (*The Winding
Stair and other poems*, 1933)

strain occasioned by Ruskin (who bade the picture-gazing public take note of Turner's 'spot upon a dead trout and the dyes upon a butterfly's wing'[65]) to be able to talk of 'a foolish sunset'. 'Art,' declares Vivian – the charming and insufferable young dilettante of Wilde's dialogue 'The Decay of Lying'[66] – 'creates an incomparable and unique effect, and, having done so, passes on to other things. Nature, upon the other hand, forgetting that imitation can be made the sincerest form of insult, keeps on repeating this effect until we all become absolutely wearied of it. Nobody of any real culture, for instance, ever talks nowadays about the beauty of a sunset. Sunsets are quite old-fashioned. They belong to the time when Turner was the last note in art. To admire them is a distinct sign of provincialism of temperament. Upon the other hand they go on. Yesterday evening Mrs Arundel insisted on my going to the window, and looking at the glorious sky, as she called it. Of course I had to look at it. She is one of those absurdly pretty Philistines to whom one can deny nothing. And what was it? It was simply a very second-rate Turner, a Turner of a bad period, with all the painter's worst faults exaggerated and over-emphasized.'

Wilde's thoughts on art look like mere *jeux d'ésprit*: an aesthetic gaily elaborated out of *bon mots* intended for the *salon*. Recently, however, Professor Ellmann has offered another explanation of the calculated waywardness of the critic's theories.[67] Wilde, he observes, was initiated into homosexual practices by Robert Ross in 1886. Ross, who admitted to this, was then seventeen and Wilde thirty-two. From this date onwards, Wilde's thinking was powerfully coloured by his practice. 'One can fancy,' he wrote in his study of the murderer-aesthete Thomas Wainwright, 'an intense personality being created out of sin.'[68] The next year, he went one better, declaring in 'The Soul of Man under Socialism'[69] that 'crime under certain conditions may be said to have created individualism'. It is certain that the criminal act (as it then was) of homosexuality released in Wilde a whole body of *pensées* innate in him perhaps, but now developed to their logical extremes. *Lord Arthur Saville's Crime* (1887), *The Portrait of Mr W. H.* (1889), *The Picture of*

[65] *Lectures upon Architecture and Painting*
[66] *Intentions*
[67] 'The Critic as Artist as Wilde' (*Encounter*, July 1967)
[68] 'Pen, Pencil, and Poison' (*The Fortnightly Review*, January 1889)
[69] *The Fortnightly Review*, February 1890

Introduction

Dorian Gray (1890), and *Intentions* (1891) constitute an apologia for perversion, a veritable philosophy *contra natura*.

The aesthetics of an amoralist – such has, in general, been the verdict of his peers on Wilde's theories of art. 'There is no such thing,' he had declared in the preface to *The Picture of Dorian Gray*, 'as a moral or an immoral book. Books are well written or badly written. That is all.'[70]

— Whether the term 'amoralist' is a fitting one for Wilde as a critic or whether the bias of his thought is, as Professor Ellmann holds, basically antinomian is a question too complexly nice to be decided here.[71] We have only to turn, however, to Baudelaire's aesthetic – particularly as set forth in his essay on Guys – to sense the difference in moral weight, in intellectual gravity, between the two men. Like those of Wilde, the theories of Baudelaire might appear to contain an element of subversion. They endanger, it is true, the ethics of profit and respectability – the values of those who, like Yeats' peasant shop-keeper, 'fumble in a greasy till/And add the halfpence to the pence/And prayer to shivering prayer, until/You have dried the marrow from the bone.'[72] Baudelaire's thought does ruthless execution on men 'born to pray and save'[73] – the 'unco guid' of Burns' day. Baudelaire, like Wilde, at times enjoyed *épatant les bourgeois*. But, even here, his so-called Satanism was, as T. S. Eliot observed, 'an attempt to get into Christianity by the back door'.[74] Orthodox, in the full sense, he certainly was not; but in his Manichean manner of thinking there is something noble, tragic and heroic.

Baudelaire's brand of Manicheism springs from an exaggerated distrust (and fear) of the organic and biological elements in life. Just as Yeats presents the work of art as transcending and mastering man's physical existence –

> A starlit or a moonlit dome disdains
> All that man is,

[70] First published in the book form of the novel, with chapters additional to those which appeared in *Lippincott's Magazine*, 1891
[71] 'The Critic as Artist as Wilde' (*Encounter*, July 1967). A short summary of Prof. Ellmann's argument, together with my comments upon it, are given in my introductory note to Wilde's contribution in this anthology
[72] 'September 1913' (*Responsibilities*, 1914)
[73] *Ibid*
[74] Introduction to Baudelaire's *Intimate Journals* (1930)

All mere complexities,
The fury and the mire of human veins.

– so Baudelaire posits the moral action, together with the work of
art, as stemming from reasoned consciousness, the archetypal
opponent of nature :

Everything beautiful and noble is the result of reason and calculation.
Crime, of which the human animal has learned the taste in his mother's
womb, is natural by origin. Virtue, on the other hand, is artificial, super-
natural, since at all times and in all places gods and prophets have been
needed to teach it to animalized humanity, man being powerless to
discover it for himself. Evil happens without effort, naturally, fatally.
Good is always the product of some art. All that I am saying about
Nature as a bad counsellor in moral matters, and about Reason as a true
redeemer and reformer, can be applied to the realms of Beauty.[76]

That this was no exercise in abstract intellection but the core of
a viable way of thinking, can be seen by the following extracts
from Baudelaire's private journals :[77]

A short formula for wisdom – toilet, prayer, work.

My humiliations have been God's graces.

The famous oft-quoted page of the journal, full of a back-to-the-
wall *ascesis*, sets out the following conscientious regimen :

Hygiene, Conduct, Method – I swear to myself to adopt from now on,
the following rules as the permanent rules of my life:
Make my prayer every morning to God, the reservoir of all strength
and all justice, and to my father, to Mariette, and to Poe as intercessors;
pray them to afford me the necessary strength to carry out all my duties,
and to grant my mother a long enough life for her to enjoy the change in
me; work all day long, or at least as much as my strength allows; trust
in God, that is to say in Justice itself, for the success of my undertaking;
every evening make a new prayer asking God for life and strength for
my mother and for me; divide my earnings into four shares, one for daily
expenses, one for my creditors, one for my friends, and one for my
mother; obey the principles of the strictest sobriety, the first of which
is to suppress all stimulants of whatever kind.

The sombre, ultimately sober, cast of his mind is confirmed by

[75] 'Byzantium'
[76] *The Painter of Modern Life*
[77] 'My Heart Laid Bare'

Gautier who recalled that 'He hated evil as a mathematical devia-
tion, and, in his quality of perfect gentleman, he scorned it as
unseemly, ridiculous, bourgeois and squalid.'[78] To hate evil because
it is ungentlemanly calls for some special understanding, some more
precise reading, of the term 'gentleman' than we generally accord
to it. Such an understanding had to hand in his key-words : 'dandy'
and 'dandyism'.

His thoughts on this subject were suggested to him by the drawings of Guys, and though there are less than four pages in
Baudelaire's study of the artist on this theme, they are central to a
right appreciation of his work – and to very much work of the
'nineties.

First, he declares that the dandy is he 'whose solitary progression
is elegance', and that 'Dandyism is a mysterious institution' – in
other words, a cult requiring qualification and initiation. In connection with this last idea, we learn that it transcends the individual;
that in it there is something binding upon the personal life of
impulse and caprice. This 'something' partakes of both an aesthetic
and moral discipline, and can best be suggested by the term
'manners'. 'Dandyism, an institution beyond the law, itself has
rigorous laws which all its subjects must strictly obey, whatever
their natural impetuosity and independence of character.'[79]

To think of a dandy is initially to envisage the embodiment of
sartorial refinement. As might be expected, Baudelaire did not fail
this test in his own person. Gautier tells us that 'his clothing consisted of an overcoat of shining black cloth, nut-coloured trousers,
white stockings, and patent leather shoes; the whole fastidiously
correct, with a stamp of almost English simplicity, intentionally
adopted to distinguish himself from the artistic folk with the soft
felt hats, the velvet waistcoats, red jackets, and strong, dishevelled
beards. Nothing was too new or elaborate about him. Charles
Baudelaire indulged in a certain dandyism, but he would do anything to take from his things the "Sunday clothes" appearance so
dear and important to the Philistine, but so disagreeable to the true
gentleman.'[80] The rejection of Bohemian costume is relevant here.
It signifies the poet's adoption of a style of dress and writing more

[78] *The Painter of Modern Life*
[79] *Ibid*
[80] *The Life and Intimate Memoirs of Charles Baudelaire*

severe and disciplined than that of Henry Murger's Romanticism.[81] In these sartorial matters, Baudelaire's example, his legend, and his theory, influenced the poets of the Rhymers Club. As Yeats tells us in his record of 'Four Years: 1887–1891' 'Our clothes were for the most part unadventurous like our conversation . . . [save himself and Le Gallienne] who wore a loose tie, and Symons who had an Inverness cape that was quite new and almost fashionable [no one] would have shown himself for the world in any costume but that of an English gentleman. "One should be quite unnoticeable,"'[82] Lionel Johnson explained to him.

In Baudelaire's understanding of dandyism, sartorial perfection was one element only. Indeed, he declared that 'at certain points, dandyism borders upon the spiritual and stoical.'[83] The implications of this seeming paradox are clarified by three further statements. The *content* of dandyism is a state of mind; its *form* is a dress and code of manners which best and most fittingly express this content. It does not consist, Baudelaire tells us, 'as many thoughtless people seem to believe, in an immoderate taste for the toilet and material elegance. For the perfect dandy these things are no more than symbols of his aristocratic superiority of mind . . . his eyes . . . are in love with *distinction* above all things.'[84]

Baudelaire also places this phenomenon within the context of history: 'Dandyism appears . . . in periods of transition when democracy is not yet all-powerful and aristocracy is only just beginning to totter and fall. . . . [It] is the last spark of heroism amid decadence. . . . Dandyism is a sunset; like the declining daystar, it is glorious, without heat and full of melancholy.'[85]

These assets and attributes of dandyism answered to the *fin-de-siècle* position in which the 'nineties writers found themselves. It was how they liked to envisage themselves, finding these fashionable philosophic props useful in their effort to dramatize their lives. 'The future belongs to the dandy,' declaimed Wilde, 'it is the dandies who are going to rule.'[86] In a number of mini-manifesto essays, Max Beerbohm endorses the theme. 'English

[81] *Scènes de la Vie Bohème* (1851)
[82] *The Trembling of the Veil* (1922)
[83] *The Painter of Modern Life*
[84] *Ibid*
[85] *Ibid*
[86] *The Picture of Dorian Gray*, 1891

society,' he gently insists, 'is always ruled by a dandy, and the more absolutely ruled the greater that dandyism is.'[87] George IV – First Gentleman of Europe, Thackeray's *bête noir* ('*He* the first gentleman of Europe! There is no stronger satire on the proud English society of that day, than that they admired George'.[88]) – becomes the favoured subject of an essay by Max. The eighteenth century – *out* for so long as the *century of prose and reason* – returns to favour in Charles Conder's fans where it features as a pastoral arcadia of choice sophistication. Beardsley illustrates Pope's *Rape of the Lock*, Pater writes on Watteau in *Imaginary Portraits* (1887), and Arthur Symons – urban elegist – finds in this painter of mortal evanescence occasion to pen an autumnal lyric on 'The dance of love's decease'.[89] Well might Max rejoice 'that Artifice, whom we drove forth, has returned among us. . . . Artifice, sweetest exile, is come into her kingdom.'[90]

In the chapter entitled 'The New Dandyism' of his book *The Eighteen Nineties* (1913), Holbrook Jackson lists an inventory of affectations offered by the authors of that decade. Commenting on Wilde's *Phrases and Philosophies for the Use of the Young*[91] – 'a little work which is a veritable philosophy of dandyism' – he remarks that 'Literature in the 'nineties ran to epigram, that poseur of syntax, and to paradox, that dandified juggler of ideas.'

The association hinted at here between style and dandyism is just. Nothing expresses and preserves the man in search of perfection and distinction so much as the mannerism of his style. The conscious dandy, as man of letters, is always the conscious stylist.

VI

One last element spoken of by Baudelaire in his essay on Guys, deserves separate attention. It is the more important because the Pre-Raphaelites failed to stress it, and because Swinburne and Pater – two seminal authorities – say little directly of it. This is the element of 'modernity' – a term becoming a key-word with Wilde, George Moore, Arthur Symons and other men of the 'nineties. It has proved, in fact, probably the most bruited term whenever

[87] 'Dandies and Dandies' (*Works*, 1896)
[88] *The Four Georges*, 1855
[89] 'For a Picture of Watteau' (*Silhouettes*, 1892)
[90] 'The Pervasion of Rouge', 1894 (*Works*, 1896)
[91] Published in *The Chameleon*, December 1894

twentieth-century art has been in question. The degree to which the notion of modernity has become central to the art of our era may be read in the title of a classic of *avant-garde* criticism – Harold Rosenberg's *The Tradition of the New* (1962). The continuity of interest in this approach is seen clearly when one recalls Baudelaire's own title of a hundred years ago: *The Painter of Modern Life*. Almost every man of letters, in fact, seems to be still saying to himself what Rimbaud said in 1873: 'One must be absolutely modern.'[92]

'By modernity,' Baudelaire tells us, he means, 'the ephemeral, the fugitive, the contingent, the half of art whose other half is the eternal and the immutable.'[93] The business of the artist, then, is 'to extract from fashion whatever element it may contain of poetry within history.'[94]

'The ephemeral, the fugitive, the contingent. . . .' In line with this definition, the 'nineties offers us a literature of transcience. 'Man is in love, and loves what vanishes,'[95] Yeats declared, describing the essence of this commemorative process of art. Earlier, in his first book *Crossways* (1889), he had distinguished the human condition in a poem called *Ephemera*: 'our souls / Are love, and a continual farewell.' Art preserves the living moment, and in the act becomes a valediction. Moods and moments become the keywords of poets, short-storyists and critics. Lord Alfred Douglas, in his *Sonnet on the Sonnet*[96] considers it the rôle of the sonneteer 'to see the moment holds a madrigal'. 'The moods of men!' enthuses Arthur Symons. 'There I find my subject, there the region over which art rules; and whatever has once been a mood of mine, though it has been no more than a ripple of the sea, and had no longer than that ripple's duration, I claim the right to render, if I can, in verse.'[97]

In fiction and the essay, this cult of mutability is reflected in the fashionable vogue for such titles as *A Man of Moods* (1896) by H. D. Lowry, *Miniatures and Moods* (1893) by G. S. Street, *Episodes* (1895) by the same writer, and *The First Step: A Dramatic*

---

[92] 'Adieu' (*Une Saison en Enfer*) 1874
[93] *The Painter of Modern Life*
[94] *Ibid*
[95] *The Shadowy Waters*, 1906
[96] *Sonnets*, 1909
[97] Preface to *London Nights* (second edition, 1896)

38

Moment (1896) by William Heinemann. The classic statement of this concern with atomized time, however, comes from the hand of Pater : 'Every moment,' he wrote, in *The Renaissance*, 'some form grows perfect in hand or face; some tone on the hills or the sea is choicer than the rest; some mood of passion or intellectual excitement is irresistibly real and attractive to us – for that moment only. . . . Not to discriminate every moment some passionate attitude to those about us, and in the very brilliancy of their gifts some tragic dividing of forces on their ways, is, on this short day of frost and sun, to sleep before evening.' Fearing that these sentences 'might possibly mislead some of those young men into whose hands it might fall', Pater removed the famous 'Conclusion' in the second edition of his book – only to reprint it, with some minor modifications, in the third! The harm, however, was already done. These few sentences, as Graham Hough observes, 'by painting a picture of dissolution and fluidity . . . set the emotional tone for what is to follow.'[98]

For all that Pater talked about 'the living moment', it was generally the living moment in the past. The chapter entitled 'Modernity' from his unfinished novel *Gaston de Latour* (1896) turns out to be an account of the impact of Ronsard's *Odes* on the debonair sixteenth-century squire who is his hero. 'Just eighteen years old, and the work of the poet's own youth, it took possession of Gaston with the ready intimacy of one's equal in age, fresh at every point; and he experienced what it is the function of contemporary poetry to effect anew for sensitive youth in each succeeding generation.'

The contemporary moment of Pater's own day was something which he shyly avoided in most of his purely imaginary studies – *The Child in the House*,[99] a disguised piece of autobiography and *Emerald Uthwart*,[100] a disguised and idealized homosexual portrait, being the only noticeable exceptions. And even when, in his critical writings, he takes a theme such as *Aesthetic Poetry*,[101] it is the medieval aspect and imagery of Pre-Raphaelitism which he stresses and not some less archaic element in contemporary verse.

[98] *The Last Romantics*
[99] *Miscellaneous Studies*, 1895
[100] *Ibid*
[101] *Appreciations*, 1889

But if Pater fought shy of focusing imagination on his own times, his younger disciples felt no such qualms. Reviewing Arthur Symons' first book of verse,[102] dedicated to him, Pater remarked that 'Mr Symons' themes are almost exclusively those of the present day, studied, as must needs happen with a very young writer, rather through literature than life.'[103] Perhaps it was because Pater believed that the substance, say, of Symons' 'The Opium-Smoker' had been 'studied . . . rather through literature than life' that he was able to endorse the volume publicly. Pater, as a thinker, was a morally dissolvant force, but he was also a very cautious man.

This make-believe, or comfortable way-out, concerning his disciples' ethical convictions, was not always vouchsafed to Pater. George Moore, for example, had gone on record autobiographically in his *Confessions of a Young Man* (1888). Here, therefore the convenient sophistry of a drama 'studied . . . rather through literature than life' could not apply. Pater accordingly wrote as follows : 'My Dear, Audacious Moore, – Many thanks for the *Confessions*, which I have read with great interest, and admiration for your originality – your delightful criticisms – your Aristophanic joy, or at least enjoyment, in life – your unfailing liveliness. Of course, there are many things in the book I don't agree with. . . . What I cannot doubt is the literary faculty displayed. "Thou cans't in such a questionable shape !" I feel inclined to say, on finishing your book : "shape" morally, I mean, not in reference to style. . . .' 'A delightful letter,' commented Moore, for whom any nice distinction between his own 'homme-moyen-sensuel-ism' and Pater's 'New Cyrenaicism' would largely be lost. Moore's Pater was the master of the sentence, the virtuoso of the semi-colon, not the subtle pseudo-traditionalist with a chill and penetrating insight into the destructive new doctrines of relativity.

Swinburne – another precursor and culture-hero of the men of the 'nineties – likewise lacked the 'modern imagination'. Living in an alcohol-stimulated dream-world with Mary Queen of Scots, Cathy Linton, Anatoria, Faustine and other 'belles Romans', the discipline of 'the holy fact',[104] which makes for a just presentation of the external world of one's day, was something he would have

---

[102] *Days and Nights*, 1889
[103] 'A Poet with Something to Say' (*Pall Mall Gazette*, 23 March 1889)
[104] *Descent into Hell* by Charles Williams

scorned to acquire. He was more interested in Dolores, a mental succubus and 'fair in the fearless old fashion',[105] than in Ada Mencken, the actual bare-backed rider with whom he had a brief liaison.

Anything like a critical statement on the nature of modernity in literature is first fully found in Arthur Symons, whose poetical practice exemplifies his theory. It is W. E. Henley whom he selects as illustrating the quality of 'modernity in verse'. 'There is,' he tells us, 'something revolutionary about all Henley's work; the very titles, the very existence, of his poems may be taken as a sort of manifesto on behalf of what is surely a somewhat new art, the art of modernity in verse. In the *London Voluntaries*, for instance, what a sense of the poetry of cities, that saner than pastoral poetry, the romance of what lies beneath our eyes, in the humanity of streets, if we have but the vision and the point of view! Here, at last, is a poet who can so enlarge the limits of his verse as to take in London. And I think that might be the test of poetry which professes to be modern: its capacity for dealing with London, with what one sees or might see there, indoors and out.'[106] Pater had written the prose-poetry of 'Beata Urbs'[107] in Roman days. Symons, taking up in his verse where Henley had left off, wrote the poetry of our own capital by no means always beautiful. Instead of Henley's London 'at the golden end of October afternoons, London cowering in Winter under the Wind-Fiend out of the poisonous east, London in all the ecstasy of Spring,'[108] he gave us 'the London of nights, the London of artificiality and of flickering gas-light.'[109] One change which Symons made in his approach to the metropolis was to drop the 'grand style' which Henley had employed and use a less literary diction, inserting here and there a well-chosen colloquialism:

> The little bed-room papered red,
> The gas's faint malodorous light,
> And one beside me in the bed,
> Who chatters, chatters half the night.[110]

[105] 'Dolores' (*Poems and Ballads*, 1865)
[106] 'Modernity in Verse' (*Studies in Two Literatures*, 1897)
[107] *Marius the Epicurean*, 1885
[108] *Arthur Symons: A Critical Biography* by Roger Lhombreaud, 1963
[109] *Ibid*
[110] 'Leves Amores II' (*London Nights*, 1895)

Another change accomplished by Symons was to step up the pace of the verse. Henley's *London Voluntaries* progress often by long loaded lines. Here, for example, is his description of the National Gallery :

> The dingy dreariness of the picture-place,
> Turned very nearly bright,
> Takes on a luminous transciency of grace,
> And shows no more a scandal to the ground.[111]

Compare this with a stanza from Symons' *City Nights: In the Train* :

> Night, and the rush of the train,
> A cloud of smoke through the town,
> Scaring the life of the streets;
> And the leap of the heart again,
> Out into the night, and down
> The dazzling vista of streets.[112]

which gives the effect of a travelling eye – a sort of mobile impressionism.

'To be modern in poetry,' continues Symons, 'to represent really oneself and one's surroundings . . . is perhaps the most difficult, as it is certainly the most interesting, of all artistic achievements.'[113] Symons notes that the other arts have attained their great modern representations, and looks to poetry to discover for itself an equivalent of these achievements. 'In music,' he suggests, 'the modern soul seems to have expression in Wagner; in painting it may be said to have taken form and colour in Manet, Degas, and Whistler; in sculpture, has it not revealed itself in Rodin?'[114] At first, one may ask what there is in common between the mystic sensualism of Wagner, the formal naturalism of Manet, the dynamic titanism of Rodin. Does their 'modernity' consist in the fact that their creations were merely contemporaries? Much as it appears so, reflection discovers a common denominator in the *impact* which these artists make, for all their difference in media and technique. This impact is more *immediate*, more present to the nerves and

[111] *London Voluntaries*, 1893
[112] *Silhouettes*
[113] 'Modernity in Verse' (*Studies in Two Literatures*)
[114] *Ibid*

42

imagination, more sensuously charged, atmospherically dense. In words which D. H. Lawrence was later to employ, the 'modernity' of these figures constitutes an art of 'the incarnate moment, the moment . . . the immediate present, the Now.'[115] Less ejaculatively, Pater puts it thus: 'The essence of all good style, whatever its accidents may be, is expressiveness;'[116] and Wagner, Manet, Degas, Whistler and Rodin, in their differing media, through diverse techniques, were seeking an expressiveness which depended, in the last resort, upon a greater sensuous appeal.

VII

Baudelaire plus Pre-Raphaelitism – the Aesthetic Movement in English poetry. These constituent influences meet in the person and work of Swinburne.

The poet's encounter with Pre-Raphaelitism occurred in the autumn of 1857. 'It was blue summer then, and always morning, and the air sweet and full of bells.' This is how Edward Burne-Jones describes the months from August to December 1857, 'when D. G. Rossetti and his disciples came down to Oxford to fresco the walls of the Union debating hall. In October young Algernon Swinburne came up for the fall term of his second year at Oxford, and on November 1 he met Rossetti, Burne-Jones, and Morris in the rooms of a friend. A few days later he went to the debating hall to watch the work.'[117]

The combination of the two prosperous undergraduates Burne-Jones and William Morris with Rossetti and his tribe of disciples resulted in what one might call a second wave of Pre-Raphaelitism. And this time, the exotic, medieval, and 'romantic' elements clearly preponderated over the naturalistic which the Pre-Raphaelite Brotherhood (by then dissolved) had earlier featured. It was certainly the archaic and subjective notes in this more technicolour Pre-Raphaelitism which appealed to Swinburne. As Barbara Charlesworth remarks of the young poet at Oxford: 'He was brought into [the Pre-Raphaelite] company immediately and dubbed "Little Carrots" [because of his aureole of red hair], and since he could not

---

[115] *New Poems*: preface to the American edition, New York 1920
[116] 'Style' (*Appreciations*)
[117] *Dark Passages: The Decadent Consciousness in Victorian Literature* by Barbara Charlesworth, U.S.A. 1965

paint even so much as a medieval animal, he set himself to the writing of Arthurian romances and border ballads.'[118]

By 1862, he was frolicking madly in the 'new Rossetti ménage at Tudor House, 16 Cheyne Walk, Chelsea, where he found installed as fellow-lodgers W. M. Rossetti, Gabriel's brother, and George Meredith, Ruskin's offer to join them having been deftly side-tracked'.[119] Along with Dante Gabriel's wife Elizabeth (who had been replaced in her husband's desires by William Morris's dark-haired spouse Jane) the house also owned to the constant presence of Fanny Cornforth (the original of 'Jenny') who possessed a prior claim on the poet. Through the house and round the garden (crammed with its strange menagerie of opossum, chameleon, wombat, armadillo, salamander, peacock, and prize white bull, whose eyes reminded D.G. of Janey Morris's), Swinburne raved and racketed, often without a stitch on him chasing Simeon Solomon – the Jewish P. R. painter, rich, fair, and handsome – in like condition.

When not disporting himself in this athletic manner, he was accumulating the verses to be featured in his 'infamous' *Poems and Ballads* (1865), which Ruskin, Rossetti, and William Bell Scott had all pleaded with him to tone down. 'I have just added,' he wrote to Charles Howell – rogue and Pre-Raphaelite P.R.O. – 'yet four more jets of boiling and gushing infamy to the perennial and poisonous fountain of Dolores.'[120]

Swinburne's attitude to his own sadistic and erotic poems was often ambiguous. While writing one of his now largely unreadable 'nationally useful' poems, 'A Song of Italy'[121] he – 'the libidinous laureate of a pack of satyrs'[122] – spoke of his venereal fantasies to William Rossetti as 'jokes and perversities'.[123]

The venereal fantasies of Baudelaire, however, were never treated by Swinburne as 'jokes'. Perhaps this was because the venereal realities in the French poet-out-number the fantasies by five to one.

---

[118] *Ibid*

[119] *A Swinburne Anthology*: Biographical Introduction by Kenelm Foss, 1955

[120] *Letters* ed. Cecil Y. Lang. 6 vols. New Haven, 1959–62

[121] *Songs before Sunrise*, 1871

[122] John Morley's anonymous review of *Poems and Ballads* in *The Saturday Review*, 4 August 1865

[123] *A Swinburne Anthology*

Introduction

In an article which introduced *Les Fleurs du Mal* to English readers, Swinburne spoke of Baudelaire's 'perfect workmanship which makes every subject admirable and respectable'.[124] It is this manner-before-matter mode of argument which distinguishes aestheticism and art-for-art's-sake.

In 1866 a rumour reached London that Baudelaire was dead. (He was in fact to die the next year.) Swinburne responded to this news with his elegy *Ave Atque Vale*,[125] a dignified and moving tribute to a man he deeply admired and believed in. As in his prose, so in his verse, Swinburne was often a discerning though diffuse critic. *Ave Atque Vale* follows the poet's familiar pattern of over-writing and under-thinking. It does, however, contain a short passage which strikingly focuses upon Baudelaire's great superiority to all his French or English disciples :

> Thou sawest, in thine old singing season, brother,
> Secrets and sorrows unbeheld of us.[126]

The penetration of Baudelaire's vision derived from two powerful faculties in the poet : an unillusioned analytic mind and a deep moral imagination. This latter quality had nothing to do with the prudential ethics or the optimism of evolutionary hopes to which Browning and Tennyson adjusted their genius with deft circumspection. Because there were neither 'words of comfort' nor vulgar hints towards 'self-help' in the poet, Baudelaire was not taken to be a 'serious' author by the English reading public. Equally, those English poets who sought to transplant his 'evil flowers' appreciated only one aspect of his imagination. Swinburne set the fashion for this in his 1862 review of *Les Fleurs du Mal*: 'Throughout the chief part of this book he has chosen to dwell mainly upon sad and strange things – the weariness of pain and the bitterness of pleasure – the perverse happiness and wayward sorrows of exceptional people. It has the languid and lurid beauty of close and threatening weather – a heavy heated temperature with dangerous hot-house scents in it; thick shadows of cloud above it, and the fire of molten light.'[127] This answers very well to the prose-poem descriptiveness

[124] *Spectator*, 6 September 1862
[125] *Poems and Ballads*: Second Series, 1878
[126] *Ibid*
[127] *Spectator*, 6 December 1862

45

in which English critics for decades to come were to picture Baudelaire's poetry: a secular hell presented in terms of a claustrophobic conservatory – forerunner of Sartre's hermetic *Huis Clos.*

The Baudelaire who discussed the nature of 'the comic in the plastic arts'[128] in the context of the Fall of Man would have sorely puzzled and tried poor Swinburne, possessed, as he was, of only two gifts: a superb and certain ear and a highly cerebralized sensuality.

In like limited fashion, the poet Symons tends to associate Baudelaire solely with clandestine sex:

> One petal of a blood-red tulip pressed
> Between the pages of a Baudelaire:
> No more; and I was suddenly aware
> Of the white fragrant apple of a breast
> On which my lips were pastured. . . .[129]

In part the weakness of the English 'nineties comes from their poets taking Verlaine, not Baudelaire as their example. Symons' deeply influential book *The Symbolist Movement in Literature* (1899) contains no study of Baudelaire, though it goes back to such earlier Romantics as Gerard de Nerval. (When Symons did publish writings on the French poet – *Baudelaire: His Prose and Poetry,* with translations, 1919; *Charles Baudelaire: A Study,* 1925; *The Letters of Charles Baudelaire to his Mother,* 1928 – he had waited too long. Like Baudelaire, he had felt pass over him 'the wind from the wing of imbecility',[130] presaging his breakdown in 1908, followed by a spell in a mental asylum, and long slow convalescence. Although he recovered, wrote and published much, his powers of thought and composition were never quite the same again.)

No better epitaph on the English 'nineties, in their failure to understand Baudelaire, could be found than Symons' last book of verse *Jezebel Mort,* published in 1931. The French poet features again and again, obsessively, maniacally, along with Verlaine, Christ and Satan, his cat Setebos, and a long-remembered unnamed mistress – the 'Bianca' – 'Lydia' of his poems:

[128] *On the Essence of Laughter,* 1855
[129] 'Hallucination: I' (*London Nights,* 1895)
[130] *My Heart Laid Bare*

When in the darkness we were hidden
What poison were we drunken of?
The poison of acts that are forbidden. . . .[131]

To receive Baudelaire in this fashion as a psychedelic stimulant, an aphrodisiac, is not enough.

The first-wave Pre-Raphaelites – the artists of the P.R.B. – were morally high-toned and predominantly Christian, being quite considerably influenced by the Christian painters of the German Nazarene Movement. Baudelaire, as has been implied, possessed the theological imagination and mind, working out his problems within the context of a Christian, if somewhat Manichean vision. Swinburne – 'an unclean imp . . . all aflame with the feverish carnality of a school-boy over the dirtiest passages of Lemprière'[132] – had not the depth or discipline of mind to comprehend Baudelaire's arguments. As Barbara Charlesworth rightly remarks, 'He had the incapacity for ideas of a genuine Barbarian [Arnold's term for the philistine English aristocrat] . . . causes not ideas interested him.'[133] Baudelaire, for Swinburne, was clearly a cause – something to be enthused about, not someone to be understood.

Whereas the first Pre-Raphaelites were Christian, Swinburne was a much-proclaimed pagan. The basis of his Hellenism, intellectually, was his study of Greek at Eton and Oxford. Temperamentally, however, his vision of Greece was more coloured by the cult of plastic beauty – Gautier's visual paganism – than by any expositions from Jowett at Balliol. And here the, at times, pagan décor of Baudelaire must have excited him also. Baudelaire of *The Pagan's Prayer* ('Voluptuousness, be thou ever my queen'); Baudelaire, with his lesbian lover – his *Femmes damnées*; Baudelaire, who loved 'those naked antique ages'[134] – all these would appeal to the erethistic poet.

Swinburne took the basically Dantean 'machinery' of Christian-ized Platonic love as presented in Rossetti's version of the *Vita Nuova* (published by him in translation, 1861) or in his imaginative portrait *Beata Beatrix* (painted a year after his wife's death), and paganized the feeling and content. By 'paganized' I imply, here,

---

[131] 'Stanzas' (*Jezebel Mort*), 1931
[132] John Morley: *The Saturday Review*, 4 August 1865
[133] *Dark Passages*
[134] *J'aime le souvenir de ces époques nues*

'degraded'. Lucien Pissarro declared that Rossetti 'painted "senti-ments" '[135] while Swinburne thought of his own *Poems and Ballads* as 'studies of passion and sensation'. The 'passions' which he studied were those of a sadistic and masochistic order as they apply to erotic experience : the 'sensations', those of the flogger or the flogged (already, before leaving Oxford, he was the author of two privately-printed works of fiction : *Lady Bum-tickler's Revels* and *The Whippingham Papers*).

In Baudelaire, he took the part for the whole, having acquired a copy of the French poet's *Les Epaves* on a visit to Paris while on vacation. *Les Epaves*, as the title suggests, were 'waif-and-stray' poems from *Les Fleurs du Mal*, excluded because of their erotic content. It was in the light of these poems that Swinburne read most of Baudelaire's work. Just as Swinburne de-spiritualized Rossetti, so he de-Christianized Baudelaire. Because of the spell of his incantatory rhythms (which, as Saintsbury recalled 'simply swept us off our legs with rapture'[136]) the Aesthetic Movement of the 'seventies had to accord him a place in its art-for-art's-sake pantheon. Aesthetic objectivity was the high aim of this school. Swinburne's rhythms more readily suggested daemonic possession than plastic beauty, and to accommodate this poet to their ranks, the artists of the Aesthetic Movement were forced to defend, as part of their programme, a position of moral indifferentism. From Swinburne, the way lay open to Wilde : 'the artist is the creator of beautiful things. . . . No artist has ethical sympathies. An ethical sympathy in an artist is an unpardonable mannerism of style.'[137]

VIII

The sociological factors involved in the acceptance and recognition of the Pre-Raphaelite Movement have seldom been considered. We know that, by 1863, Rossetti 'now society's pet as a painter, was making £4,000 a year',[138] and Professor Hough tells us that 'Rossetti, Hunt and their fellows sold their pictures to the new business magnates,'[139] particularly in the industrial towns of the Midlands and the North. He notes, too, that such transactions make

[135] *Rossetti* by Lucien Pissarro (n.d.)
[136] *A Swinburne Anthology*, selected by Kenelm Foss
[137] *The Picture of Dorian Gray* : the preface
[128] *A Swinburne Anthology*, selected by Kenelm Foss
[139] *The Last Romantics*

for 'an excellent illustration of the paradoxical nature of the movement – for pre-Raphaelitism was in part a protest against towns like
Liverpool, yet it was gladly welcomed by them.'[140]

Quentin Bell, in his Slade Lectures at Oxford, observed that 'the
"hard-edge" school of Pre-Raphaelitism had become well established
and was exerting a powerful influence upon British painting by
1860',[141] and that, three years earlier, Rossetti had launched a
second wave of the movement when decorating the Oxford Union
– a more exotic variation of the original P.R.B. *putsch* and one even
more financially remunerative.

An assessment which interestingly summarizes the social-economic
causes of this success was made by the contemporary critic F. H. W.
Myers on the occasion of a posthumous exhibition of Rossetti's
pictures at Burlington House in 1883. His essay 'Rossetti and the
religion of Beauty'[142] – 'written from a point of view of by no means
exclusive sympathy with the movement' – begins by admitting to
'a new strain of thought and emotion within the pale of our artistic
orthodoxy'. Myers agrees that though 'many critics, whose ethical
point of view demands respect, continue to find in Rossetti's works
an enigma not worth the pains of solution, and to decry them as
obscure, fantastic, or even as grossly immoral in tendency . . .
assuredly the "aesthetic movement" is not a mere fashion of the
day – the modish pastime of nincompoops and charlatans.' Myers'
testimony is the more of importance because it is delivered from a
position which is neither that of the *Punch*-drunk philistine nor
the posturing 'greenery-yallery' *avant-garde*. Myers is in line with
the moral-approach-to-art mid-Victorian critics, and exemplifies the
uneasiness of the largely traditional humanists when confronted
with the new art-for-art's-sake phenomenon.

He considers, first, the changes in society making for a new
popularity of art. 'We have . . . only,' he tells us, 'to look around . . .
to perceive that – whether or not the conditions of the modern
world are favourable to artistic *excellence* – all the main forces of
civilization are tending towards artistic *activity*. The increase of
wealth, the diffusion of education, the gradual decline of the
military, the hieratic, the aristocratic ideals – each of these causes

[140] *Ibid*
[141] *Victorian Artists*, 1967
[142] *Essays: Modern* by F. H. W. Myers, 1897

removes some obstacles from the artist's path or offers some fresh prize to his endeavours. Art has outlived both the Puritans and the Inquisition; she is no longer deadened by the spirit of self-mortification, nor enslaved by a jealous orthodoxy. The increased wealth of the world makes the artist's life stable and secure, while it sets free a surplus income so large that an increasing share of it must almost necessarily be diverted to some form of aesthetic expenditure.'

Myers notes that, here, but more particularly in America, 'a need is felt of some kind of social distinction – some new aristocracy – based on differences other than those of birth and wealth.' He believes that the artist and the art-nourished minority may come to form this 'new aristocracy' – an *'optimacy* of passion and genius . . . which is coming into existence as a cosmopolitan gentility among the confused and fading class-distinctions of the past'.

All this strikingly, reflectively, corroborates what Max Beerbohm had so casually chronicled in his picture of society in 1880 : 'It was felt that the aristocracy could not live by good-breeding alone. The old delights seemed vapid, waxen. Something vivid was desired. And so the sphere of fashion converged with the sphere of art, and revolution was the result.'[143]

The essence of Pre-Raphaelite appeal, however, lay in the nourishment it offered to the forces of feminism. 'In this renaissance,' noted Max, 'the keenest students of the exquisite were women.'[144] Rossetti's art – both in painting and poetry – coincided with, and assisted at, the birth of a new feminine type : sensitive, cultivated, very largely leisured, and educated as never before. 'The steady rise in the status of women,' observed Myers, 'that constant deepening and complication of the commerce between the sexes which is one of the signs of progressive civilization; all this is perpetually teaching and preaching . . . the powers of womanhood to all sections of the community.'[145] Not unnaturally, this new womanhood welcomed an art which showed her in its mirror as an infinitely interesting being : elusive, intense, mysterious, the subject of a worshipping cult.

Myers rightly describes Rossetti's paintings as 'the sacred pictures

[143] '1880' (*Works*)
[144] *Ibid*
[145] *Essays: Modern*

of a new religion; forms and faces which bear the same relation to that mystical worship of beauty . . . as the forms and faces of a Francia or a Leonardo bear to the medieval mysteries of the worship of Mary or of Christ.'[146] These esoteric icons of a subtle feminism, created by a desirous male mind, fascinated numerous women, who thereupon set about the task of reproducing in their own persons the charm which confronted them on the painter's canvas. As Myers observed of Rossetti's picture-types : 'All . . . have something in common, some union of strange and puissant physical loveliness with depth and remoteness of gaze. They range from demon to angel – as such names may be interpreted in a Religion of Beauty – from Lilith, whose beauty is destruction, and Astarte, throned between the Sun and the Moon in her sinister splendour, to the *Blessed Damozel* and the maiden "pre-elect type", type of the love whose look regenerates and whose assumption lifts to heaven. But all have the look – characteristic of Rossetti's faces as the mystic smile of Leonardo's – the look which bids the spectator murmur –

> What netherworld gulf-whispers does she hear,
> In answering echoes from the planisphere,
> Along the wind, along the estuary?'[147]

In this passage, one is given the two grounds of appeal which Rossetti's feminine images possessed : first, a distinctive physical comeliness stamped with no obvious 'come-hither' allure; and, secondly, a supra-physical characteristic – the suggestion of commerce with 'the other world' whether of angels or of demons. Such a portrayal of feminine power and appeal naturally enough flattered the women who felt the dimension of the self, their armoury of means, increased by such study.

The impact of 'the Pre-Raphaelite women' on a young distinguished stranger to these shores is beautifully described in the following passage of a letter from Henry James, newly arrived in London, to his sister Alice. He had been with friends to visit William Morris and his wife in Queen's Square, Bloomsbury :

Oh, ma chère, such a wife ! *Je n'en reviens pas* – she haunts me still. A figure cut out of a missal – out of one of Rossetti's or Hunt's pictures – to

[146] *Ibid*
[147] *Ibid*

say this gives but a faint idea of her, because when such an image puts on flesh and blood, it is an apparition of fearful and wonderful intensity. It's hard to say whether she's a grand synthesis of all the pre-Raphaelite pictures ever made – or they a 'keen analysis' of her – whether she's an original or a copy. In either case she is a wonder. Imagine a tall lean woman in a long dress of some dead purple stuff, guiltless of hoops (or of anything else, I should say) with a mass of crisp black hair heaped into great wavy projections on each of her temples, a thin pale face, a pair of strange sad, deep, dark Swinburnian eyes, with great thick black oblique brows, joined in the middle and tucking themselves away under her hair, a mouth like the 'Oriana' in our illustrated Tennyson, a long neck, without any collar, and in lieu thereof some dozen strings of outlandish beads – in fine complete. On the wall was a nearly full-length portrait of her by Rossetti, so strange and unreal that if you hadn't seen her you'd pronounce it a distempered vision, but in fact an extremely good likeness.[148]

As Myers observed, one explanation of 'the mystery which attaches to the female form' in Rossetti is that it is 'in some way a transformation of sexual passion'.[149] The women who admired Rossetti's pictures recognized this readily. They saw their glamour, their market-value, their marriageability heightened by this art, and accordingly subscribed gladly to the cult.

But although 'the delight in beauty alloyed with appetite and strengthened by that alloy'[150] was clearly the starting-point of Rossetti's painting of women, another element was present there which gave the feminine spectator a fuller interest in herself, a higher respect for the range of her effects. To Rossetti, remarks Myers, 'his beloved seems not as herself alone, "but as the meaning of all things that are," her voice recalls a prenatal memory, and her eyes "dream against a distant goal" '.[151] To the strong but refined sexual attraction, which Rossetti's female appreciators discovered in his painting of their likenesses, there was added this rarer appeal – the sense of woman as a vehicle of the divine; a creature affording man the means of identification with the cosmos. Rossetti's paintings thus constituted a splendid advertisement for

[148] To Miss Alice Fanes, 10 March 1869. *The Letters of Henry James*, selected and edited by Percy Lubbock, 1920
[149] *Essays: Modern*
[150] *Ibid*
[151] *Ibid*

woman. To employ the language of the cinema, this was a double-feature programme.

Physically, Rossetti's women were 'stunners' (the current Pre-Raphaelite slang), their sensuous attributes rendered with a haunting tactile fascination by Rossetti. As Edward Lucie-Smith tells us, 'his picture "The Blue Bower" was praised by a critic in *The Athenaeum* for "the marvellous fleshliness of the flesh!"' Swinburne described "Sibylla Palmfera" as "ripe and firm of flesh", and used very similar language, for that matter, about Rossetti's poetry, saying of it that "no nakedness could be more harmonious, more consummate in its fleshly sculpture".'[152] Psychologically, his women were enigmas; ideally intriguing, not the least to their own sex. The common assumption has been that they were the nineteenth-century counterparts of Dante's Beatrice – loving guides through some inner purgatory up towards the mountain-top of light; and it is certainly the Italian poet's *Vita Nouva* which provided Rossetti with the basis of his iconography, both in painting and in verse. Quentin Bell, in his Oxford Slade Lectures, has wittily refuted this assumption, however. He considers Rossetti, at first, as 'essentially decorative and liturgical'. About the second term he admits to having misgivings. ' "Devotional",' he writes, 'might have been better but Rossetti is not exactly devout. He believes in nothing and yet he is altogether enchanted by the act of worship. . . . Rossetti looks for a shrine on which he can lavish all his art and all his ingenuity, the deity of which, Mary, Beatrice, Guinevere, Astarte Syriaca, is so protean as to be non-existent. He is not religious but he is profoundly mythophiliac. His cult makes no demands either on faith or on morality, it implies no articles of belief and no rules of conduct. It is the religion of a man who wants something passionately and can only express his wants by way of incantation. What Rossetti wanted, to put it crudely, was girls.'[153]

Having performed a Strachey-like autopsy on the legend of Rossetti's spirituality, Quentin Bell presses on, beyond the stage of debunking, to reach some more subtle truth on the far side. 'But that [the fact he 'wanted girls'] is to put it much too crudely, for in Rossetti the hearty commonsensical carnality which leads him to

---

[152] *Dante Gabriel Rossetti* by Edward Lucie-Smith (*The Listener*, 15 June 1967)
[153] *Victorian Artists*

find such names as Guggums and Jumbo for his various "stunners", is balanced by an opposite tendency to relegate them to the "Gold Bar of Heaven" – in some of his drawings they seem almost sexless, almost ghostlike, it is the face not the body, that captures our attention.'[154]

Strange as it may seem, this interpretation of the attitude behind the paintings explains, not why Rossetti failed, but why he succeeded with the art-loving public. The Victorians did *not* want fresh versions of Beatrician love on the Dantean model. They *did* want, however, in the 'sixties and 'seventies, an *erotic* passion *romantically* expressed. They were quite prepared that this should bear all the appearance of a religion of beauty spiritualized into a beatific dream',[155] provided that the beautitude proved upon examination to be the envelope of physical bliss. Rossetti's paintings solved the dilemma : how to be sensual *and* refined.

IX

The intention of Myers in writing his essay on *Rossetti and the Religion of Beauty* was to exorcize the Movement – to sprinkle all its visionally amorous totems with the holy water of Platonic humanism. About this task, he was not quite happy. 'This aesthetic paradise of the well-to-do might,' he conceded, prove impermanent, 'something to be convulsed by an invasion from the rough world without' (a conjecture which the Boer Wars showed to be correct). *Fin-de-siècle* aestheticism died to such jingoistic strains as 'Good-bye Dolly' and Kipling's 'The Absent-minded Beggar'. (He had already knocked aetheticism hard – hard, that is, by philistine standards – in 'The Mary Gloster' in 1894. The dying self-made ship-owner is speaking to his son :

> The things I knew was proper you wouldn't thank me to give,
> And the things I knew was written you said was the way to live.
> For you muddled with books and pictures, an' china an' ethchin's
> and fans;
> And your rooms at college was beastly – more like a whore's than a
> man's.)

Again, Myers was not certain 'what encouragement the moralist

[154] *Ibid*
[155] *Ibid*

can find in this counter-wave of art and mysticism'.[156] Place Rossetti's poems beside those of Sidney or Lovelace, and, he declared, they 'seem the expression of a century which is refining itself into quietism and mellowing into decay'.

But if Myers was troubled with doubts and suspicions, he also proved unperceptive. 'There is,' he wrote of Rossetti's work, 'no trace in him of this deliberate worship of Baal and Ashtoreth; no touch of the cruelty which is the characteristic note of natures in which the sexual instincts have become haunting and dominant.'[157] This is certainly to see only what one wishes; for nothing is clearer in Rossetti's painting than the change which occurs in the female image. It is a transition from docility ('Ecce Ancilla Domine', 1850), from beatific exaltation ('Beata Beatrix', 1863), from wistful sadness ('The Bower Meadow', finished 1872), to baleful beauty ('Astarte Syriaca', 1877), and sultry narcissism ('The Bower Meadow', 1883).

Arthur Symons, in his essay on *The Rossettis*,[158] noticed the change which came over the painter. 'As his intentions overpower him,' he wrote, 'as he became the slave and no longer the master of his dreams [steeped in chloryl, Symons might have added], his pictures became no longer symbolic. They become idols. Venus growing more and more Asiatic as the moon's crescent begins to glitter above her head, and her name changes from Aphrodite into Astarte, loses all the freshness of the waves from which she was born, and her own sorcery hardens into a wooden image painted to be the object of savage worship.' Rossetti's dreams, concludes Symons, 'are no longed content to be turned into walking realities . . . but . . . remain lunar, spectral, a dark and unintelligible menace.'

For Symons, with the smallest store of self-knowledge and his own 'fatal initiation'[159] into madness, the 'menace might well seem unintelligible'. For our own post-Freudian ear, however, the menace is quite lucidly located. To the guilty and remorseful middle-ageing amourist, eroticism and the feminine image are becoming synonymous with danger and destruction. All of Rossetti's visual indica-

---

[156] 'Rossetti and the Religion of Beauty' (*Essays: Modern*)
[157] *Ibid*
[158] *Dramatis Personae*, 1923, U.S.A.
[159] *Arthur Symons: A critical Biography by Roger Lhombreaud*

tions meet in the unfinished poem 'The Orchard Pit'[160] – a poem
which carried forward the *femme fatale-vampire-succubus* presence
of Keats' 'La Belle Dame' and Coleridge's 'Christabel', details from
which appear in 'The Orchard Pit'. The significant images, however, establish a clear connection between the notion of woman and
death. This is how Rossetti describes the siren who sings to him
from 'the screening apple-branch' above the pit in the orchard :

> Life's eyes are gleaming from her forehead fair,
>> And from her breasts to the ravishing eyes of Death.

and this is how he envisages the destructive-erotic process :

> My love I call her, and she loves me well;
>> But I love her as in the maelstrom's cup
> The whirled stone loves the leaf inseparable
> That clings to it round all the circling swell
> And that the last same eddy swallows up.

What we find in Rossetti's work is the emergence of a *darkling
Venus* – a feminine image moving from the benign to the malign,
the submissive to the devouring. Nor was this developing image one
which was personal to Rossetti alone. 'The second generation of
Pre-Raphaelites is haunted by a female figure – by a feminine
principle,' Quentin Bell remarks '– which dominates Rossetti's work
and the work of his disciple Burne-Jones, and through them their
followers', who included Simeon Solomon and Aubrey Beardsley.

Quentin Bell has commented on the paradox in Burne-Jones'
work. On the one hand, its high-mindedness, on the other, its
'repulsive' and 'shockingly indecent' characteristics. The *Pygmalion*
sequence of frescoes in Birmingham, he describes as 'a kind of
hymn to sexuality in art. The sculptor creates an image of marble,
he adores it and the goddess turns it into a real live woman – made
of soap. Pygmalion is also made of soap and one recoils at the idea
of their sad, cold, slimy, saponaceous embraces. . . . Burne-Jones's
purity is negative, he is so horribly anxious *not* to be impure, he is
determined that everything shall be kept on the elevated plane of
High Art and it is precisely this anxiety which produces an overwhelmingly prurient effect.'[161]

This nullifying contradiction in Burne-Jones's work (a desire to

[160] *Poems* ed. Oswald Doughty, 1957
[161] *Victorian Artists*

express beauty in terms of the erotic negated by an insistence on ladylike gentility) is described by Quentin Bell as 'one of the diseases of the century, particularly of the mid-century'. Another way of putting this would be to say that Burne-Jones resisted the sensibility of his time. The most effective artists working within the convention of second-wave Pre-Raphaelitism succumbed to an image of the *darkling Venus*. It is the explicit or sensed presence of this which gives to their productions a psychological unity, an atmospheric haunting. In rejecting the call of Venus Pandemos, Burne-Jones – for all his technical talents – emasculated and nullified his expression.

No such negation bound, for long, the more sensitized imagination of Beardsley. The more fully he yields up his fancy to portraying a darkling Venus, the more his art gains in malefic charm and power. As I noted on another occasion, 'looking through his work one sees the seraphic Burne-Jones type of woman, deriving from Botticelli, in the process of becoming, via Rossetti, the satanic. One can trace this development from the early 'Adoremus Te', with its dark-haired angel creature with a zither, through the 'Head with a Wreath of Grapes and Vine Leaves' with the large half-closed eyes and puffy lower lids, its well-shaped but camel nose, and full bottom lip, to 'The Snare of Vintage', where the women with their towering grape-decked coiffures, eager and predatory, have caught their startled male victims; 'Messalina returning from the Bath', the study of a heavy-thewed maenad with a lowering look of pent-up lust on her face, completes the stages of feminine sensuality,'[162] as portrayed in this artist's work.

The darkling Venus is an image discovered readily in the drama, fiction and poetry of the 'eighties and 'nineties. Wilde's Salome ('daughter of Sodom', 'daughter of an incestuous mother'), with her obsessive and repetitive refrain 'I will kiss thy mouth, Jokanaan, I will kiss thy mouth,' represents the darkling Venus to perfection. The erotic chimera in Wilde's poem 'The Sphinx' (1894) – 'half woman and half animal' – is another, even more fantastic symbol of the same presence. The short stories of Ella D'Arcy and George Egerton both abound in figures of the destructive woman.[163] In

[162] *Aubrey Beardsley's Erotic Universe* with an introduction and illustrations selected by Derek Stanford, 1967
[163] *Short Stories of the 'Nineties: A Biographical Anthology* edited by Derek Stanford, 1968

George Moore's first experimental autobiography she features as 'the Lilith of old', 'a terrible malady', 'the woman of thirty'. Of the relationship of this being with 'the young man of refined man', Moore concludes, 'she shall haunt his wife's face and words (should he seek to rid himself of her by marriage), a bitter-sweet, a half-welcome enchantment; she shall consume and destroy the strength and spirit of his life, leaving it desolation, a barren landscape, burnt out and faintly scented with the sea. Fame and wealth shall slip like sand from him. She may be set aside for the cadence of a rhyme, for the flowing line of a limb, but when the passion of art has raged itself out she shall return to blight the peace of the worker.'[164]

X

In the imagination of the 'nineties, the darkling Venus is complemented by another image – that of Ganymede.

The image of Ganymede is stamped over most of Wilde's later work, and was recognized as such. What was by no means recognized, however, in all its plenary physical detail, was much the same image in Walt Whitman's verse. That Whitman was of great importance to men of letters from Rossetti to the 'nineties can be seen by the names of just these few writers who devoted an essay or study to his work: William Michael Rossetti'[165] Swinburne,[166] Stevenson,[167], Havelock Ellis,[168] Symonds,[169] and Wilde.[170] All these men were conscious stylists; all of them influenced in their own practice by notions deriving from the Aesthetic Movement. The attraction which these two art-minded generations felt for Whitman and his work (the work of a declared non-perfectionist) constitutes an interesting paradox. 'I round and finish little . . . and could, consistently with my scheme,'[171] the American poet cheerfully admitted; and, again, 'No one will get to my verses who insists

---

[164] *Confessions of a Young Man*, 1888
[165] *Poems of Walt Whitman*, selected and edited by W. M. Rossetti, 1868
[166] 'Whitmania' (*Studies in Prose and Poetry*), 1894
[167] 'Walt Whitman' (*Familiar Studies of Men and Books*), 1882
[168] 'Whitman' (*The New Spirit*), 1890
[169] 'Democratic Art, with special reference to Walt Whitman' (*Essays Speculative and Suggestive*), 1890
[170] 'The Gospel According to Walt Whitman' (*A Critic in Pall Mall*), 1919 and *Walt Whitman: A Study* 1893
[171] *November Boughs*

upon viewing them as a literary performance . . . or as aiming mainly towards art and aestheticism.'[172] In the light of these statements, it is surprising to hear the self-styled aesthetic impressario Wilde telling his readers that 'in his very rejection of art Walt Whitman is an artist'.[173]

On the face of it, Wilde seems to have been won by a recognition of Whitman's utmost individualism, his unashamed personalism – his *culte de moi*. Wilde, no doubt, had arrived at the point at which he regarded his life and himself as finer works of art than his writings (he put, he said, his genius into living and his talent into writing). We noted Professor Ellmann's theory that Wilde's initiation into homosexual practice in 1886 led to a quickening of his personality soon to be reflected in a number of equally quickened antinomian compositions. It is significant, then, that Wilde speaks of Whitman as 'having obtained [in his hospital nursing throughout the Civil War] the necessary stimulus for the quickening and awakening of the personal self, someday to be endowed with universality'.[174] He quotes, too, with obvious approval, the following declaration of Whitman, obviously aware how well it would fit certain features of his own existence : 'Defiant of ostensible literary and other conventions, I avowedly chant "the great pride of man in himself".'[175]

Again, he quotes Whitman as saying that '*Leaves of Grass* . . . has mainly been the out-croppings of my own emotional and other personal nature – an attempt, from first to last, to put a *Person* . . . freely, fully and truly on record'.[176] One may hazard that what excited Wilde here was Whitman's *gesture of exposure*. The fall of Wilde and his conduct at the time of the collapse of his case against Queensberry rather suggests that he was compulsively impelled to expose his own life. 'On at least two occasions,' as one writer on Wilde has remarked, 'he might have avoided the abyss that yawned before him, but he was perhaps too vain, too much the artist to turn and flee, to turn and flee from the stage. If he was egocentric, he

[172] *Ibid*
[173] 'The Gospel According to Walt Whitman' (*Pall Mall Gazette*, 25 January 1889)
[174] *Ibid*
[175] *November Boughs*
[176] *Ibid*

was also consistent, even when confronted by a hostile and jeering audience, he followed the dramaturgic rules.'[177]

Wilde, in his review of Whitman's book *November Boughs* had cited the poet as saying that '*Leaves of Grass* is avowedly the song of Sex and Amativeness, and even Animality – *though meanings that do not usually go along with these words are behind all, and will duly emerge*' [my italics]. Despite this significant passage, it is to be doubted whether the English authors who wrote upon him – with the exception of Wilde and Symonds – realized that Whitman was a pioneering poet of homosexuality. Havelock Ellis, who published an excellent study of him, in his book *The New Spirit* (1890) hardly recognized the fact. As he recounted later, in his autobiography, 'At that time I had no real practical knowledge of inborn sexual inversion of character. In every essay I had written on Walt Whitman . . . I had passed over the homosexual strain in Whitman, in a deprecatory footnote, as negligible'.[178]

But if the medically-trained 'professional' mind of Havelock Ellis missed the substance of Whitman's poetry, it was detected (and elucidated) by the 'amateur' – in both senses – mind of J. A. Symonds. The essence of his findings – in so far as he publicly expressed them – are to be discovered in chapter four and five of his book *Walt Whitman: A Study* (1893). Pre-dating Edward Carpenter's *Love's Coming of Age* by three years and *The Intermediate Sex* by fifteen, it remains – for all its hair-splitting and hedging – the first attempt by a non-scientific, humanely-cultured, nineteenth-century mind to deal with the theme of homosexual love as reflected in contemporary literature.

Other sexual instincts pressing for expression are to be seen in the images of the *hermaphrodites* and the *demi-vierge*. While the art of Simeon Solomon and Beardsley provides numerous examples of the former, its representation in literature, in this country, is exceedingly rare. On the Continent, however, its presentation flourished; and Professor Mario Praz has enumerated some of its more bizarre manifestations in the chapter entitled 'Byzantium' of his famous compendium *The Romantic Agony* (1933). A more recent examination of the theme is conducted by A. J. L. Busst in

[177] *The Works of Oscar Wilde*, edited, with an introduction by G. F. Maine, 1948
[178] *My Life*, 1940

his essay 'The Image of the Androgyne in the Nineteenth Century'.[179]

As might be expected, the *demi-vierge* is no entire stranger to our creative verse and prose, the most condensed and dramatic portrayal probably being present in Arthur Symons' poem 'Bianca':[180]

> I set my lips on hers; they close
> Into a false and phantom rose;
> Upon her thirsting lips I rain
> A flood of kisses, and in vain;
> Her lips inexorably close.
>
> Through her closed lips that cling to mine,
> Her hands that hold me and entwine,
> Her body that abandoned lies,
> Rigid with sterile ecstasies,
> A shiver knits her flesh to mine.

Then-current morality interpreted the sexual behaviour implicit in these images as constituting clear transgressions of nature. This led to their stigmatization as perverse, not in-born, patterns of conduct. The practitioners or defenders of such activities were thus led to associate 'the perverse' with 'the artificial', and 'the artificial' with art. As has been shown, it was Wilde who stage-managed this aesthetic with most brazen efficacy. 'The first duty of life,' he wrote, in an *avant-garde* Oxford magazine, 'is to be as artificial as possible. What the second duty is no one has as yet discovered.'[181]

XI

An extension of the sense of sex and of style – such, I suggested, were the characteristics of the art and literature of the 'nineties and of their reflection in the writings of its critics. By way of evidence to support the first half of my statement, I have offered certain factors and features which seem to have a bearing on the case. And now as to the second half – an extension of the sense of style.

It is easy to see, on short reflection, the connection between a sense of sex and style. Both of them represent a quickening of the

[179] *Romantic Mythologies*, edited by Ian Fletcher, 1967
[180] *London Nights*
[181] 'Phrases and Philosophies for the Use of the Young' (*Chameleon*, December 1894)

personality; a deeper, fuller, alerted awareness; a keener expressiveness of the whole being. Carefully to cultivate these two senses was, surely, in Pater's language 'To burn always with [a] hard gem-like flame.'[182] Psychologist and elegist of the 'Nineties Movement, Pater had prospectively defined the condition, the limitations of man; and based his great question of conduct upon it. 'A counted number of pulses only,' he had written in his 'Conclusion', 'is given to us of a variegated, dramatic life. How may we see in them all that is to be seen in them by the finest senses?' Pater himself had little doubt but that the answer lay in passion : 'ecstasy and sorrow of love . . . various forms of enthusiastic activity . . . [and finally] the poetic passion, the desire of beauty, the love of art for its own sake.'[183]

Cultivation of both the sense of sex and of style had been facilitated by a fresh liberating current of thought. A freer enjoyment of them both hangs upon the prevailing presence of an epicurean attitude in society. Such an attitude – slowly growing in strength from the mid-point of the century – was by no means absent in the 'nineties. The 'larger latitude'[184] concerning sex in literature is reflected, for example, in G. S. Street's essay on the duke of Buckingham. Joining in the general *avant-garde* attack on the Victorian table-leg taboo, he remarks of Buckingham's poems : 'The sum of indecency in them . . . is small; they are rather frank than gross . . . only a race essentially indelicate could have invented a delicacy that consists merely in ignoring the common facts of physical existence – a delicacy to be acquired by the coarsest and most vulgar mind in the world, and one that is in itself a mode of coarseness.'[185]

Just as there was a Puritan view-point which censored the sense of sex in writing, so too in the nineteenth century there existed a Puritan attitude to style. The 'life is real, life is earnest' school regarded style as frivolous, a mode of luxury probably suspect, a wanton and subversive *voluptas*. Nor was style solely under the ban of these moralizers of letters : the utilitarian hacks of speech looked with equally severe eye upon it. 'Depreciation of "writing",' Remy de Gourment informs us, '– that is, writing as an art – is a precaution taken from time to time by worthless writers. . . . They

[182] 'Conclusion' (*The Renaissance: Studies in Art and Poetry*) 1873
[183] *Ibid*
[184] 'Greville Fane' (1893) (*The Middle Years*, 1917)
[185] 'Zimri the Writer' (*Miniatures and Moods*, 1893)

declare that their ideas are rare enough not to need fine clothing; that the newest richest imagery is merely the veil thrown by vanity over the emptiness of the thought; that what matters, after all, is the substance and not the form, the spirit and not the letter, the thing and not the word; and they can continue like this a long time, for they have at their command a whole flock of facile commonplaces which, however, fool nobody. . . . There are two sorts of writers : the writers who write and the writers who do not write – just as there are voiceless singers and singers with voices.'[186]

The sense of sex, the sense of style : both of these brought a greater sense of immediacy into literature. A third quality making for immediacy also – particularly in the handling of ideas – was the prized Gallic element of *esprit* as reflected in wit and elegance in writing. Even the abstract-minded J. M. Robertson pays his tribute in kind to it when contributing a note on 'German Criticism' (1888). '*Esprit,*' he writes, 'is still the appanage of the French. It is not withheld, let us humbly suggest, from another neighbouring race, and it flourishes on the other side of the Atlantic among a population certainly well dashed with German; but the united Fatherland continues to present to literary Europe that colossal simplicity of literary method which presumably moved Abbé Bouhours to raise his celebrated problem ['whether it is possible for a German to have *esprit*'].'

German influences in literature and thought had dominated English cultural life to well beyond the first half of the century. The great reputation of Goethe and Schiller, of the writers associated with the *Aufklarung,* followed by those of the *Sturm und Stress*; the intensive Germanizing work of Coleridge, de Quincey and Carlyle; the fact, too, that France had been our late enemy in the Napoleonic Wars – all these factors emphasize the teutonic roots of our inheritance.

This tendency received further encouragement when the young Queen Victoria married Prince Albert of Saxe-Coburg in 1840. A man of distinct intelligence, Albert was naturally concerned to concrete Britain's tie with German culture, a policy he largely succeeded in maintaining till his death in 1861.

From the time of France's defeat at the hands of Prussia in 1870, Anglo-German interchange lapsed. By the 'eighties, Germany

[186] 'Of Style or Writing' (1899) (*The Culture of Ideas,*)

equalled us in technological achievement; and, little by little, was to forge ahead. Political and cultural closeness to France slowly replaced our German affinities, till the former were cemented by the signing of the *Entente Cordiale* on 28 April 1904.

Paris now became, in Henry James' phrase (though in another context), 'the great good place'.[187] As pilgrims to the shrine of Symbolism – respectfully eager to touch the hem of the robes of the high priests Verlaine and Mallarmé – came Symons, Gosse, and Havelock Ellis (Wilde and George Moore having bent the knee before them). 'I no longer recall,' wrote Ellis in his chapter 'Early Impressions of Paris', 'how contact with Mallarmé was secured, but I well remember climbing up with Symons to the little apartment in the Rue de Rome, the neatly kept home of a family man of fine taste who had to exercise a rigid economy. It was Tuesday evening, his reception day, and he opened the door to us, a small quiet man with a pleasant smile, a figure at once arousing a sympathetic response. These famous Tuesday evening gatherings – at that period the social focus of French poetic art – correspond to nothing in London.'[188] Other doors which opened in Paris to Symons, Ellis, and Englishmen of talent were those of Huysmans, Remy de Gourmont, Rodin, de Regnier, and Odilon-Redon.

If Paris was the capital of *ésprit*, it was also the city where a *ruling in taste* might often be held to supersede a moral judgment. To numerous English writers, and readers, this *priority of the aesthetic* was both a liberating and refining condition. Part of this liberation derived from the Paphian possibilities of the place. 'My Paris,' wrote Symons in a poem by that name,

> is a land where twilight days
> Merge into violet nights of black and gold;
> Where, it may be, the flower of dawn in cold:
> Ah, but the gold nights, and the scented ways![189]

A *fin-de-siècle* capital of sex, just a few hours away across the water – however misleading this notion might be – was a belief which the young English writer needed to entertain in his family quarrel with Mrs Grundy. That it was also the capital of style, that prim lady herself was forced to admit.

[187] 'The Great Good Place' (1900)
[188] *From Rousseau to Proust*, 1935, N.Y.
[189] 'Paris' (*London Nights*, 1895)

WALTER PATER

1839-94

Walter Horatio Pater was born on 4 August 1839 at Shadwell, a district between Stepney and Wapping in the East End of London, and died at Oxford on 30 July 1894.

His life was not outwardly eventful. Proceeding from King's School, Canterbury (vividly recalled by him in his stormy 'Emerald Uthwart'[1]), to Queen's College, Oxford, he became a Fellow of Brasenose in 1864, after a short period of private tutoring. Apart from a spell of eight years in London where he resided during the vacations at 12 Earl's Terrace, Kensington, and an annual holiday for five or six weeks abroad, travelling in France and Italy, Oxford remained his home.

Pater did not marry. His two sisters kept house for him whether in London or Oxford, and accompanied him when he visited the Continent. Reserved and shy as he certainly was, Pater occasionally moved among handsome and attractive young men such as the painter Simeon Solomon; and the few pages on him in Rupert Croft-Cooke's *Feasting with Panthers* leave one in no doubt as to his emotional inclinations.

Biographies of Pater are not numerous. Of them should be singled out the two-volume *Life* by Thomas Wright – 'One of the (unintentional) comic masterpieces of our literature,'[2] but full of early indispensable material – and A. C. Benson's portrait of him in the English Men of Letters series (1906), a work of both charm and discernment. Among studies concentrating on the elements of Pater's thought, Graham Hough's brilliant thirty-page chapter in his book *The Last Romantics* (1947) can hardly be bettered, while for a quick

---

[1] *Miscellaneous Studies* (1895)
[2] *Walter Pater* by Ian Fletcher (Writers and their Work series) 1959

overall assessment Ian Fletcher's monograph *Walter Pater*, a British Council pamphlet, is to be recommended.

Although Pater was a man whose essential nature was largely hidden, there are many passing glimpses of him in the writings of his day, whether by sympathizers, cool observers, or critics. We see him, in George Moore's *Confessions of a Young Man*, giving only 'a rapid sign of recognition' as his disciples accosted him when out walking (in London) before hastening away 'composing his slowly moving rhythms', or 'at André Raffalovich's dinner-table, two very full-blown roses on either side of him, composing always'.[3] More detachedly, Frederick Wedmore paints him in a short story, 'standing with bowed head and folded hands in exquisite politeness' listening to the cockney songs of Albert Chevalier warbled by 'gifted youth' in 'a house on the north side of the Park'.[4] Less amiably, W. H. Mallock presents him, in terms of caricature, as Mr Rose in his novel *The New Republic*, 1877. Mr Rose's 'two topics are self-indulgence and art'. He 'always speaks in an undertone', telling us that he rather looks upon 'life as a chamber which we decorate as we would decorate the chamber of the woman or the youth that we love'. He also shows 'undue interest in certain books of a curious character, including the *Cultes Secrets des Dames Romaines* which occupy a locked compartment of his hosts' bookcase'.[5] Pater, by the way, was not to be drawn, remarking urbanely that he was 'pleased to be called Mr Rose – the rose being the queen of flowers'.[6]

Pater's life as an author – so far as concerns his preserved writings – begins with the essay 'Diaphaneité'[7] (dating from 1864) and ends with the unrevised undelivered lecture on Pascal[8] upon which he was working at the time of his death. Any time after 1873, when his *Studies in the History of the Renaissance* appeared in book-form, Pater was regarded as a famous or infamous character, according to the ideas of the individual reader. For good or ill, from this point forward, he was a recognized contributary force in the culture of his time.

[3] Preface to *Confessions of a Young Man*, new edition, 1904
[4] 'The Vicar of Pimlico' (*English Episodes*, 1894)
[5] *The Aesthetic Adventure* by William Gaunt (1945)
[6] *Ibid*
[7] First published in *Miscellaneous Studies*, 1895
[8] 'Pascal', first published in *Miscellaneous Studies*

'Pater's reputation,' writes Ian Fletcher, 'was at its height in the twenty years after his death [i.e. 1894–1914].'[9] Throw in the initial years of the decade in which he died, and his influence will be seen to be the determining factor in the writing of the 'nineties. A cloud of witnesses attest to his status, of which the following may be taken as representative. For Wilde, the *Studies in the History of the Renaissance* became 'the golden book of spirit and sense, the holy writ of beauty' while Pater's fourth book *Appreciations* (1899) is described by him as 'an exquisite collection of exquisite essays . . . all of them absolutely modern in the true meaning of the term modernity'.[10] Reviewing the third edition of *Marius the Epicurean* in 1892, Le Gallienne dubs it 'The Book Beautiful'.[11] Commenting the following year on Pater's *Plato and Platonism*, he notices in it 'that gracious union of the austere and the sensuous so characteristic of Mr Pater's writing', 'the temperate beauty'[12] pervading all his work. Lionel Johnson, pronouncing a valedictory, claims that 'he stands quite alone'. For him, Pater is a 'master of irony and pity'; a creative artist who took criticism, and so manipulated it that in 'his effective hands it issued with the charm of profoundly imaginative thought, clothed in a language of triumphant nicety'.[13] For Symons – performing the same office, and on whom one half of Pater's mantle descended – *Studies in the History of the Renaissance* is a book in which 'prose seemed to have conquered a new province'. 'Nothing in it is left to inspiration; but it is all inspired.'[14]

Nor is it only the writings of Pater which receive veneration from the men of the 'nineties. Making do as best they might with his somewhat recessive nature, the members of his cult loyally subscribe to the charm of Pater's personality. 'He was the most lovable of men,' declares Symons, 'the most fascinating; the most generous and helpful of private friends, and in literature a living counsel of perfection.'[15] Only Johnson – who inherited the other half of Pater's cloak – can equal this eulogy, to the strains of verse. Writing of

[9] *Walter Pater*
[10] 'Mr Pater's Appreciations', *Spectator*, 22 March 1890 (*A Critic in Pall Mall*, 1919)
[11] *Retrospective Reviews*, vol. I (1896)
[12] *Ibid*
[13] 'Walter Pater' (*Post Liminium*, 1911)
[14] 'Walter Pater' (*Studies in Two Literatures*, 1897)
[15] *Ibid*

him in 1902, the year of his own death, Johnson commemorates him as 'Scholarship's constant saint'; 'that unforgettably most gracious friend'.[16]

In a very real sense, Pater *was* the 'nineties in a way no other figure (save Beardsley) can lay claim to. Much less at the social centre (though he still retained his London house until 1893) than his erstwhile disciple Wilde, he was still that 'mauve decade's'[17] *eminence grise*, the almost sequestered source of its doctrine.

Probably the two main causes of this were, one, his hold upon literary youth, through the influence of his presence and teaching at Oxford, in addition to the initial and continuing appeal of his *Studies in the History of the Renaissance*; and, two, his comparatively greater intellectual prowess in terms of philosophical throught. Neither were such thinking processes for Pater mere academic or pedagogic labours. As Lionel Johnson rightly remarked, his was 'a passionately pensive soul';[18] and the formulation of his analysis of man's condition derived from the pathos of his own isolation, which he thought of as that of humankind itself. The generalizations of Pater's thought served, indeed, to set the psychological boundaries within which the men of the 'nineties could elaborate their largely elegiac art: 'Not to discriminate every moment some passionate attitude in those about us, and in the very brilliancy of their gifts some tragic dividing of forces on their ways, is, on this short day of frost and sun, to sleep before evening.'[19]

With the passing of the century, some diminution of excited reverence towards Pater slowly became apparent. From 1895 (with the trial and disgrace of Wilde) onwards, the aestheticism of the 'nineties suffered a number of setbacks and defeats. Symons' short-lived periodical *The Savoy* closed down in 1896 for want of adequate financial support. *The Yellow Book* followed it the following year, and Beardsley's death in 1898 dealt the decadent ideal a staggering blow. 1900 saw the decease of Wilde and Dowson; and against such losses could only be set a single renovating event: the publication in 1899 of Symons' abracadabra to some of the esoteric prose and poetry of France – *The Symbolist Movement in Literature*.

[16] 'Walter Pater' (*Post Liminium*)
[17] *The Mauve Decade* by Thomas Beer
[18] 'Walter Pater', 1902
[19] Conclusion to *Studies in the History of the Renaissance*, 1873

By 1906 Pater's shade is beginning to receive less ceremonious handling. Reviewing A. C. Benson's book on the master, the flippant and witty Ronald Ross does not fear to indite some few detracting touches. Of *Marius the Epicurean*, he confesses that 'dullness is by no means its least fault',[20] and that '*Emerald Uthwart* is frankly very silly'.[21] More critically, he places Pater in a new, and larger, perspective. 'Pater,' he writes, 'is an aside in literature, and that is why he was sometimes overlooked, and may be so again in ages to come. Though he is the greatest master of prose the century produced, he can be regarded as part of the structure of English prose. He is, rather, one of the ornaments, which often last, long after a structure has perished.'[22]

More mildly and restrainedly, Havelock Ellis in 1914 scales down the proportions of the cult-image, speaking of 'Pater, who was exquisite, even a magician, yet scarcely great'.[23] Ellis distinguishes between two chief modes of expression in fine English prose : 'the liquid style that flows, and the bronzed marmoreal style that is moulded or carved',[24] and sets Pater with Bacon and Landor ('the artistically deliberate men') as opposed to Newman, Ruskin, or Jeremy Taylor ('the lyrically impetuous men').[25]

It is not, however, till we come to T. S. Eliot's pronouncement on Pater in 1930 that we have the spectacle of a major literary critic speaking upon him – whether to agree or disagree – *without respect*. '*Marius* itself,' asserts Eliot, 'is incoherent; its method is a number of fresh starts, its contents is a hodge-podge of the learning of the classical don, the impression of the sensitive holiday visitor to Italy, a prolonged flirtation with the liturgy.'[26] The same cavalier note of dismissal informs his statement about *Studies in the History of the Renaissance* when he tells us that 'I do not believe that Pater, in this book, has influenced a single first-rate mind of a later generation [a post-'nineties or post-1918 generation]'.[27]

Eliot's essay marked the nadir of Pater's reputation; and with the ending of the Second World War, his work became the subject of positive interest, of qualified approval, or critical assent. That

[20] 'Mr Benson's *Pater*' (*Masques and Phases*, 1909)
[21] *Ibid*   [22] *Ibid*
[23] *Impressions and Comments: First Series*, 1914
[24] *Ibid*   [25] *Ibid*
[26] 'Arnold and Pater' (*The Eighteen-eighties* ed. Walter de la Mare, 1930)
[27] *Ibid*

old disguised art-for-art's-saker Richard Aldington edited a generous *Selected Works* in 1948, a volume which was followed in 1949 by Derek Patmore's slimmer choice of *Selected Writings.* These two useful editions, in the post-war's general dearth of books, helped to keep Pater circulating at a popular level. In 1949 Graham Hough effectively replied to Eliot's High Church sneer at Pater in his work *The Last Romantics.* Lord David Cecil in a Cambridge lecture[28] – published in 1955 – sought to uphold Pater's value in a more conventional academic context. In 1959 Frank Kermode's *Romantic Image* demonstrated, in passing, 'the importance of Pater as a source for the assumptions behind modern criticisms of poetry'.[29] In the same year Ian Fletcher published his excellent short pamphlet monograph,[30] while Barbara Charlesworth included a thoughtful chapter on Pater's *aesthetics of memory* and their relation to his ideal of style and form ('a certain firmness of outline, that touch of the worker in metal'[31]) in her *Dark Passages: The Decadent Consciousness in Victorian Literature* (Milwaukee, 1965). Finally, we may take Geoffrey Tillotson's short essay on Pater, in *Critics who have Influenced Taste* published the same year, as indicating the gathering strength of his status today. 'We are coming,' writes Tillotson, 'to see that there is more to Pater than blue china and the hard gemlike flame.' His intellect, Tillotson insists, 'is princely' before going on to state his relationship to the twentieth-century novel. 'There is,' Tillotson declares, 'first-rate poeticalness in the phrasing of his criticism, as in the fiction he wrote. His fiction and criticism together help the novel to shed what was not aesthetic, so that in James, and later in a more feminine way in Virginia Woolf, the novel came as near to Keats as to Defoe or Fielding. If, as Arnold saw, the future of poetry was to be immense, Pater saw that the poetry of the future would take the form of prose. And there has been much in twentieth-century literature to fulfil this prophecy.'

The complex precision of Pater's style had probably contributed much to the concealment – in many readers' eyes – of his distinctive mode of thought. In his thinking, Pater manipulates and repeats a

[28] *Walter Pater: The Scholar-Artist*
[29] *Walter Pater* by Ian Fletcher
[30] *Ibid*
[31] *Marius the Epicurean*, 1885

few basically simple ideas, of which the most important are two : the relativity of all things, and the subjectivity of the artist and the receiver of his art. Temperament, not external fact, becomes the criterion of experience; and art is seen as the world viewed through a temperament and edited, instinctively, by such viewing. What Pater established for criticism is, indeed, something closely parallel to what Kierkegaard established for philosophy : the unmeaning nature of the language of abstraction (as represented by Hegelian thought) and the substitution of a point of view confessedly personal and individual. One can profitably compare Pater's essay on Coleridge, published in 1866, with Walter Lourie's translation of Kierkegaard's *The Point of View for My Work as an Author* (including 'Two Notes' about 'The Individual' and 'On My Work as an Author') published in 1939.

From Pater's acceptance of the notions of relativity and subjectivity, there follows his artistic and dramatic desire to create incarnate points of view, specific observation-posts from which the arts are examined in his writings. It is this which gives diversity of form to his creative criticism : 'appreciations', 'imaginary portraits', and the atmospheric perspective of poets or thinkers presented in his two novels. Thus, among others, we have Watteau and his art viewed from the vantage-point of Jean-Baptiste Pater's sister ('A Prince of Court Painters', *Imaginary Portraits*, 1887), or an impression of Ronsard and his verse as they appeared to a young bishop's page and clerk-in-orders of the sixteenth century (chapter III, 'Modernity', *Gaston de Latour*, 1896), or the same young gentleman's encounter with the work of Montaigne (chapter V, 'Suspended Judgment', *Gaston de Latour*), or with the person and thought of Giordano Bruno (chapter VII, 'The Lower Pantheism', *Gaston de Latour*).

As Eliot admitted of Pater, 'he had a visual imagination' and 'a taste for painting and the plastic arts'[32] (qualities which no great Victorian critic – with the exception of Ruskin – prior to himself possessed). It was this which gave vividness to his style, making possible the assessment of art (with its imagistic expression) in terms of the critic's own *language of images*. Wilde, who took this to be the proper and attractive procedure of the critic, put the matter thus : 'To convey ideas through the medium of images has always

[32] 'Arnold and Pater' (*The Eighteen-Eighties* ed. Walter de la Mare)

been the aim of those who are artists as well as thinkers in literature.'[33]

One other feature in Pater's thought leading to a greater degree of sensuous diction in literature was the oft-quoted notion from his 'Giorgione' essay that *'all art constantly aspires to the condition of music'*.[34] Pater's adumbration of this idea may be said to have provided the art-for-art's-sake movement with its own formal theory – often misunderstood by writers favourable or unfavourable to it. John Addington Symonds, for example, challenged it in an essay 'Is Music the Type or Measure of all Art?'[35] (included in this anthology and discussed in the prefatory notice to Symonds).

It is, of course, an extension of the sense of style which is most manifest in Pater's criticism. That other aspect of the time, an extension or pervasion of the sense of sex, is not *overtly* evident in Pater. On the other hand, Geoffrey Tillotson claims that 'whenever Pater approached the human body in his writing he approached it as one who seemed to be using writing as a substitute of some sort of faint sexual experience, indeed for some sort of mischievous faint homosexual experience'.[36] Arthur Symons, whose criticism assumes the *impressionist* aspect of Pater, sometimes produces much the same feeling, though of a heterosexual nature. Lionel Johnson – the other disciple, and a largely repressed homosexual himself – conserves the *intellectual* side of Pater, writing with an animated scholarly decorum.

MODERNITY[1]

[The Poetry of Ronsard]

The book was none other than Pierre de Ronsard's 'Odes', with *'Mignonne! allons voir si la Rose'*, and 'The Skylark' and the lines

[33] 'Mr Pater's Imaginary Portraits', *Pall Mall Gazette*, 11 June 1887 (*A Critic in Pall Mall*, 1919)   [34] *Studies in the History of the Renaissance*
[35] *Essays Speculative and Suggestive*, 1890
[36] *Critics who have influenced taste*. (ed. A. P. Ryan, 1965)
[1] In Chapter III, 'Modernity', of his posthumously-published novel *Gaston de Latour* (1896), Pater describes how a bishop's young page of the sixteenth century receives from one of his friends a gift of Ronsard's *Odes*. It is Gaston's 'intellectual springtime' and, in the following passage, Pater describes the impression which the book makes upon him.

to April – itself verily like nothing so much as a jonquil, in its golden-green binding and yellow edges and perfume of the place where it had lain – sweet, but with something of the sickliness of all spring flowers since the days of Proserpine. Just eighteen years old, and the work of the poet's own youth, it took possession of Gaston with the ready intimacy of one's equal in age, fresh at every point; and he experienced what it is the function of contemporary poetry to effect anew for sensitive youth in each succeeding generation. The truant and irregular poetry of his own nature, all in solution there, found an external and authorized mouthpiece, ranging itself rightfully, as the latest achievement of human soul in this matter, along with the consecrated poetic voices of the past.

Poetry! Hitherto it had seemed hopelessly chained to the bookshelf, like something in a dead language, 'dead, and shut up in reliquaries of books', or like those relics 'one may only see through a little pane of glass', as one of its recent 'liberators' had said. Sure, apparently, of its own 'niche in the temple of Fame', the recognized poetry of literature had had the pretension to defy or discredit, as depraved and irredeemably vulgar, the poetic motions in the living genius of to-day. Yet the genius of to-day, extant and forcible, the wakeful soul of present time consciously in possession, would assert its poetic along with all its other rights; and in regard to the curiosity, the intellectual interest, of Gaston, for instance, it had of course the advantage of being close at hand, with the effectiveness of a personal presence. Studious youth, indeed, on its mettle about 'scholarship', though actually of listless humour among books that certainly stirred the past, makes a docile act of faith regarding the witchery, the thaumaturgic powers, of Virgil, or may we say of Shakespeare? Yet how faint and dim, after all, the sorrows of Dido, of Juliet, the travail of Æneas, beside quite recent things felt or done – stories which, floating to us on the light current of to-day's conversation, leave the soul in a flutter! At best, poetry of the past could move one with no more directness than the beautiful faces of antiquity which are not here for us to see and unaffectedly love them. Gaston's demand (his youth only conforming to pattern therein) was for a poetry, as veritable, as intimately near, as corporeal, as the new faces of the hour, the flowers of the actual season. The poetry of mere literature, like the dead body, could not bleed, while there was a heart, a poetic heart, in the living world, which beat, bled, spoke with irresistible power. Elderly people, Virgil in hand, might assert professionally that the contemporary age, an age, of course, of little people and things, deteriorate since the days of their own youth, must necessarily be unfit for poetic uses. But then youth, too, had its perpetual part to play, protesting that, after all said, the sun in the air, and in its own veins, was still found to be hot, still begetting, upon both alike, flowers and fruit; nay! visibly new flowers, and fruit richer than ever. Privately, in fact, Gaston had conceived of a poetry more thaumaturgic than could be anything of earlier standing than himself. The age renews itself; and in immediate derivation from it a novel poetry also grows superb and large, to fill a certain mental situation made ready in advance. Yes! the acknowledged, and, so to call it, legitimate, poetry of literature was but a thing he might sip at, like some sophisticated rarity in the way of wine, for example, pleasing the acquired taste. It was another sort of poetry, unexpressed, perhaps inexpressible, certainly not hitherto made known in books, that must drink up and absorb him, like the joyful air – him, and the earth, with its deeds, its blossoms, and faces.

In such condition of mind, how deeply, delightfully, must the poetry of Ronsard and his fellows have moved him, when he became aware, as from age to age inquisitive youth by good luck does become aware, of the literature of his own day, confirming – more than confirming – anticipation! Here was a poetry which boldly assumed the dress, the words, the habits, the very trick, of contemporary life, and turned them into gold. It took possession of the lily in one's hand, and projecting it into a visionary distance, shed upon the body of the flower the soul of its beauty. Things were become at once more deeply sensuous and more deeply ideal. As at the touch of a wizard, something more came into the rose than its own natural blush. Occupied so closely with the visible, this new poetry had so profound an intuition of what can only be felt, and maintained that mood in speaking of such objects as wine, fruit, the plume in the cap, the ring on the finger. And still that was no dubious or generalized form it gave to flower or bird, but the exact pressure of the jay at the window; you could count the petals – of the exact natural number; no expression could be too faithful to the precise texture of things; words, too, must embroider, be twisted and spun, like silk or golden hair. Here were real people, in their real, delightful attire, and you understood how they moved; the visible was more visible than ever before, just because soul had come to its surface. The juice in the flowers, when Ronsard named them, was like wine or blood. It was such a coloured thing; though the grey things also, the cool things, all the fresher for the contrast – with a freshness, again, that seemed to touch and cool the soul – found their account there; the clangorous passage of the birds at night foretokening rain, the moan of the wind at the door, the wind's self made visible over the yielding corn.

It was thus Gaston understood the poetry of Ronsard, generously expanding it to the full measure of its intention. That poetry, too, lost its thaumaturgic power in turn, and became mere literature in exchange for life, partly in the natural revolution of poetic taste, partly for its faults. Faults and all, however, Gaston loyally accepted it; those faults – the lapse of grace into affectation, of learning into pedantry, of exotic fineness into a trick – counting with him as but the proof of faith to its own dominant positions. They were but characteristics, needing no apology with the initiated, or welcome even, as savouring of the master's peculiarities of perfection. He listened, he looked round freely, but always now with the ear, the eye, of his favourite poet. It had been a lesson, a doctrine, the communication of an art – the art of placing the pleasantly aesthetic, the welcome, elements of life at an advantage, in one's view of it, till they seemed to occupy the entire surface; and he was sincerely grateful for an undeniable good service.

And yet the gifted poet seemed but to have spoken what was already in Gaston's own mind, what he had longed to say, had been just going to say; so near it came, that it had the charm of a discovery of one's own. That was an illusion, perhaps; it was because the poet told one so much about himself, making so free a display of what though personal was very contagious; of his love-secrets especially, how love and nothing else filled his mind. He was in truth but 'love's secretary', noting from hour to hour its minutely changing fortunes. Yes! that was the reason why visible, audible, sensible things glowed so brightly, why there was such luxury in sounds, words, rhythms, of the new light come on the world, of that wonderful freshness. With a masterly appliance of what was near and familiar, or again in the way of bold innovation, he found new words for perennially new things, and the novel accent awakened long-slumbering associations. Never before had words, single words, meant so much. What expansion, what liberty of heart, in speech : how associable to music, to singing, the written lines ! He sang of the lark, and it was the lark's voluble self. The physical beauty of humanity lent itself to every object, animate or inanimate, to the very hours and lapses and changes of time itself. An almost burdensome fulness of expression haunted the gestures, the very dress, the personal ornaments, of the people on the highway. Even Jacques Bonhomme at his labour, or idling for an hour, borrowed from his love, homely as it was, a touch of dignity or grace, and some secret of utterance, which made one think of Italy or Greece. The voice of the shepherd calling, the chatter of the shepherdess turning her spindle, seemed to answer, or wait for answer – to be fragments of love's ideal and eternal communing.

It was the power of 'modernity', as renewed in every successive age for genial youth, protesting, defiant of all sanction in these matters, that the true 'classic' must be of the present, the force and patience of present time. He had felt after the thing, and here it was – the one irresistible poetry there had ever been, with the magic word spoken in due time, transforming his own age and the world about him, presenting its every-day touch, the very trick one knew it by, as an additional grace, asserting the latent poetic rights of the transitory, the fugitive, the contingent. Poetry need no longer mask itself in the habit of a by-gone day : Gaston could but pity the people of by-gone days for not being above-ground to read. Here, was a discovery, a new faculty, a privileged apprehension, to be conveyed in turn to one and to another, to be propagated for the imaginative regeneration of the world. It was a manner, a habit of thought, which would invade ordinary life, and mould that to its intention. In truth, all the world was already aware, and delighted. The 'school' was soon to pay the penalty of that immediate acceptance, that intimate fitness to the mind of its own time, by sudden and profound neglect, as a thing preternaturally tarnished and tame, like magic youth, or magic beauty, turned in a moment by magic's own last word into withered age. But then, to the liveliest spirits of that time it had seemed nothing less than 'impeccable', after the manner of the great sacred products of the past, though in a living tongue. Nay! to Gaston for one, the power of the old classic poetry itself was explained by the reflex action of the new, and might seem to justify its pretensions at last.

(FROM 'GASTON DE LATOUR', 1896)

OSCAR WILDE

1854-1900

Oscar Fingal O'Flahertie Wills Wilde was born in Dublin on 15 October 1854. His father, knighted for his services to medicine, was a distinguished surgeon but a man of notoriously depraved living. His mother, who wrote under the name of 'Spesanza' in a magazine of the 'Young Ireland' party, was a woman of presence but vain and proud. She was also the author of a book of poems.

At the Portora School in Enniskillen, where he received part of his education, Wilde was recognized as a brilliant talker, but his special turn consisted in giving extremely quaint imitations of holy people in stained-glass-window attitudes, 'his power of twisting his limbs into weird contortions' – as Sir Edward Sullivan, a contemporary of Wilde at school, recalled – 'being very great'. At Trinity College, Dublin, his classical triumphs of his schooldays continued. In 1874 he won the gold medal for Greek, and proceeded to Magdalen College, Oxford, just one day after his twentieth birthday, winning the Newdigate Prize with his poem *Ravenna* and a First in 'Greats' in 1878.

The marks of the bibliophile and the dandy were already recognizable in him, as a school contemporary of his remarked: 'We noticed that he always like to have editions of the classics that were of stately size with large print. . . . He was more careful of his dress than any other people.'[1] It is not difficult to extend these hands until they point towards that Dandyism ('an attempt to assert the absolute modernity of beauty')[2] and that 'new Hedonism'[3] which were the marks of his narcissistic hero in *The Picture of Dorian Grey* (1890).

Leaving Oxford, he became self-appointed leader of the Aesthetic School. He visited America on a lecture tour (1882), telling the

[1] *Oscar Wilde: His Life and Confessions* by Frank Harris, 1938
[2] *The Picture of Dorian Gray*   [3] *Ibid*

78

customs officers in New York that he had nothing to declare but
his own genius. Back in London in 1883, he set out to capture the
provincial public with expositions of THE HOUSE BEAUTIFUL – a
high-falutin' phrase for interior decoration. In 1884 he married
Constance Lloyd, the daughter of a well-to-do Dublin barrister.
They had two children, Cyril and Vyvyan, and for them he wrote
his book of fairy stories *The Happy Prince and Other Tales* (1888).
The year before this he had become editor of *Woman's World*, a
magazine whose standard he raised till it became the equivalent,
say, of today's *Nova* or *The Queen*. Professor Richard Ellman, in a
fascinating article, has suggested that the crucial date in the life
and career of Wilde was 1886, when Ronald Ross boasted that at
the age of seventeen, he had seduced the older man into homosexual practices. The bearings of this upon Wilde's writing have
been assessed by Professor Ellman ('The Critic as Artist as Wilde,'
Encounter, July 1967) while Montgomery Hyde has exhaustively
chronicled the events which led to his trial in 1895, his imprisonment with hard labour for two years, and his death in Paris on
30 November 1900, at the age of forty-six.

Perhaps the best brief impression of Wilde is that which Max
Beerbohm noted down in a private character book : 'Luxury – gold-
tipped matches – hair curled – Assyrian – wax statue – huge rings
– fat white hands – not soigné – feather-bed – pointed fingers –
ample scarf – Louis Quinze cane – vast malmaison – cat-like tread
– heavy shoulders – enormous dowager – or schoolboy – way of
laughing with hand over mouth – stroking chin – looking up side-
ways – jollity overdone – But real vitality. . . . Effeminate, but
vitality of twenty men. Magnetism – authority – Deeper than repute
or wit – Hypnotic.'[4]

Wilde's first ambitious critical essay was the university-exercise
piece *The Rise of Historical Criticism*. It is not a work deserving
inclusion in the canon; but its repudiation of absolute values which
may have derived from the first part of Pater's essay on Coleridge
('Modern thought is distinguished from ancient by its cultivation
of the "relative" spirit in place of the "absolute". . . . To the
modern spirit nothing is, or can be rightly known except relatively
and under conditions.'[5])

[4] *Max Beerbohm: Letters to Reggie Turner*, ed. Rupert Hart-Davis, 1964
[5] Walter Pater: 'Coleridge' (*Westminster Review*, January 1866)

If, as Robert Ross remarked, 'the interpretation of the Essay is sometimes obscure',[6] its acceptance of the comparative and relative spirit of inquiry can be seen as moving towards the formulation of that a-moralist criticism which Wilde practised in his maturity.

Perhaps the origin of such a criticism in English literature is first to be found in Charles Lamb's essay 'On the Artificial Comedy of the Last Century'. As far back as 1822, reflecting upon Restoration drama, Lamb declared : 'I confess for myself (with no great delinquencies to answer for) I am glad for a season to take an airing beyond the diocese of the strict conscience – not to live always in the precincts of the law courts – but now and then, for a dream while or so, to imagine a world with no meddling restrictions.' Seeking to adjust his own nineteenth-century conscience, and that of his readers, to these acrobatics of infamy which the Restoration audience considered 'good theatre', Lamb distinguished between the necessary shackles of practical living and the freedom provided by art. The doings of the characters of Wycherley and Congreve take place, for Lamb, in a *moral vacuum*. 'They have,' he maintained, 'got out of Christendom into . . . the utopia of gallantry, where pleasure is duty, and the manners perfect freedom. It is altogether a speculative scheme of things, which has no reference whatsoever to the world that is.' This is well on the way to the aesthetes' a-moral credo contained in the preface to *The Picture of Dorian Gray* though more subtle than such glib aphorisms as 'Those who find ugly meanings in beautiful things are corrupt without being charming' or 'No artist has ethical sympathies. An ethical sympathy in an artist is an unpardonable mannerism of style.'

Wilde's intellectual attitude has generally been thought of as stemming from Pater, but it is important to stress the difference between them. In *De Profundis*, Wilde acknowledges his debt to Pater's volume on the Renaissance, referring to it as 'that book which was to have such a strange influence over my life.'[7] 'It is my golden book,' he once told Yeats, 'I never travel anywhere without it; but it is the very flower of decadence : the last trumpet should have sounded the moment it was written.'[8]

[6] *Oscar Wilde's Collected Works*, ed. Robert Ross, Boston, 1921.
[7] *The Letters of Oscar Wilde*, ed. Rupert Hart-Davis, 1962
[8] 'The Trembling of the Veil' (*Autobiographies*, 1926)

It is probably statements of this latter order which disquieted Pater who, according to Robert Ross, 'did not hesitate to express disapprobation [of Wilde] to private friends.'[9] Reviewing *The Picture of Dorian Gray*, Pater blandly criticized the 'dainty Epicurian theory' of his disciple. 'A true Epicurean,' he stated, 'aims at a complete though harmonious development of man's entire organism. To lose the moral sense, therefore, for instance, the sense of sin and righteousness, as Mr Wilde's hero – his heroes seem bent on doing as speedily, as completely as they can, is to lose, or lower organization, to become less complex, to pass from a higher to a lower degree of development.'[10]

Yeats and Symons both believed that Wilde was the sort of man forced to live, turn by turn, through different aspects of his personality. Wilde certainly thought of himself in such a way – a living proof of his own 'Truth of Masks'. 'I am so glad you like that strange many coloured book of mine [*The Picture of Dorian Gray*],' he wrote to an admirer Ralph Payne : 'it contains much of me in it. Basil Hallward is what I think I am : Lord Henry, what the world thinks of me : Dorian what I would like to be – in other ages, perhaps.'[11] Wilde's tendency to live in 'a fragment of himself and to dramatize that fragment', as Yeats expressed it, is probably responsible for the fact that his best criticism – 'The Decay of Lying' and 'The Critic as Artist' (*Intentions*) are both written in dialogue form.

The speakers in these two dialogues – Cyril, Vivian, Gilbert and Ernest – are young men of leisure and taste, and there is something of the Oscar-Alfred Douglas tone about their relationship. As dialogic art, these essays in critical conversation are undoubtedly the brightest thing in this *genre* written in English. Beside them Landor's *Imaginary Conversations*, for all their magniloquence, are heavy as dreadnoughts. Wilde's dialogues have tempo, mood and wit; a ready flexibility of mind and a nimble manoeuvring power of argument. The positions which Wilde seeks to discredit are : one, the notion of Nature as a criterion ('One touch of Nature will make the whole world kin, but two touches of Nature will destroy any work of art'); and, two, the idea of fiction as a realistic art-form

[9] Oscar Wilde: *Collected Works*, ed. Robert Ross, Boston, 1910
[10] 'A Novel by Mr Wilde' (*Uncollected Essays*, Portland, Maine, 1903)
[11] *The Letters of Oscar Wilde,* ed. Rupert Hart-Davis

('No great artist ever sees things as they really are. If he did, he would cease to be an artist'). Wilde opposes to 'unimaginative realism' the concept of an 'imaginative reality'. The positions which Wilde seeks to establish are likewise two : the notion that, through the activity of the imagination, art transcends both the truth of fact and the diocese of moral opinion. It is answerable only to Beauty. In a like manner, criticism should be creative – 'the record of one's own soul. . . . The highest criticism deals with art not as expressive but as impressive purely.' Related to these attitudes are those of the French author Anatole France who, in his famous dictum, defined criticism as 'the adventure of [one's] soul among masterpieces,'[12] and an American professor, Joel Elias Spingarm, who turned from the academic examination of Renaissance critical theory to writing his witty monograph entitled *Creative Criticism* (1917). Another American, James Haneker, must also be numbered among the tribe of Oscar with such impressionistic explorations as *Promenades of an Impressionist* (1910).

Last in the line of Wildean critics comes Oscar's intimate friend Robert Ross. In the dedication to his volume *Masques and Phases* (1909) he tells us 'there are essays in my book cast in the form of fiction, criticism cast in the form of parody; and a vein of high seriousness sufficiently obvious, I hope, behind the masques and phases of my jesting'. One has moved a long way from Walter Pater with his murmured reverence for art in this book. A bright and brittle jagged punning dominates the prose, and we are approaching the intellectual farce of Huxley's writing in the post-war Jazz Age.

MR PATER'S APPRECIATIONS
[*Speaker*, 22 March 1890]

When I first had the privilege – and I count it a very high one – of meeting Mr Walter Pater, he said to me, smiling, 'Why do you always write poetry? Why do you not write prose? Prose is so much more difficult.'

[12] *La Vie littéraire* 1888–1892

Oscar Wilde

It was during my undergraduate days at Oxford; days of lyrical ardour and of studious sonnet-writing; days when one loved the exquisite intricacy and musical repetitions of the ballade, and the villanelle with its linked long-drawn echoes and its curious completeness; days when one solemnly sought to discover the proper temper in which a triolet should be written; delightful days, in which, I am glad to say, there was far more rhyme than reason.

I may frankly confess now that at the time I did not quite comprehend what Mr Pater really meant; and it was not till I had carefully studied his beautiful and suggestive essays on the Renaissance that I fully realized what a wonderful self-conscious art the art of English prose-writing really is, or may be made to be. Carlyle's stormy rhetoric, Ruskin's winged and passionate eloquence, had seemed to me to spring from enthusiasm rather than from art. I do not think I knew then that even prophets correct their proofs. As for Jacobean prose, I thought it too exuberant; and Queen Anne prose appeared to me terribly bald, and irritatingly rational. But Mr Pater's essays became to me 'the golden book of spirit and sense, the holy writ of beauty'. They are still this to me. It is possible, of course, that I may exaggerate about them. I certainly hope that I do; for where there is no exaggeration there is no love, and where there is no love there is no understanding. It is only about things that do not interest one, that one can give a really unbiassed opinion; and this is no doubt the reason why an unbiassed opinion is always valueless.

But I must not allow this brief notice of Mr Pater's new volume to degenerate into an autobiography. I remember being told in America that whenever Margaret Fuller wrote an essay upon Emerson the printers had always to send out to borrow some additional capital 'I's', and I feel it right to accept this transatlantic warning.

Appreciations, in the fine Latin sense of the word, is the title given by Mr Pater to his book, which is an exquisite collection of exquisite essays, of delicately wrought works of art – some of them being almost Greek in their purity of outline and perfection of form, others mediæval in their strangeness of colour and passionate suggestion, and all of them absolutely modern, in the true meaning of the term modernity. For he to whom the present is the only thing that is present, knows nothing of the age in which he lives. To realize the nineteenth century one must realize every century that has preceded it, and that has contributed to its making. To know anything about oneself, one must know all about others. There must be no mood with which one cannot sympathize, no dead mode of life that one cannot make alive. The legacies of heredity may make us alter our views of moral responsibility, but they cannot but intensify our sense of the value of Criticism; for the true critic is he who bears within himself the dreams and ideas and feelings of myriad generations, and to whom no form of thought is alien, no emotional impulse obscure.

Perhaps the most interesting, and certainly the least successful, of the essays contained in the present volume is that on *Style*. It is the most interesting because it is the work of one who speaks with the high authority that comes from the noble realization of things nobly conceived. It is the least successful, because the subject is too abstract. A true artist like Mr Pater is most felicitous when he deals with the concrete, whose very limitations give him finer freedom, while they necessitate more intense vision. And yet what a high ideal is contained in these few pages! How good it is for us, in these days of popular education and facile journalism, to be reminded of the real scholarship that is essential to the perfect writer, who, being a true lover of words for their own sake, a minute and constant observer of their physiognomy,' will avoid what is mere rhetoric, or ostentatious ornament, or negligent misuse of terms, or ineffective surplusage, and will be known by his tact of omission, by his skilful economy of means, by his selection and self-restraint, and perhaps above all by that conscious artistic structure which is the expression of mind in style. I think I have been wrong in saying that the subject is too abstract. In Mr Pater's hands it becomes very real to us indeed, and he shows us how, behind the perfection of a man's style, must lie the passion of a man's soul.

As one passes to the rest of the volume, one finds essays on Wordsworth and on Coleridge, on Charles Lamb and on Sir Thomas Browne, on some of Shakespeare's plays and on the English kings that Shakespeare fashioned, on Dante Rossetti, and on William Morris. As that on Wordsworth seems to be Mr Pater's last work, so that on the singer of the *Defence of Guenevere* is certainly his earliest, or almost his earliest, and it is interesting to mark the change that has taken place in his style. This change is, perhaps, at first sight not very apparent. In 1868 we find Mr Pater writing with the same exquisite care for words, with the same studied music, with the same temper, and something of the same mode of treatment. But, as he goes on, the architecture of the style becomes richer and more complex, the epithet more precise and intellectual. Occasionally one may be inclined to think that there is, here and there, a sentence which is somewhat long, and possibly, if one may venture to say so, a little heavy and cumbersome in movement. But if this be so, it comes from those side-issues suddenly suggested by the idea in its progress, and really revealing the idea more perfectly; or from those felicitous after-thoughts that give a fuller completeness to the central scheme, and yet convey something of the charm of chance; or from a desire to suggest the secondary shades of meaning with all their accumulating effect, and to avoid, it may be, the violence and harshness of too definite and exclusive an opinion. For in matters of art, at any rate, thought is inevitably coloured by emotion, and so is fluid rather than fixed, and, recognizing its dependence upon the moods and upon the passion of fine moments, will not accept the rigidity of a scientific formula or a theological dogma. The critical pleasure, too, that we receive from tracing, through what may seem the intricacies of a sentence, the working of the constructive intelligence, must not be overlooked. As soon as we have realized the design, everything appears clear and simple. After a time, these long sentences of Mr Pater's come to have the charm of an elaborate piece of music, and the unity of such music also.

I have suggested that the essay on Wordsworth is probably the most recent bit of work contained in this volume. If one might choose between so much that is good, I should be inclined to say it is the finest also. The essay on Lamb is curiously suggestive; suggestive indeed, of a somewhat more tragic, more sombre figure, than men have been wont to think of in connection with the author of the *Essays of Elia*. It is an interesting aspect under which to regard Lamb, but perhaps he himself would have had some difficulty in recognizing the portrait given of him. He had, undoubtedly, great sorrows, or motives for sorrow, but he could console himself at a moment's notice for the real tragedies of life by reading any one of the Elizabethan tragedies, provided it was in a folio edition. The essay on Sir Thomas Browne is delightful, and has the strange, personal, fanciful charm of the author of the *Religio Medici*, Mr Pater often catching the colour and accent and tone of whatever artist, or work of art, he deals with. That on Coleridge, with its insistence on the necessity of the cultivation of the relative, as opposed to the absolute spirit in philosophy and in ethics, and its high appreciation of the poet's true position in our literature, is in style and substance a very blameless work. Grace of expression and delicate subtlety of thought and phrase, characterize the essays on Shakespeare. But the essay on Wordsworth has a spiritual beauty of its own. It appeals, not to the ordinary Wordsworthian with his uncritical temper, and his gross confusion of ethical and æsthetical problems, but rather to those who desire to separate the gold from the dross, and to reach at the true Wordsworth through the mass of tedious and prosaic work that bears his name, and that serves often to conceal him from us. The presence of an alien element in Wordsworth's art is, of course, recognized by Mr Pater, but he touches on it merely from the psychological point of view, pointing out how this quality of higher and lower moods gives the effect in his poetry 'of a power not altogether his own, or under his control'; a power which comes and goes when it wills, 'so that the old fancy which made the poet's art an enthusiasm, a form of divine possession, seems almost true of him'. Mr Pater's earlier essays had their *purpurei panni*, so eminently suitable for quotation, such as the famous passage on *Mona Lisa*, and that other in which Botticelli's strange conception of the Virgin is so strangely set forth. From the present volume it is difficult to select any one passage in preference to another as specially characteristic of Mr Pater's treatment. This, however, is worth quoting at length. It contains a truth eminently suitable for our age :

That the end of life is not action but contemplation – *being* as distinct from *doing* – a certain disposition of the mind : is, in some shape or other, the principle of all the higher morality. In poetry, in art, if you enter into their true spirit at all, you touch this principle in a measure; these, by their sterility, are a type of beholding for the mere joy of beholding. To treat life in the spirit of art is to make life a thing in which means and ends are identified : to encourage such treatment, the true moral significance of art and poetry. Wordsworth, and other poets who have been like him in ancient or more recent times, are the masters, the experts, in this art of impassioned contemplation. Their work is not to teach lessons, or enforce rules, or even to stimulate us to noble ends, but to withdraw the thoughts for a while from the mere machinery of life, to fix them, with appropriate emotions, on the spectacle of those great facts in man's existence which no machinery affects, 'on the great and universal passions of men, the most general and interesting of their occupations, and the entire world of nature' – on 'the operations of the elements and the appearances of the visible universe, on storm and sunshine, on the revolutions of the seasons, on cold and heat, on loss of friends and kindred, on injuries and resentments, on gratitude and hope, on fear and sorrow.' To witness this spectacle with appropriate emotions is the aim of all culture; and of these emotions poetry like Wordsworth's is a great nourisher and stimulant. He sees nature full of sentiment and excitement; he sees men and women as parts of nature, passionate, excited, in strange grouping and connection with the grandeur and beauty of the natural world: – images, in his own words, 'of men suffering, amid awful forms and powers.'

Certainly the real secret of Wordsworth has never been better expressed. After having read and re-read Mr Pater's essay – for it requires re-reading – one returns to the poet's work with a new sense of joy and wonder, and with something of eager and impassioned expectation. And perhaps this might be roughly taken as the test or touchstone of the finest criticism.

Finally, one cannot help noticing the delicate instinct that has gone to fashion the brief epilogue that ends this delightful volume. The difference between the classical and romantic spirits in art has often, and with much over-emphasis, been discussed. But with what a light sure touch does Mr Pater write of it! How subtle and certain are his distinctions! If imaginative prose be really the special art of this century, Mr Pater must rank amongst our century's most characteristic artists. In certain things he stands almost alone. The age has produced wonderful prose styles, turbid with individualism, and violent with excess of rhetoric. But in Mr Pater, as in Cardinal Newman, we find the union of personality with perfection. He has no rival in his own sphere, and he has escaped disciples. And this, not because he has not been imitated, but because in art so fine as his there is something that, in its essence, is inimitable.

Appreciations, with an Essay on Style. By Walter Pater, Fellow of Brasenose College. (Macmillan and Co.)

(FROM 'A CRITIC IN PALL MALL', 1919)

JOHN ADDINGTON SYMONDS

1840-93

John Addington Symonds, poet, critic, historian and apostle of homosexual love, was born on 5 October 1840 at Clifton, near Bristol. His father – a distinguished medical practitioner ('open at all pores to . . . art . . . science [and] literature') – was the author of *Miscellanies* (a volume of studies on such varied subjects as 'Nightmares' and 'Tooth-Ache') published posthumously, with an introduction by his son in 1871.

'He was born and brought up in the lap of culture,' wrote Richard Le Gallienne with a touch of envy in 1895. 'His Clifton home was rich in spiritual, intellectual, and artistic influences; all the most approved Harrovian and Oxonian apparatus for the production of men of genius was brought to bear upon him. . . . He was a "young gentleman" with nothing to think of but the development of his soul and his aesthetic faculties.'[1] So far, so good; but Le Gallienne also noted the sinister omens, the Saturnian side: 'His nerves were terribly against him. He suffered from terrifying and exhausting nightmares, was perplexed with strange trance-like visitations, and worn with aesthetic sensibilities morbidly keen, when even quite young: besides he was not beautiful in personal appearance, and thus suffered at times from painful self-consciousness.'[2]

Symonds's 'chequered and morally perturbed existence' was set down by him in a private autobiography in 1889. His literary executor Horatio Brown made discreet use of this when he published

[1] *J. A. Symonds*: 'H. F. Brown's Biography (*Retrospective Reviews*, 1896)
[2] *Ibid*

his two-volume *John Addington Symonds: A Biography* (1895),
'composed,' as Arthur Symons noted, 'with so careful and so successful a reticence'.[3] On his death in 1926, Brown bequeathed Symonds'
Manuscript Memoirs to the London Library with a fifty-year
embargo on their release for publication. When Phyllis Grosskurth
was preparing her sensational scholarly life of the poet, she was
permitted to read these, but to quote from them *verbatim* only
such passages as Brown had himself quoted. Even so, her book
John Addington Symons: A Biography (1964) is one of the most
illuminating twentieth-century post-Freudian studies of any
Victorian figure we possess. Due largely to Miss Grosskurth's work,
we see Symonds no longer merely as 'a late nineteenth-century
aesthete, a minor Pater'[4] but 'a man hidden behind a mask, a writer
who . . . suffered the tormented struggle of a homosexual within
Victorian society'.[5] Although Symonds' life cannot be said to lie
fully open to us till the publication in 1976 of his secret self-account
presumably takes place, Miss Grosskurth's life and the massive two-
volume *Letters of John Addington Symonds* edited by Herbert M.
Schueler and Robert L. Peters (1967, Detroit) give us substantial
material for a just portrait.

Any claim for Symonds to stand specifically as 'a critic of the
'nineties' appears, at first, somewhat uncertain. Unlike most of the
figures commonly considered within that category, he published
more work in the 'seventies and the 'eighties than in the decade in
question. His first pieces – unsigned articles for *The Saturday
Review*, paid for at the rate of £12 each – commenced appearing
in December 1862 when he was still an undergraduate. This gave
Symonds a four-year edge on Pater, whose first article entitled
'Coleridge' was published in the *Westminster Review* for January
1866. By 1890 (when his bulky *Essays Speculative and Suggestive*
were published), Symonds could talk of having 'sent some twenty-
nine volumes out'.[6] Even so, the 'nineties was a productive period
as far as fresh books by him were concerned. Along with the two-
volume *Essays*, there came the two-volume *Memoirs of Count Carlo
Gozzi* in the same year. This was followed by the privately-printed

[3] 'John Addington Symonds (*Studies in Two Literatures*, 1897)
[4] *John Addington Symonds: A Biography*
[5] *Ibid*
[6] Preface [by Horatio Brown] to *Essays Speculative and Suggestive*, third
edition, 1907

short book of 104 pages *A Problem in Modern Ethics* (1891), dealing with the history and nature of homosexuality, with some suggestions as to an amendment of the laws. In 1893, the year of his death, Symonds published no less than three works : the two-volume *Life of Michelangelo Buonarroti*, the brief but indicative *Walt Whitman: A Study*, and *In the Key of Blue and Other Prose Essays*, 'a book so typical in some ways of the 'nineties,' as Holbrook Jackson terms it, 'that it might well have been written by one of the younger generation'.[7]

Like John Gray's *Silverpoints*, Symonds' *In the Key of Blue* was one of those volumes of the 'nineties which owed its *cachet* to the nice combination between book-designer and author. Published by Elkin Matthews and John Lane, its light-blue and ivory-coloured cover carried a design of hyacinth and laurel by Charles Rickett, founder of the Vale Press and co-editor with Charles Shannon of the artistic periodical *The Dial*. Symonds' opening piece, which bore the title of the book, was what, in the parlance of the time, used to be referred to as a colour-study. 'The nomenclature of colour in literature,' wrote Symonds, 'has always puzzled me. It is easy to talk of green, blue, yellow, red. But when we seek to distinguish the tints of these hues, and to accentuate the special *timbre* of each, we are practically left to suggestions founded upon metaphor and analogy. We select some object in nature – a gem, a flower, an aspect of the sky or sea – which possesses a particular quality which we wish to indicate. We talk of grass-green, apple-green, olive-green, emerald-green, sage-green, jade-green; of sapphire, forget-me-not, turquoise, gentian, ultra-marine, sky-blue; of topaz, gold, orange, citron; of rose and cherry, ruby and almandine, blood and flame. Or else we use the names of sub-stances from which the pigments are compounded : as yellow-ochre, burnt-sienna, cadmium, lamp-black, verdigris, vermilion, madder, cinnabar.' To a fond fan of Gautier, enamoured of his *'emaux et camées'* and the painterly adjectives describing his travels in Spain, this would have seemed very much the 'new wave'. Perhaps such a reader would be reminded, too, of those inventories of exquisite objects – jewels, embroideries, and ecclesiastical vestments – which feature in chapter XI of *The Picture of Dorian Gray*, published in book form only two years earlier than Symonds' volume.

[7] *The Eighteen Nineties* (1913)

John Addington Symonds

In addition to its study in the diction of colour, the essay has a further, and formal, interest, being – as Le Gallienne called it – 'an intermezzo in prose and verse'.[8] The first verse passage seeks to give a series of colour-impressions of a certain Venetian gondolier wearing his blue blouse as he ferries across the lamp-lit waters :

> Pitch-dark! you were the one thing blue;
> Four tints of pure celestial hue:
> The larkspur blouse by tones degraded
> Through silken sash of sapphire faded,
> The faintly floating violet tie,
> The hose of lapis-lazuli. . . .

But it was not solely the gondolier's blue blouse in which Symonds was interested. Along with another intermezzo essay in prose and verse entitled 'Clifton and a Lad's Love', 'In the Key of Blue' dealt with what Le Gallienne, with nice euphemism, described as 'an idyll of friendship'.[9] Ian Fletcher has remarked on a growing literature with homosexual undertones as represented by that Oxford magazine of the 'eighties *The Dark Blue*. The homosexual theme was developed in two further Oxford periodicals : *The Spirit Lamp* and *The Chameleon*, both of them undergraduate publications. It was, among others, the readership of such magazines that hailed Symonds' volume as a triumph of advanced opinion and taste.

Well, Symonds might be in the vanguard of opinion; but what of his presentation of it – his *art*? Reviewing the volume *In the Key of Blue*, Le Gallienne commented that neither of the two essays in question 'appear to indicate the possibilities of the intermezzo form – the verse in each case being merely set amid the prose, and not blossoming out of it, by irresistible impulse, as though one talking should suddenly break out into song'.[10] Such a criticism would have been nothing new to Symonds, who held the deepest doubts about his own performance as an artist. 'I have written,' he confessed, 'few good paragraphs, and possibly no single perfect line.'[11] For one who desired to stand among the small elect fashioners of art, this was a sad admission; and it is this recurring measure of imperfection as to means which makes Symonds something of an anomaly when judged by his peers among the men of the 'nineties.

[8] 'J. A. Symonds: *In the Key of Blue*' (*Retrospective Reviews*, 1896)
[9] *Ibid*   [10] *Ibid*
[11] *John Addington Symonds: A Biography* by Horatio F. Brown

Wilde, reviewing Symonds' most ambitious work, his seven-volume *Renaissance in Italy,* faulted him as an historian as Le Gallienne had done as a literary essayist. Speaking of the first five volumes, Wilde remarked that 'Mr Symonds has regarded the past rather as a picture to be painted than as a problem to be solved'.[12] He noted his too constant 'desire to represent life at all costs under dramatic conditions',[13] but conceded that in Symonds' final two volumes 'the art of the picturesque chronicler is completed by something like the science of the true historian'.[14] Yet even here, Wilde notes 'the rhetoric and over-emphasis of his style'.[15]

Symons and Le Gallienne both saw and commented upon the flawed aspect of Symonds' work. 'Passionate,' wrote the latter, 'to be a literary creator, an original poet, he had to rest content with being a sensitive and catholic critic.'[16] Le Gallienne, with his usual generosity, over-estimates him here when he calls Symonds 'a great critic of art and literature'.[17] 'There is no corner of history,' Le Gallienne declared, 'on which the human spirit has left its impress that is not eloquent to him and to which he is without some answering sympathy.'[18] Le Gallienne was right in locating the *humanistic* element in Symonds' make-up, but wrong in believing that its functioning made him 'a great critic'. Too often the workings of this sympathy were spasmodic, prejudiced, or too enthusiastic. Then, too, there was a further factor, referred to by one writer as 'Symonds' sophistry'.[19] Symonds tells us that this term had been coined by a hostile critic to describe the point of view expressed by him in the last chapter of his *Studies in the Greek Poets: Second Series* (1876). Briefly one can say that the sophistry consisted of a justification of any such cultural attitude as seemed to further or facilitate erotic love between man and man. His essay on the little-known Victorian poet Edward Cracroft Lefroy is full of these partly specious appreciations and value-judgments. Thus, he praises Lefroy's poetic thinking which teaches us, he declares, how 'to be a Christian without asceticism, and a Greek without sensuality',[20]

---

[12] 'Mr Symonds' *History of the Renaissance*' (*A Critic in Pall Mall*)
[13] *Ibid*   [14] *Ibid*
[15] *Ibid*   [16] *Retrospective Reviews*, 1896
[17] *Ibid*   [18] *Ibid*
[19] 'Edward Cracroft Lesroy' (*In the Key of Blue*)
[20] *Ibid*

a piece of deception and dishonesty since to be *a sensual Greek* was the end which Symonds desired to attain.

On the other hand, it was the real or fancied vibration, indicative of homosexual interest, which most stimulated Symonds, leading him to choose such a subject for critical exploration. Of all subjects treated by him, the best instance of the above is to be found in his short book on Whitman – a poet deeply dear to Symonds on account of his *cult of comrades*. Necessarily, his study may be read as implicit propaganda for homosexual love.

Just how limited was Symonds' adherence to the ideals of the 'nineties can be seen in his criticism of Pater's central doctrine of form, pronounced in his essay on Giorgione, namely that 'all art continually aspires towards the condition of music'.[21] Pater's belief that 'the highest and most complete form of poetry artistically is that in which 'we are least able to detach the matter from the form'[22] is challenged by Symonds who defends an earlier Victorian point of view : that intellect or spirituality should be the controlling factor in a work of art.

As with Havelock Ellis, it is Symonds' sense of sex in literature which aligns him with the critics of the 'nineties; and it is, of course, his special distinction that his own intuitions were for sexual inversion. One is not perhaps surprised to hear Swinburne speaking of him, after his death on 19 April 1893 at Davos Platz, Switzerland, as 'the Platonic amorist of blue-breeched gondoliers'[23] – so characteristic a gesture of the pot calling the kettle black.

SEX IN THE POETRY OF WALT WHITMAN

[Chapters IV and V of J. A. Symonds' book *Walt Whitman: a study*, 1893]

The transition from Personality to Sex offers no difficulty. Sex, the passions, the affections, love, are clearly the main things in life.

[21] *Studies in the History of the Renaissance*
[22] *Ibid*
[23] *The Swinburne Letters,* ed. Cecil Y. Lang (Harvard, 1959–62)

In his treatment of Love, Whitman distinguishes two broad kinds of human affection; the one being the ordinary sexual relation, the other comradeship or an impassioned relation between man and man. The former he describes as 'amativeness', the latter as 'adhesiveness'. There is no reason why both forms of emotion should not co-exist in the same person. Indeed, Whitman makes it plain that a completely endowed individuality, one who, as Horace might have said, is 'entirely rounded and without ragged edges', will be highly susceptible of both. The exact bearing of amativeness and adhesiveness upon one another, and upon the spiritual nature of the individual, has been fully expressed in the following poem :

> Fast-anchored eternal O love! O woman I love!
> O bride! O wife! More resistless than I can tell,
>   the thought of you!
> Then separate, as disembodied or another born,
> Ethereal, the last athletic reality, my consolation,
> I ascend, I float in the regions of your love, O man,
> O sharer of my roving life.

Since this is the most condensed and weighty of Whitman's utterances upon the subject of love, every word in it may be supposed to have been carefully considered. It is not therefore insignificant to notice that, in the edition of 1860–61, 'primeval' stood for 'fast-anchored' in the first line, and 'the purest born' for 'or another born' in the third line.

The section of his complete works which deals exclusively with sexual love, is entitled *Children of Adam*. The frankness and the rankness of the pieces composing this chapter called down a storm of insults, calumnies, unpopularity, on Whitman. Yet the attitude which he assumed as poet and prophet demanded this frankness, while the spirit of his treatment deprived the subject-matter of its rankness.

His originality consisted, I have said, in giving the idealism of poetry and powerful emotion to the blank results of modern science. Now it is in the very nature of science to consider nothing as 'common or unclean', to accept all the facts presented to its vision with indifference, caring for nothing in the process of analysis except the proof of reality, the elucidation of truth. Science, in her wise impartiality, regards morbid phenomena, disease and decay,

crime and aberration, as worthy of attention, upon the same lines
as healthy and normal products. She knows that pathology is an
indispensable adjunct to the study of organic structure.

Sharing the scientific spirit in his quality of poet, Whitman was
not called to celebrate what is unhealthy and abnormal in humanity.
That is a proper subject for the laboratory. The poet's function
is to stimulate and to invigorate. It is his duty to insist upon what
is wholesome, the things in life which conduce to organic growth,
the natural instincts and normal appetites upon which the continua-
tion of the species, the energy of the individual, the welfare of the
family, the fabric of the commonwealth, eventually rest. Feeling
thus, and being penetrated with the scientific spirit, Whitman was
justified in claiming the whole of healthy manhood and womanhood for his province. To exclude sex from his account of human
nature would have been absurd; for it is precisely sex by which
men and women are differentiated; sex which brings them into
mutual relations of amativeness; sex which determines the preserva-
tion and the future of the species. The inspiration which prompted
him, first among modern poets, to penetrate the blank results of
science with imagination and emotion, led him inevitably to a frank
treatment of sexual relations. Each portion of the healthy human
body had for a thinker of his type to be considered 'sweet and
clean'. He could not shrink from the facts of paternity and
maternity, these being the most important both for men and women,
and through them for society at large. For him 'the parts and poems
of the body' are not 'of the body only, but of the soul' – indeed
'these are the soul'. Following the impulse which forced him to
insist upon a vigorous and healthy personality or self as the
fundamental integer of human life, he proceeded to impress upon
his nation the paramount duty of maintaining a robust and healthy
breed. Scientific pathology may be left to deal with abnormalities
and diseases. The social conscience is sufficiently, if dimly,
acquainted with those evils. For the poet, who has accepted the
scientific point of view, it is enough to indicate their wrongness.
But he enjoys the privilege of proclaiming the beauty and the
goodness of functions and organs which constitute the central reality
of human life. To recognize the dignity of sex, to teach personalities,
both male and female, that they have the right to take a pride in it,
and that this pride is their duty, was for a poet of Whitman's

stamp a prime consideration. Those mediæval lies regarding sexual sinfulness, those foolish panegyrics of chaste abstinence, those base insinuations of foul-minded priests, had to be swept away – not by polemic or vituperation, but by a plain proclamation of the truth which had been veiled from sight so long. Delicacy in matters of sex had become indelicacy by a false habit of envisaging the fact. All falsehood is inconsistent with science and injurious to the best interests of society.

Having entered upon this region with the objects I have hinted at – a recognition of fundamental truths, an acceptance of scientific as opposed to the theological principles, a deep sense of personality, and a conviction that the maintenance of the breed at its highest level of efficiency is a prime condition of national well-being – Whitman naturally treated the ordinary sexual relations with a breadth and simplicity which appear to more sophisticated minds as brutal. He does not shrink from images and descriptions, from metaphors and phrases, as closely borrowed from the facts of sex as are his pictures of the outer world, or his transcripts from the occupations of mankind. Sex, being for him so serious and excellent a thing, has the right to equal freedom of speech with sunrise or sun-setting, the stars in their courses, the woods and fields, the industries of carpenter or typesetter, the courage of soldiers, the inevitable fact of death. Therefore he speaks plainly about many things which hitherto were tacitly ignored in poetry, or were touched upon by seekers after obscene literary effects. It is not inconsequent that he should have been accused of indecency, because the things he talked of had so long been held to be indecent. Wishing to remove the stigma of indecency and obscenity, which he rightly considered due to conventionally imported prejudices, he had to face the misconstruction of those who could not comprehend his real intention.

Whitman thought and wrote habitually, not with people of culture, refined tastes, literary and social traditions in view, but for the needs and aspirations of what he called 'the divine average'. He aimed at depicting robust and sane humanity in his verse. He wanted to brace character, and to create through his art-work a type applicable to all sorts and conditions of men, irrespective of their previous differentiation by specific temperament or class-association. For this reason, his treatment of the sexual relations will be felt by some persons not only to be crudely frank in detail, but also to lack delicacy in its general outlines. The overwhelming attractions of sex, swaying the physique of men and women, are broadly insisted upon. The intercourse established in matrimony is regarded not so much as an intellectual and moral union, but as an association for mutual assistance in the labours of life, and for the production of noble human specimens. It is an Adamic hygienic view of marriage, satisfying the instincts of the primeval man. Take this passage, in which he describes the qualities of the help-mate for his typical male :

Without shame the man I like knows and avows the deliciousness of his
  sex,
Without shame the woman I like knows and avows hers.
Now I will dismiss myself from impassive women,
I will go stay with her who waits for me, and with those women that
  are warm-blooded and sufficient for me;
I see that they understand me, and do not deny me:
I see that they are worthy of me – I will be the robust husband of these
  women.
They are not one jot less than I am,
They are tanned in the face by shining suns and blowing winds,
Their flesh has the old divine suppleness and strength,
They know how to swim, row, ride, wrestle, shoot, run, strike, retreat,
  advance, resist, defend themselves,
They are ultimate in their own right – they are calm, clear, well-possessed
  of themselves.
I draw you close to me, you women !
I cannot let you go, I would do you good,
I am for you, and you are for me, not only for our own sake, but for
  others' sake;
Envelop'd in you sleep greater heroes and bards,
They refuse to awake at the touch of any man but me.

It is obvious, from this slightly humorous, but pregnant, passage, that Whitman abandoned those dregs of mediæval sentimentalism and platonism, which, filtering through the middle-class minds of an unchivalrous modern age, have resulted in commonplace notions about 'the weaker and the fairer sex', 'woman's mission to console and elevate', the protection rendered by the stronger to the frailer', 'the feminine ornament of our homes' – notions and phrases which the active-minded and able-bodied woman of the present day repudiates and from the thraldom of which she is rapidly working out her way toward freedom. Whitman, to use a phrase of Clough, looked upon love as 'fellow-service'. He recognized the woman's right to share alike with man in labour and in privilege. And it was not for nothing, as appears from some sentences in the quotation, that he spoke in another place about 'the athletic American matron'*.

A theory of sexual relations, so primitive, so archetypal, so based and planted on the primal needs and instincts, must of necessity lack much of delicacy and fine gradations. It is, however, bracing to return to this from the psychological studies of the modern French school, from such silly and nauseous lucubrations as Bourget's *Physiologie de l'Amour Moderne,* from all that stifling literature of *L'Amour Coupable,* which lands us at last in nothing better than what Whitman calls 'the sly settee, and the unwholesome adulterous couple'.

There is an Aeschylean largeness, a Lucretian energy, in Whitman's *Children of Adam.* Sex is once again recognized; not in its aspect of the boudoir, the alcove, the brothel; but as the bass-note of the world, the universal Pan, unseen, yet omnipresent, felt by all, responded to by all, without which the whole vast symphony of things would have for man no value. By subtle associations, he connects the life of nature, in dewy forests and night-winds, in scents of fruits and pungent plants, in crushed herbs, and the rustling of rain-drenched foliage against our faces, with impressions of the sexual imagination. He finds the choicest images to shadow forth the acts of sex.

The hairy wild bee that murmurs and hankers up and down – that gripes the full-grown lady-flower, curves upon her with amorous firm legs, takes his will of her, and holds himself tremulous and tight till he is satisfied.

That is audacious, in spite of its consummate style, a critic will exclaim. But the same critic, being accustomed by habit to the exercise, reads with equanimity the long-drawn paragraphs and chapters which lay bare the latest secrets of the 'sly settee'. The boudoir, the alcove, the brothel, have come to be recognized as legitimate subjects for analytical art. Even Bourget, even Catulle

* In the preface to the 1872 edition of *Leaves of Grass,* Whitman asserts that this book 'is, in its intentions, the song of a great composite *democratic individual,* male or female'.

Mendès, are accepted and acclaimed. From these taints of the city and civilization Whitman calls us away. He says in passing:

> Have you seen the fool that corrupted his own live body? or the fool that corrupted her own live body?
> For they do not conceal themselves, and cannot conceal themselves.

Here and there he returns to this point and repeats the warning. He insists upon the truth that sins against the body, self-contamination, uncleanly lusts and refinements of sensuality, carry their own punishments. But he knows that their analysis in literature, except for the professed pathologist and psychiatrist, is harmful to the manhood of a nation; whereas the rehabilation of healthy and legitimate functions restores the natural man to a sense of his own dignity and responsibility. Nor does Whitman neglect that superflux of sense, which also claims a part in human life, that phallic ecstasy of which the pagan poets sang. A much-criticized piece from *Children of Adam* puts the matter very plainly. It is called *Native Moments*, and need not be enlarged upon. Were we not expressly told by him that it is useless to extract a coherent system from his utterances, we might be puzzled to explain the logical connection of that poem with the rest of the section. I take it that he recognized the right and the necessity of 'native moments' in that free play of the normal senses which he is upholding. Only, the ground-thoughts which penetrate the whole of his work upon this topic, the pervading essence whereof will remain longest with those who have imbibed its spirit, are expressed in lines like these:

> If any thing is sacred, the human body is sacred,
> And the glory and sweet of a man is the token of manhood untainted;
> And in man or woman, a clean, strong, firm-fibred body is beautiful as the most beautiful face.

If Aeschylus could come again, he would recognize Whitman's treatment of Aphrodite as akin to these lines of his own:

> Love throbs in holy heaven to wound the earth;
> And love still prompts the land to yearn for bridals.
> The rain that falls in rivers from the sky,
> Impregnates earth, and she brings forth for men
> The flocks and herds and life of teeming Ceres;
> The bloom of forests by dews hymeneal
> Is perfected: in all which things I rule.

If we are to have sex handled openly in literature – and I do not see why we should not have it, or how we are to avoid it – surely it is better to be in the company of poets like Aeschylus and Whitman, who place human love among the large and universal mysteries of nature, than to dwell with theologians who confound its simple truth with sinfulness, or with self-dubbed 'psychologues' who dabble in its morbid pruriencies.

The section of Whitman's works which deals with adhesiveness, or the love of comrades, is fully as important, and in some ways more difficult to deal with, than his *Children of Adam*. He gave it the title *Calamus*, from the root of a water-rush, adopted by him as the symbol of this love.* Here the element of spirituality in passion, of romantic feeling, and of deep enduring sentiment, which was almost conspicuous by its absence from the section on sexual love, emerges into vivid prominence, and lends peculiar warmth of poetry to the artistic treatment. We had to expect so much from the poem quoted by me at the commencement of this disquisition. There Whitman described the love of man for woman as 'fast-anchored, eternal'; the thought of the bride, the wife, as 'more resistless than I can tell'. But for the love of man for man he finds quite a different class of descriptive phrases: 'separate, disembodied, another born, ethereal, the last athletic reality, my consolation'. He hints that we have left the realm of sex and sense, and have ascended into a different and rarer atmosphere, where passion, though it has not lost its strength, is clarified. 'Largior hic aether, et campos lumine vestit purpureo'.

This emphatic treatment of an emotion which is usually talked about under the vague and formal term of friendship, gives peculiar importance to *Calamus*. No man in the modern world has expressed so strong a conviction that 'manly attachment', 'athletic love', 'the high towering love of comrades', is a main factor in human life, a virtue upon which society will have to lay its firm foundations, and a passion equal in permanence, superior in spirituality, to the sexual affection. Whitman regards this emotion not only as the 'consolation'

* Its botanical name is Acorus Calamus. We call it 'sweet-rush' or 'sweet sedge' of the individual, but also as a new and hitherto unapprehended force for stimulating national vitality.

There is no softness or sweetness in his treatment of this theme. His tone is sustained throughout at a high pitch of virile enthusiasm, which, at the same time, vibrates with acutest feeling, thrills with an undercurrent of the tenderest sensibility. Not only the sublimest thoughts and aspirations, but also the shyest, most shame-faced, yearnings are reserved for this love. At one time he exclaims:

O I think it is not for life that I am chanting here my chant of lovers – I
    think it must be for Death,
For how calm, how solemn it grows, to ascend to the atmosphere of
    lovers,
Death or life, I am then indifferent – my soul declines to prefer,
I am not sure but the high soul of lovers welcomes death most;
Indeed, O Death, I think now these leaves mean precisely the same as
    you mean;
Grow up taller, sweet leaves, that I may see! Grow up out of my breast!
Spring away from the concealed heart there!
Do not fold yourselves so, in your pink-tinged roots, timid leaves!
Do not remain down there so ashamed, herbage of my breast!

The leaves are Whitman's emotions and the poems they engender; the root from which they spring is 'manly attachment', 'athletic love', symbolized for him in the blushing root of the pond-calamus which he plucked one day and chose to be the emblem of the love of lovers:

O here I last saw him that tenderly loves me – and returns again, never
    to separate from me,
And this, O this shall henceforth be the token of comrades – this Calamus-
    root shall,
Interchange it, youths, with each other! Let none render it back!

At another time, in minor key, he writes as follows:

O you when I often and silently come where you are, that I may be with
    you;
As I walk by your side, or sit near, or remain in the same room with
    you,
Little you know the subtle, electric fire that for your sake is playing within
    me.

These extracts were necessary, because there is some misapprehension abroad regarding the precise nature of what Whitman meant by *Calamus*. His method of treatment has, to a certain extent, exposed him to misconstruction. Still, as his friend and commentator, Mr Burroughs, puts it : 'The sentiment is primitive, athletic, taking form in all manner of large and homely out-of-door images, and springs, as any one may see, directly from the heart and experience of the poet.' The language has a passionate glow, a warmth of devotion, beyond anything to which the world is used in the celebration of friendship. At the same time the false note of insincerity or sensuousness is never heard. The melody is in the Dorian mood – recalling to our minds that fellowship in arms which flourished among the Dorian tribes, and formed the chivalry of pre-historic Hellas.

In the preface to the 1880 edition of *Leaves of Grass* and *Two Rivulets*, Whitman gives his own explanation of *Calamus*, and of the feelings which inspired that section of his work.

Something more may be added – for, while I am about it, I would make a full confession. I also sent out *Leaves of Grass* to arouse and set flowing in men's and women's hearts, young and old, endless streams of living, pulsating love and friendship, directly from them to myself, now and ever. To this terrible, irrepressible yearning (surely more or less down underneath in most human souls), this never-satisfied appetite for sympathy and this boundless offering of sympathy, this universal democratic comradeship, this old, eternal, yet ever-new interchange of adhesiveness, so fitly emblematic of America, I have given in that book, undisguisedly, declaredly, the openest expression. Besides, important as they are in my purpose as emotional expressions for humanity, the special meaning of the *Calamus*, cluster of *Leaves of Grass* (and more or less running through the book and cropping out in *Drum Taps*), mainly resides in its political significance. In my opinion, it is by a fervent accepted development of comradeship, the beautiful and sane affection of man for man, latent in all the young fellows, north and south, east and west – it is by this, I say, and by what goes directly and indirectly along with it, that the United States of the future (I cannot too often repeat) are to be the most effectually welded together, intercalated, annealed into a living union.

This being so, Whitman never suggests that comradeship may occasion the development of physical desire. On the other hand,

he does not in set terms condemn desires, or warn his disciples
against their perils. There is indeed a distinctly sensuous side to
his conception of adhesiveness. To a Western Boy he says :

If you be not silently selected by lovers, and do not silently select lovers,
Of what use is it that you seek to become elect of mine?

Like Plato, in the *Phaedrus*, Whitman describes an enthusiastic
type of masculine emotion, leaving its private details to the moral
sense and special inclination of the individuals concerned.

The poet himself appears to be not wholly unconscious that there
are dangers and difficulties involved in the highly-pitched emotions
he is praising. The whole tenor of two carefully-toned compositions, entitled *Whoever you are, Holding me now in hand*, and
Trickle, Drops, suggest an underlying sense of spiritual conflict.
The following poem, again, is sufficiently significant and typical
to call for literal transcription :

Earth, my likeness!
Though you look so impassive, ample and spheric there,
I now suspect that is not all;
I now suspect there is something fierce in you, eligible to burst forth;
For an athlete is enamoured of me – and I of him,
But toward him there is something fierce and terrible in me, eligible to
   burst forth,
I dare not tell it in word – not even in these songs.

The reality of Whitman's feeling, the intense delight which he
derives from the personal presence and physical contact of a beloved
man, find luminous expression in *A Glimpse, Recorders ages hence,
When I heard at the Close of Day, I saw in Louisiana a Live-Oak
growing, Long I thought that Knowledge alone would suffice me,**
O Tan-faced Prairie Boy*, and *Vigil Strange I kept on the Field one
Night.†*
It is clear then that, in his treatment of comradeship, or the
impassioned love of man for man, Whitman has struck a key-note,
to the emotional intensity of which the modern world is
unaccustomed. It therefore becomes of much importance to discover

* Not included in the *Complete Poems and Prose*. It will be found in
Leaves of Grass, Boston, 1860–61
† The two last are from *Drum-Taps*

the poet-prophet's *Stimmung* – his radical instinct with regard to the moral quality of the feeling he encourages. Studying his works by their own light, and by the light of their author's character, interpreting each part by reference to the whole and in the spirit of the whole, an impartial critic will, I think, be drawn to the conclusion that what he calls the 'adhesiveness' of comradeship is meant to have no interblending with the 'amativeness' of sexual love. Personally, it is undeniable that Whitman possessed a specially keen sense of the fine restraint and continence, the cleanliness and chastity, that are inseparable from the perfectly virile and physically complete nature of healthy manhood. Still we have the right to predicate the same ground-qualities in the early Dorians, those founders of the martial institution of Greek love; and yet it is notorious to students of Greek civilization that the lofty sentiment of their masculine chivalry was intertwined with much that is repulsive to modern sentiment.

Whitman does not appear to have taken some of the phenomena of contemporary morals into due account, although he must have been aware of them. Else he would have foreseen that, human nature being what it is, we cannot expect to eliminate all sensual alloy from emotions raised to a high pitch of passionate intensity, and that permanent elements within the midst of our society will imperil the absolute purity of the ideal he attempts to establish. It is obvious that those unenviable mortals who are the inheritors of sexual anomalies, will recognize their own emotion in Whitman's 'superb friendship, exalté, previously unknown', which 'waits, and has been always waiting, latent in all men', the 'something fierce in me, eligible to burst forth', 'ethereal comradeship', 'the last athletic reality'. Had I not the strongest proof in Whitman's private correspondence with myself that he repudiated any such deductions from his *Calamus*, I admit that I should have regarded them as justified; and I am not certain whether his own feelings upon this delicate topic may not have altered since the time when *Calamus* was first composed.

These considerations, do not, however, affect the spiritual quality of his ideal. After acknowledging, what Whitman omitted to perceive, that there are inevitable points of contact between sexual anomaly and his doctrine of comradeship, the question now remains whether he has not suggested the way whereby abnormal instincts may be moralized and raised to higher value. In other words, are those exceptional instincts provided in *Calamus* with the means of their salvation from the filth and mire of brutal appetite? It is difficult to answer this question; for the issue involved is nothing less momentous than the possibility of evoking a new chivalrous enthusiasm analogous to that of primitive Hellenic society, from emotions which are at present classified among the turpitudes of human nature.

Let us look a little closer at the expression which Whitman has given to his own feelings about friendship. The first thing that strikes us is the mystic emblem he has chosen for masculine love. That is the water-plant, or scented rush, called CALAMUS, which springs in wild places, 'in paths untrodden, in the growth by margins of pond-waters'. He has chosen these 'emblematic and capricious blades' because of their shyness, their aromatic perfume, their aloofness from the patent life of the world. He calls them 'sweet leaves, pink-tinged roots, timid leaves', 'scented herbage of my breast'. Finally, he says :*

> Here my last words, and the most baffling,
> Here the frailest leaves of me, and yet my strongest-lasting.
> Here I shade down, and hide my thoughts – I do not expose them,
> And yet they expose me more than all my other poems.

The manliness of the emotion which is thus so shyly, allegorically indicated, appears in the magnificent address to soldiers at the close of the great war, *Over the Carnage rose Prophetic a Voice.*† Its tenderness emerges in the elegy on a slain comrade :‡

> Vigil for boy of responding kisses (never again on earth responding):
> Vigil for comrade swiftly slain – vigil I never forget, how as day brightened,
> I rose from the chill ground, and folded my soldier well in his blanket,
> And buried him where he fell.

Its pathos and clinging intensity transpire through the last lines of the following piece, which may have been suggested by the

* This I cannot find in *Complete Poems and Prose*. It is included in the Boston edition, 1860–61, and the Camden edition, 1876
† *Drum-Taps. Complete Poems*, p. 247.
‡ *Ibid.* p. 238

legends of David and Jonathan, Achilles and Patroclus, Orestes and Pylades : *

When I peruse the conquered fame of heroes, and the victories of mighty generals,
I do not envy the generals,
Nor the President in his Presidency, nor the rich in his great house;
But when I read of the brotherhood of lovers, how it was with them,
How through life, through dangers, odium, unchanging, long and long,
Through youth, and through middle and old age, how unfaltering, how affectionate and faithful they were,
Then I am pensive – I hastily put down the book, and walk away, filled with the bitterest envy.

But Whitman does not conceive of comradeship as a merely personal possession, delightful to the friends it links in bonds of amity. He regards it eventually as a social and political virtue. This human emotion is destined to cement society and to render commonwealths inviolable. Reading some of his poems, we are carried back to ancient Greece – to Plato's *Symposium,* to Philip gazing on the sacred band of Thebans after the fight at Chaeronea.†

I dream'd in a dream, I saw a city invincible to the attacks of the whole of the rest of the earth;

* *Leaves of Grass. Complete Poems,* p. 107. Since writing the above, I have been privileged to read a series of letters addressed by Whitman to a young man, whom I will call P., and who was tenderly beloved by him. They throw a flood of light upon *Calamus,* and are superior to any commentary. It is greatly to be hoped that they may be published. Whitman, it seems, met P. at Washington not long before the year 1869, when the lad was about eighteen years of age. They soon became attached. Whitman's friendship being returned with at least equal warmth by P. The letters breathe a purity and simplicity of affection, a *naïveté* and reasonableness, which are very remarkable considering the unmistakable intensity of the emotion. Throughout them, Whitman shows the tenderest and wisest care for his young friend's welfare, helps him in material ways, and bestows upon him the best advice, the heartiest encouragement, without betraying any sign of patronage or preaching. Illness soon attacked Walt. He retired to Camden, and P., who was employed as 'baggage-master on the freight-trains' of a railway, was for long unable to visit him. There is something very wistful in the words addressed from a distance by the ageing poet to this 'son of responding kisses'. I regret that we do not possess P.'s answers. Yet, probably, to most readers, they would not appear highly interesting; for it is clear he was only an artless and uncultured workman.
† *Complete Poems,* p. 109. Compare 'I hear it was charged against me', ibid, p. 107

John Addington Symonds

I dream'd that was the new City of Friends
Nothing was greater there than the quality of robust love – it led the rest;
It was seen every hour in the actions of the men of that city,
And in all their looks and words.

And again :*

I believe the main purport of These Slates is to found a superb friendship,
    exalté, previously unknown,
Because I perceive it waits, and has been always waiting, latent in all men.

And once again : †

Come, I will make the continent indissoluble;
I will make the most splendid race the sun ever yet shone upon;
I will make divine magnetic lands,
    With the love of comrades,
      With the life-long love of comrades.
I will plant companionship thick as trees all along the rivers of America,
    and along the shores of the great lakes, and all over the prairies;
I will make inseparable cities, with their arms about each other's necks;
    By the love of comrades,
      By the manly love of comrades.
For you these from me, O Democracy, to serve you *ma femme!*
For you, for you I am trilling these songs.

We may return from this analysis to the inquiry whether anything like a new chivalry is to be expected from the doctrines of
Calamus, which shall in the future utilize for noble purposes some
of those unhappy instincts which at present run to waste in vice and
shame. It may be asked what these passions have in common with
the topic of Whitman's prophecy? They have this in common with
it. Whitman recognizes among the sacred emotions and social
virtues, destined to regenerate political life and to cement nations,
an intense, jealous, throbbing, sensitive, expectant love of man for
man : a love which yearns in absence, droops under the sense of
neglect, revives at the return of the beloved : a love that finds honest
delight in hand-touch, meeting lips, hours of privacy, close personal
contact. He proclaims this love to be not only a daily fact in the
present, but also a saving and ennobling aspiration. While he

* *Complete Poems*, p. 110
† Camden edition, 1876, p. 127. *Complete Poems*, p. 99. Compare
Democratic Vistas, Complete Prose, p. 247, note

expressly repudiates, disowns, and brands as 'damnable' all 'morbid inferences' which may be drawn by malevolence or vicious cunning from his doctrine, he is prepared to extend the gospel of comradeship to the whole human race. He expects democracy, the new social and political medium, the new religious ideal of mankind to develop and extend 'that fervid comradeship', and by its means to counterbalance and to spiritualize what is vulgar and materialistic in the modern world. 'Democracy', he maintains, 'infers such loving comradeship, as its most inevitable twin or counterpart, without which it will be incomplete, in vain, and incapable of perpetuating itself'.*

If this be not a dream, if he is right in believing that 'threads of manly friendship, fond and loving, pure and sweet, strong and life-long, carried to degrees hitherto unknown', will penetrate the organism of society, 'not only giving tone to individual character, and making it unprecedentedly emotion, muscular, heroic, and refined, but having deepest relations to general politics' – then are we perhaps justified in foreseeing here the advent of an enthusiasm which shall rehabilitate those outcast instincts, by giving them a spiritual atmosphere, an environment of recognized and healthy emotions, wherein to expand at liberty and purge away the grossness and the madness of their pariahdom?

This prospect, like all ideals, until they are realized in experience, may seem fantastically visionary. Moreover, the substance of human nature is so mixed that it would perhaps be fanatical to expect from Whitman's chivalry of 'adhesiveness', a more immaculate purity than was attained by the mediæval chivalry of 'amativeness'. Nevertheless that mediæval chivalry, the great emotional product of feudalism, though it fell short of its own aspiration, bequeathed incalculable good to modern society by refining and clarifying the crudest of male appetites. In like manner, this democratic chivalry, announced by Whitman, may be destined to absorb, control, and elevate those darker more mysterious, apparently abnormal appetites, which we know to be widely diffused and ineradicable in the ground-work of human nature.

Returning from the dream, the vision of a future possibility, it will, at any rate, be conceded that Whitman has founded comrade-

* These prose passages are taken from *Democratic Vistas*, cited above, p. 94, note

ship, the enthusiasm which binds man to man in fervent love, upon a natural basis. Eliminating classical associations of corruption, ignoring the perplexed questions of a guilty passion doomed by law and popular antipathy to failure, he begins anew with sound and primitive humanity. There he discovers 'a superb friendship, exalté, previously unknown'. He perceives that 'it waits, and has been always waiting, latent in all men'. His method of treatment, fearless, and uncowed by any thought of evil, his touch upon the matter, chaste and wholesome and aspiring, reveal the possibility of restoring in all innocence to human life a portion of its alienated or unclaimed moral birthright.

It were well to close upon this note. The half, as the Greeks said, is more than the whole; and the time has not yet come to raise the question whether the love of man for man shall be elevated through a hitherto unapprehended chivalry to nobler powers, even as the barbarous love of man for woman once was. This question at the present moment is deficient in actuality. The world cannot be invited to entertain it.

(FROM 'WALT WHITMAN : A STUDY', 1893)

ARTHUR SYMONS

1865 - 1945

Arthur William Symons, poet and critic, was born at Milford Haven
in the county of Pembrokeshire on 21 February 1865. His father
was a Methodist minister and his mother, who enjoyed a public
hanging, was said by her son to be unstable. Instability certainly
developed in him. Visiting Italy with his wife in 1908, he
experienced a total mental breakdown from which his recovery was
gradual and never complete.

The tale of his descent into the maelstrom and of his incarceration
was told by Symons himself in his confessions: *A Study in
Pathology*. This is, in many ways, a moving document; but less
precise in its delineation than the fine account which Symons left
of his earlier experience in *A Prelude to Life*.[1]

So far the fullest account of him is to be found in *Arthur Symons:
A Critical Biography* by Roger Lhombreaud (1963). Writing in 1957
on the development of modern poetics, Professor Frank Kermode
found Symons a 'crucial' figure. In the same year Dame Edith
Sitwell spoke of him in the *Sunday Times* as 'a great critic of the
1890s and 1900s'. To Dr Ian Fletcher in 1953 he appeared as 'a
good minor poet, an excellent minor translator, a major critic'.[2]
Despite these encomia, he remains out of print. It is time a selection
of his best work was republished.

Historically, Symons's development as a critic begins with his
defence of impressionism. The relevant documents here are the
prefaces he wrote to his first two books of verse,[3] an article published

---

[1] *Spiritual Adventures*, 1905
[2] *The Complete Poems of Lionel Johnson*
[3] *Silhouettes*, revised edition 1896; *London Nights*, second edition 1896

in *Harper's* magazine on 'The Decadent Movement in Literature'[4]
and a causerie entitled 'Impressionistic Writing'.[5]

In the last of these, impressionistic literature is described as the
art of phenomenalism – a visual phenomenalism deftly edited. 'The
first thing,' writes Symons, 'is to see, and with an eye which sees
all; and then to write, from a selecting memory, and as if one's
only business were to write.' The aim of such writing should be –
truth to the artistic eye rather than truth to reality.

The essence of Symons's thought as a critic is to be discovered
in his essay 'The Decadent Movement in Literature'. Symons and
a caricature-idea of Decadence had been attacked by Richard
Le Gallienne, and Symons felt himself called upon to answer. He
had been associated with the Decadents and referred to in terms
of this group. It was necessary, to him, to define these terms in
words he would be prepared to accept. In this essay, he begins,
strategically, by linking Decadence with Impressionism and
Symbolism (dogs without existing bad names). These latter two, he
tells us, are 'two main branches' of the Decadent movement and
have more in common than one supposes. 'What both seek is not
general truth merely, but *la verité vrai*, the very essence of truth –
the truth of appearance to the senses, of the visible world to the
eyes that see it; and the truth of spiritual things to the spiritual
vision. The Impressionists . . . would flash upon you . . . an image
of what you have just seen, just as you have seen it. . . . The
Symbolists would flash upon you the "soul" of that which can be
apprehended only by the soul – the finer sense of things unseen,
the deeper meaning of things evident. And both Symbolism and
Impressionism call for a new style, an entire new creative psychology.
This endeavour after perfect truth to one's impression, to one's
intuition . . . has brought with it, in its revolt from ready-made
impressions and conclusions, a revolt from the ready-made of
language, from the bondage of traditional form, of a form become
rigid.'

Mention of the word Symbolism carries one forward to Symons's
famous book *The Symbolist Movement in Literature* published in
1899. As Symons sees it, the outward characteristics of Symbolism
are those of an anti-movement. 'This revolt against exteriority,

[4] 1893, reprinted in *Dramatic Personae*, 1923, New York
[5] *Dramatis Personae*

against rhetoric, against a materialistic tradition,' he terms it. Zola and the realists had 'tried to build in brick and mortar inside the covers of a book'. Leconte de Lisle and the Parnassians with their 'literature of form' had in their verse 'turned the world to stone'. Led by the Symbolists, literature was passing, reasoned Symons, from an art of appearance to an art of essence. 'Description is banished that beautiful things may be evoked, magically.'

But the key-word in Symons's master-plan of Symbolism is 'Mysticism', behind which lies the influence of Yeats. 'I speak often in this book of Mysticism,' writes Symons to his friend in the Dedication. 'It will be no surprise to you, for you have seen me gradually finding my way, uncertainly but inevitably, in that direction.'

To associate Symons in any exact fashion with the theoretical aspect of modern poetics is certainly no easy matter. The attempt, however, has been made by Professor Frank Kermode who finds him to be 'a crucial figure'. 'He,' asserts Professor Kermode, 'more explicitly and more influentially than any of his contemporaries, saw how to synthesize the earlier English tradition – particularly Blake – . . . with Pater and those European Symbolists he knew so well.'[6] Such a claim might take some showing; but Professor Kermode is not content. He wishes also to suggest that Symons's part in the revival of Donne (along with his interest in the Jacobean dramatists and the Symbolists) 'makes intelligible a habit that came to dominate the twentieth-century criticism in its historical phase'.[7] 'Intelligible' perhaps is rather a misnomer. Nowhere did Symons praise the 'metaphysical conceit' as a type of figurative expression nor suggest that in some way it anticipated Symbolist procedure. Indeed, he disapproved of Donne's method. 'Just as he drags into his verse,' wrote Symons, 'words that have had no time to take colour from men's association of them with beauty, so he puts his "naked thinking heart" into verse as if he were setting forth an argument. He gives us the real thing, as he would have been proud to assure us. But poetry will have nothing to do with real things, until it has translated them into a diviner world. . . . He would make poetry speak straight. Well, poetry will not speak straight, in the way Donne wished it to, and under the goading that his restless

[6] *The Romantic Image*
[7] *Ibid*

intellect gave it.'[8] There is precious little in this passage of the 'modern' approach to Donne which finds in the Metaphysical poet 'a mechanism of sensibility which could devour any kind of experience'.[9]

Professor Kermode is on a safer wicket when he claims that Symons saw the dangers of Symbolism as well as its achievements. Like Yeats, he was always aware of the limits of communication. He knew that a work of art must preserve the balance between communication and expression; and that the artist who becomes his one and only reader has somehow failed in his task and duty. Because the expressionist element was more developed in Symbolist verse than in other poetries, Symons understood how it could easily fall prey to obscurity. Of Mallarmé's most difficult last phase he wrote as follows: 'A new image occurs to him, rarer, subtler, than the one he has used; the image is transferred. By the time the poem has reached, as it seems to him, a flawless unity, the steps of the progress have been only too effectually effaced; and while the poet, who has seen the thing from the beginning, still sees the relation of point to point, the reader, who comes to it only in its final stage, finds himself in a not unnatural bewilderment. Pursue this manner of writing to its ultimate; start with an enigma, and then withdraw the key of the enigma; and you arrive, easily, at the frozen impenetrability of those latest sonnets, in which the absence of all punctuation is a scarcely recognizable hindrance.'[10]

To maintain, as Professor Kermode does, that Symons sought to synthesize Blake and the Symbolists is something not readily evident. What is more apparent is that Symons saw the short-comings of Blake's method just as he saw the limitations of Mallarmé. Of the former's *Prophetic Books* he observed: 'He is concerned now only with his message . . . and he has ceased to accept any mortal medium, or to allow himself to be penetrated by the sun-light of earthly beauty, he has lost the means of making that message visible to us. It is a miscalculation of means, a contempt for possibilities: not, as people were once hasty enough to assume, the irresponsible rapture of madness.'[11] 'A miscalculation of means,

[8] 'Donne' (*Figures of Several Centuries*) 1916
[9] 'The Metaphysical Poets' (*Selected Essays*) by T. S. Eliot, 1932
[10] 'Stéphane Mallarmé' (*The Symbolist Movement in Literature*) 1899
[11] 'William Blake' (*The Romantic Movement in English Poetry*) 1909

a contempt for possibilities' – a good deal of modern poetry, inscribed in its wayward subjective shorthand, could be written off in those two phrases. Symons, in the van of the 'nineties, would prove a conservative influence today.

More fruitful, in general approach, is Mr Graham Hough's *Image and Experience* (1960) in which he has sought to trace the connection between the Symbolist and Imagist movements. Taking this notion as its point of departure, Derek Stanford's essay on *Arthur Symons and Modern Poetics*[12] might also be mentioned here.

If one's interest lay in Symbolism alone, it is not certain that Symons would prove the surest guide. For a picture of the lives of these French authors, and a general impression and survey of their work, for this one can safely resort to him. But if one is wanting some deeper sense, some greater spiritual insight into the principles behind their art, then Yeats is a finer authority. However, the critical acumen of Yeats, at his best, is still to be explored.

It happens though that Symons's writings on the Symbolists make up only a portion of his work. In *Studies in Two Literatures* (1897) there are essays on Walter Pater, Coventry Patmore, William Morris, Christina Rossetti, John Addington Symonds, Stevenson and others, as well as sketches of non-Symbolist French writers: Zola, Gautier, Constant, Maupassant. *Studies in Prose and Verse* (1904) contains important appreciations of three leading contemporaries: Yeats, Wilde and Dowson; in addition to fine essays on Balzac and Merimée. Next comes his encyclopaedic *The Romantic Movement in English Poetry* (1909), a compendium of able reference and comment on over ninety figures belonging to this period, a work as significant in scholarship as it is in criticism.

'Arthur Symons,' recalled Yeats, 'more than any man ever known, could slip as it were into the mind of another.'[13] It was this responsive receptivity which made him the sensitive critic that he was. One of the factors of this receptivity was the absence in him of any moral censure. 'Criticism,' states Symons, 'is a valuation of forces, and it is indifferent to their direction. It is concerned with them only as force, and it is concerned in its kind and degree.'[14]

[12] *The Southern Review*, Spring 1966
[13] 'The Trembling of the Veil' (*The Tragic Generation*)
[14] 'On Criticism' (*Dramatis Personae*)

The laws of such criticism will be the laws of a kind of physics of purely aesthetic motion, and this, of course, works two ways, producing two different and opposed results. In the first case, it ensures for the critic a generous catholicism of response; in the second, it deprives him of the security of a point of view. From his other writings, one is left with the impression that Symons possessed little self-knowledge. In the last resort, he literally did not know who he was; and after his recovery from madness, he knew even less than before.

Because he lacks a real standpoint, Symons can never be approached as one approaches Dr Johnson, for the moral sense of some author in question. And just as he lacks a moral point of view, so, too, he is without intellectual belief, something definite and formulated. Behind his 'appreciations' there is no firm structure of ideas, social, religious or philosophical. His criticism of literature takes place within a cultural context consisting almost solely of travel, languages, and the arts. Of the varied life of society, and of man's other activities and studies – politics, history, philosophy and science – he appears to possess no interest and no knowledge. He has nothing but his sensibility; lonely, discriminating, exquisite. All his writing is one man's record – that of one man hardly aware of the social ties which bind him to the body of mankind within a common culture.

In a generation of impressionist critics, Symons was the impressionist *par excellence*. He was also the impressionist in painful isolation. Lionel Johnson had, to temper his impressions, a sense of tradition, vast learning, and the Church. Richard le Gallienne had his journalistic sense, a sense of the public and of the main chance. The one was protected by his scholarship; the other by his vulgarity. Symons must, in the words of his own poem

> Sole with himself, his single burden bear
> All the day long until the night's release.

Like the speaker in *The Waste Land*, Symons could say of his impressions, hoarded into verse and prose, 'These fragments I have shored against my ruins.'[16] They were the communicable portion of the man.

[15] 'Credo' (*London Nights*)
[16] *Collected Poems 1909–1935* by T. S. Eliot

IMPRESSIONISTIC WRITING

Impressionistic writing requires the union of several qualities; and to possess all these qualities except one, no matter which, is to fail in impressionistic writing. The first thing is to see, and with an eye which sees all, and as if one's only business were to see; and then to write, from a selecting memory, and as if one's only business were to write. It is the interesting heresy of a particular kind of art to seek truth before beauty; but in an impressionistic art concerned, as the art of painting is, with the revelation, the re-creation, of a coloured and harmonious world, which (they tell us) owes its very existence to the eyes which see it, truth is a quality which can be attained only by him who seeks beauty before truth. The true impressionist may be imagined as saying: 'Suppose I wish to give you an impression of the Luxembourg Gardens, as I see them when I look out of my window, will it help to call up in your mind the impression of those glimmering alleys and the naked darkness of the trees, if I begin by telling you that I can count seven cabs, half another at one end, and a horse's head at the other, in the space between the corner of the Odéon and the houses on the opposite side of the street; that there are four trees and three lamp-posts on the pavement; and that I can read the words "Chocolat Menier", in white letters, on a blue ground, upon the circular black kiosk by the side of the second lamp-post? I see those things, no doubt, unconsciously, before my eye travels as far as the railings of the garden; but are they any essential part of my memory of the scene afterward?'

I have turned over page after page of clever, ingenious summarizing of separate detail in a certain book, but I have found nowhere a page of pure beauty; all is broken, jagged, troubled, in this restless search after the broken and jagged outlines of things. It is all little bits of the world seen without atmosphere, and, in spite of many passages which endeavour to draw a moral from clouds, gas, flowers and darkness, seen without sentiment. When the writer describes to us 'the old gold and scarlet of hanging meat; the metallic green of mature cabbages; the wavering russet of piled potatoes; the sharp white of fly-bills, pasted all awry'; we can not doubt that he has seen exactly what he describes, exactly as he describes it, and, to a certain extent, we too see what he describes to us. But he does not, as Huysmans does in the *Croquis Parisiens*, absolutely force the sight of it upon us, so that we see it, perhaps with horror, but in spite of ourselves we see it. Nor does he, when some vague encounter on the road has called up in him a 'sense of the ruthless nullity of life, of the futile deception of effort, a bitter revolt against the extinction of death, a yearning after faith in a vague survival beyond', convey to us the impression which he has felt in such a way that we, too, feel it, and feel it to be the revelation of the inner meaning of just that landscape, just that significant moment. He has but painted a landscape, set an inexpressive figure in the background, and ticketed the frame with a motto which has nothing to do with the composition.

In this book the writer has not, it seems to me, succeeded in his intention; but I have a further fault to find with the intention itself. It is one of the discreditable signs of the haste and heedlessness of our time that artists are coming to content themselves, more and more, with but sketching out their pictures, instead of devoting themselves to the patient labour of painting them; and that they are anxious to invent an excuse for their idleness by proclaiming the superiority of the unfinished, instinctive first draught over the elaborated, scarcely spontaneous work of finished art. A fine composition may, in the most subtle and delicate sense, be slight : a picture of Whistler, for example, a poem of Verlaine. To be slight, as Whistler, as Verlaine, is slight, is to have refined away, by a process of ardent, often of arduous, craftsmanship, all but what is most essential in outward form, in intellectual substance. It is because a painter, a poet of this kind, is able to fill every line, every word, with so intense a life, that he can afford to dispense with that amplification, that reiterance, which an artist of less passionate vitality must needs expend upon the substance of his art. But it is so easy to be brief without being concise; to leave one's work unfinished, simply because one has not the energy to finish it ! This book, like most experiments in writing prose as if one were writing sonnets, is but a collection of notes, whose only value is that they may some day be worked into the substance of a story or an essay. It has not yet been proved – in spite of the many interesting attempts which have been made, chiefly in France, in spite of *Gaspard de la Nuit*, Baudelaire's *Petits Poèms en Prose*, and

Mallarmé's jewelled fragments – that prose can, quite legitimately, be written in this detached, poetic way, as if one were writing sonnets. It seems to me that prose, just because it is prose, and not poetry – an art of vaguer, more indeterminate form, of more wandering cadences – can never restrict itself within those limits which give the precision of its charm to verse, without losing charm, precision, and all the finer qualities of its own freedom.

In France, as in England, there are two kinds of poetical reputation, and in France these two kinds may be defined as the reputation of the Latin Quarter and the reputation of the boulevards. In England a writer like Francis Thompson was, after all, known to only a very narrow circle, even though many, in that circle, looked on him as the most really poetical poet of his generation. In France, Vielé-Griffin is greatly admired by the younger men, quite as much, perhaps, as De Régnier, but he is not read by the larger outside public which has, at all events, heard of De Régnier. These fine shades of reputation are not easily recognized by the foreigner; they have, indeed, nothing to do with the question of actual merit; but they have, all the same, their interest, if only as an indication of the condition and tendency of public opinion.

If we go further, and try to compare the actual merit of the younger French and English poets, we shall find some difficulty in coming to any very definite conclusion. To certain enthusiasts for exotic things, it has seemed as if the mere fact of a poem being written in French gives it an interest which it could not have had if it had been written in English. When the poem was written by Verlaine or by Mallarmé, yes; but now that Verlaine and Mallarmé are gone? Well, there is still something which gives, or seems to give, French verse an advantage over English. The movement which began with Baudelaire, and culminated in Verlaine, has provided, for every young man who is now writing French verse, a very helpful kind of tradition, which leaves him singularly free within certain definite artistic limits. It shows him, not a fixed model, but the suggestion of innumerable ways in which to be himself. All modern French verse is an attempt to speak straight, and at the same time to speak beautifully. *'L'art, mes enfants, c'est d'être absolument soimême,'* said Verlaine, and all these poets who are writing *vers libre*, and even those who are not writing *vers libre*, are content to be absolutely themselves, and to leave externalities perhaps even too much alone. What we see in England is exactly the contrary. We have had our traditions, and we have worn them out, without discovering a new form for ourselves. When we try to be personal in verse, the personal emotion has to mould anew every means of expression, every time; and it is rarely that we succeed in so difficult a task. For the most part we write poems for the sake of writing poems, choosing something outside ourselves to write about, and bringing it into permanent relation with ourselves. Our English verse-writers offer us a ballad, a sonnet, an eclogue; and it is a flower without a root, springing from no deep soil in the soul. The verse is sometimes excellent verse, but it is not a personal utterance; it is not a mood of a temperament, but something outside a temperament. In France, it is true, we often get the temperament and nothing else. And, in France, all these temperaments seem stationary; they neither change nor develop; they remain self-centred, and in time we become weary of seeing their pale reflections of themselves. Here, we become weary of poets who see everything in the world but themselves, and who have no personal hold upon the universe without. Between the too narrowly personal and a too generalized impersonality, there remains, in France and in England, a little exquisite work, which is poetry. Is it important, or even possible, to decide whether there is a little more of it to be found in the books of English or of French poets?

(FROM DRAMATIS PERSONAE, 1923, New York)

W. B. YEATS

1865-1939

William Butler Yeats – the laureate of the Celtic Twilight and a deep, subtle, unacademic critic – was born on 13 June 1865 at Sandymount, near Dublin. There have been a number of good and full biographies of Yeats, among which should be noted Richard Ellman's *Yeats: The Man and the Masks* (1948) and Norman Jeffares' *W. B. Yeats: Man and Poet* (1949). Among critical examinations of the poet's work T. R. Henn's *The Lonely Tower* (1950) and P. Ure's *Toward a Mythology: Studies in the Poetry of Yeats* (1946) should certainly be mentioned.

Yeats' achievement, as a critic of the 'nineties, lies in two fields : his attempt to provide the Celtic Renaissance with a rough and ready working-body of ideas, as bearing on contemporary Irish letters; and his formulation of Symbolism – a French and Continental poetic – largely in terms of the Irish background and his occult studies.

Yeats' imaginative roots – as 'Reveries over Childhood and Youth'[1] (1914) makes plain – lay in Ireland and Irish experience. One has only, however, to read the next section of his autobiographical sequence[2] – 'Four Years 1887–91' – to see that his first *intellectual* ideas came to him, via his father, from English literature and painting. This latter element constituted what can be referred to as Yeats' Pre-Raphaelite inheritance – a body of shadowy subjective notions which it was his initial task to adapt to the culture of Irish folk-lore, popular tales and poetry. Both, after all, were anti-rationalist and anti-materialist in their assumptions. Both, consciously or instinctively, posited beauty and the inward life as,

---

[1] *Autobiographies*, 1926
[2] 'The Trembling of the Veil', 1922 (*Autobiographies*)

perhaps, the two 'goods' of human existence. It was mainly that, while the Pre-Raphaelite artists focused on individual experience (an experience seemingly solipsist in some cases), the creators and tellers of Irish tales had developed their fantasies against the national background of a complete society.

The first fruits of Yeats' work in this field are three collections of stories, each with accompanying introduction: *Fairy and Folk Tales of the Irish Peasantry* (1888), *Representative Irish Tales* (1891), and *Irish Fairy Tales* (1892). Yeats' spirit of working here was that of the mythologist, not the anthropologist. This is another way of saying that his approach was not scientific but aesthetic. He was not detachedly seeking to uncover the detailed culture-patterns of a people, but rather for the remnants of a spoken or popular literature which should be the basis for a great written literature of his own day. Yeats' positive way of looking for what he wanted to find is suggested, very distinctly, in his introduction to *Fairy and Folk Tales of the Irish Peasantry*. 'The various collections of Irish folk-lore,' he wrote, 'have from our point of view, one great merit, and from the point of view of others, one great fault. They have made their work literature rather than science, and told us of the Irish peasantry rather than of the primitive religion of mankind, or whatever else the folk-lorists are on the gad after. To be considered scientists they should have tabulated all their tales in forms like grocers' bills – item the fairy kind, item the queen. Instead of this they have caught the very voice of the people, the very pulse of life, each giving what was most noticed in his day.'

In 1893 Yeats published his own collection of tales, many from the Sligo district where his family had their roots, under the title of *The Celtic Twilight*. It is what must be described as semi-documentary literature, slight, apparitional, yet often humorous. The wording of the title, however, caught on, and the 'Celtic Twilight' now became a phrase to describe that body of writers who were engaged in presenting the Irish imagination, whether in fresh creative literature or through folk-lore and mythologies of the past.

What came to be known as the Celtic Twilight Movement was, then, the literary and imaginative equivalent, in the cultural arena, of Irish Nationalism. 'It was the death of Parnell [1891],' Yeats recalled later, 'that convinced me that the movement had come for work in Ireland, for I knew that for a time the imagination of young men would turn from politics.'[3] Yeats' desire was to purify imaginative Irish verse and prose from the clouds of patriotic rhetoric which made it a mere humble, if frenetic, servant of politics. Nor was Yeats the only one who lamented the domination of Irish literature by the standards of oratory. Dedicating his *Early Poems and Stories* (1925) to his friend Ashe King, Yeats wrote how he 'remembered a lecture you delivered in the year 1894 to the Dublin National Literary Society; a denunciation of rhetoric, and of Irish rhetoric most of all' – a point some 'patriots' did not receive kindly – adding that 'a distaste for rhetoric was a chief characteristic of my generation'.

The main instrument which Yeats forged to strengthen and clarify the Irish artistic conscience already existed in rough untutored form – 'a little . . . society of young people, clerks, shop-boys, and shop-girls . . . [who] got the giggles.'[4] This somewhat unpromising body was known as 'The Southwark Irish Literary Society', whose committee he invited in 1892 to his father's house in Bedford Park, London W.4, 'and there proposed a new organization, "The Irish Literary Society",' which – with T. W. Rolleston's help – 'was founded and joined by every London-Irish author and journalist'.[5] In the same year, Yeats was over in Dublin, founding a society there called 'The Irish National Literary Society', 'and affiliating it with certain Young Ireland Societies in country towns which seemed anxious to accept its leadership. I had definite plans.'[6]

The first piece of writing by Yeats under the aegis of this group convoked by him was an article on the society, in which he posed the question: 'Can we not write literature to the great passion of patriotism and ennoble both thereby?'[7] One thing which Yeats clearly sought to do was to separate the appeal of contending parties. 'Amidst the clash of party against party,' he wrote, 'we have tried to put forward a nationality that is above party, and

[3] 'Four Years: 1887–1891' (*Autobiographies*, 1926)
[4] 'Ireland After Parnell' (*Autobiographies*)
[5] *Ibid*
[6] *Ibid*
[7] 'The Irish National Literary Society' 1892 (*W. B. Yeats: Selected Criticism*, ed. A Norman Jeffares, 1964)

amid the oncoming roar of a general election we have tried to assert these everlasting principles of love and of truth and love of country that speak to men in solitude and in the silence of the night.'[8] The truths that 'speak to men in solitude and in the silence of the night' are not the 'truths' of political parties : they are the truths of the spirit or Symbolist truths. 'No sooner,' wrote the Belgian Symbolist Maeterlinck, 'are the lips still than the soul awakes, and sets forth on its labours !')[9]

The most reflective account, however, of what Yeats would have the Celtic Movement stand for is to be found in an article 'Ireland and the Arts' (1901), containing the condensed substance of the pan-Celtic theories propounded by him in the 'nineties. He says that in Ireland the writers will find 'two passions ready to their hands, love of the Unseen Life and love of country'. Again, one sees Yeats at his task of seeking to give the programme of Symbolism (with its stress on the inward and invisible) a specific Irish slanting.

The article is of interest, too, for the way in which Yeats differentiates his thinking from that of the typical *fin-de-siècle* aesthete. He criticizes that exclusive aestheticism which was still operating in English literature, a position which Yeats knew well enough from the example of many of his friends to assess quite accurately. The aesthetic author, Yeats maintained, was 'too proud, too anxious to live alone with the perfect'. The artist, he thought, should be both proud and humble. He must learn to find his 'passion among the people', and to preach and baptize the popular imagination.

Symbolism, along with the Celtic Imagination, had long been Yeats's leading interest. Unlike Arthur Symons – customarily hailed as the custodian of the Symbolist mystique – Yeats' apprenticeship to Symbolist thought had been arduous and methodical. As early as February 1889 we find him writing to Katharine Tynan announcing the project : 'You will be surprised to hear what I am at besides the new play; a commentary on the mystical writings of Blake. A friend is helping me or perhaps I should say I am helping him, as he knows Blake much better than I do, or anyone else perhaps. It should draw notice – be a sort of red flag above the

---

[8] *Ibid*
[9] 'Silence' (*The Treasure of the Humble* 1897)

waters of oblivion – for there is no clue printed anywhere to the mysterious "Prophetic Books" – Swinburne and Gilchrist found them unintelligible.'[10] This was the task undertaken with the poet Edwin J. Ellis and finally published in 1893 as *The Works of William Blake*. The payment which each author received from its publisher, the bookseller Quaritch, for this three-volume venture was 'thirteen large paper copies . . . worth at the smallest £3 apiece'.

Yeats had received his passion for Blake as part of the Pre-Raphaelite inheritance. Blake had long been a cult, almost a church, with the Pre-Raphaelites since William and Dante Gabriel Rossetti purchased a manuscript book of the poet from the British Museum on 30 April 1847.

Other products of his Blakeian studies were his selection of the poems of Blake (1893) and his articles *William Blake and the Imagination* and *William Blake and His Illustrations to the Divine Comedy*, both of which appeared in 1897.

Yeats has described the poetic and intellectual excitement which he shared with his friend Arthur Symons between 1895 and 1900. He has told us how they shared chambers in Fountain Court, Temple, together; and how the translations which Symons made from the French of Verlaine and Mallarmé influenced certain of the pieces in his own book of verse *The Wind among the Reeds* (1899). The interchange of thought between these two men, however, was not a one-way traffic only; and when read side by side, in their respective critical writings, the same ideas are often found re-echoed or re-phrased. Comparing Yeats' volume of essays *Ideas of Good and Evil* (1903) with Symons' volume of critical studies *The Symbolist Movement in Literature* (1899), one has the feeling that here are two books by co-authors. Nor is the date of book-publication a clue to the first enunciation of these notions, since the constituent contents in both volumes had appeared, in most cases, in various periodicals as far back as 1895 or earlier. Some of this combined intellectual activity has been examined by Dr Ian Fletcher in an article[11] contributed to *London Magazine*; but Yeats, in this phase of his career, still remains a highly important, largely unstudied critic.

Symbolism's debt to Yeats as a theorist is too complicated an

[10] *W. B. Yeats: Letters to Katharine Tynan* ed. B. McHugh, 1953
[11] 'Symons, Yeats and the Demonic Dance' (*London Magazine*, June 1960)

issue for more than an oblique glance at here. Perhaps one might possibly say, however, that whereas Symons appears as the delicate and often just assessor of individual authors and their books, it is Yeats – among the British *literati* – who contributed most to Symbolism's stock of general ideas.

Yeats, as has been said, studied William Blake as a prolegomenon to his acquaintance with certain ideas of French Symbolism, but long before there had been Shelley, and in his indicative essay 'The Philosophy of Shelley's Poetry', he tells us that when he was a boy in Dublin 'I was one of a group who rented a room in a mean street to discuss philosophy. . . . I thought that whatever of philosophy has been made poetry is alone permanent, and that one should begin to arrange it in some regular order, rejecting nothing as the make-believe of the poets.'[12]

Shelley and Blake – unlike the French Symbolists whom Symons studied, with the possible exception of Mallarmé – were philosophical or entological poets, and in examining their structure of ideas, Yeats was strengthening his untutored but temperamental bent for general ideas. ('I was full of thought, often very abstract thought,'[13] he wrote of himself in 1891, noting that his co-poets of the Rhymers' Club, Lionel Johnson and Herbert Horne, opposed 'all ideas, all generalizations that can be explained and debated.'[14])

When we contrast the impression which these few casual statements present of Yeats' mentality as a critic with Symons' remark that the true critic 'studies origins in effects', we pass from the kind of personality to whom ideas are essential to one for whom only sensations are valid (we recall how tiresomely Symons retells us that 'I am one of those for whom the visible world exists').

Nowhere in Symons does one encounter any such personal definition of the Symbol as that which Yeats offered in his highly pertinent essay 'On Magic' (1900) : 'A symbol is indeed the only possible expression of the same invisible essence, a transparent lamp about a spiritual flame.'[15] Yeats's trafficking with magic dated from the 'eighties when he attended Madame Blavatsky's soirées at

[12] 'The Philosophy of Shelley's Poetry', 1900 (*Yeats: Selected Criticism* ed. A. Norman Jeffares, 1964)
[13] 'Trembling of the Veil' (*Autobiographies*)
[14] *Ibid*
[15] *Essays and Introductions*, 1961

Norwood and Macgregor Mathis initiated him in a Charlotte Street studio into the Society of 'The Hermetic Students'. Those who read the poet's *Autobiographies* and carefully study the brilliant essay 'On Magic' will see the bearings which his occult activities had upon his literary ideas, for it is no exaggeration to describe Magic as Applied or Practical Symbolism.

THE SYMBOLISM OF POETRY

I

Symbolism, as seen in the writers of our day, would have no value if it were not seen also, under one 'disguise or another, in every great imaginative writer', writes Mr Arthur Symons in *The Symbolist Movement in Literature*, a subtle book which I cannot praise as I would, because it has been dedicated to me; and he goes on to show how many profound writers have in the last few years sought for a philosophy of poetry in the doctrine of symbolism, and how even in countries where it is almost scandalous to seek for any philosophy of poetry, new writers are following them in their search. We do not know what the writers of ancient times talked of among themselves, and one bull is all that remains of Shakespeare's talk, who was on the edge of modern times; and the journalist is convinced, it seems, that they talked of wine and women and politics, but never about their art, or never quite seriously about their art. He is certain that no one who had a philosophy of his art, or a theory of how he should write, has ever made a work of art, that people have no imagination who do not write without forethought and afterthought as he writes his own articles. He says this with enthusiasm, because he has heard it at so many comfortable dinner-tables, where someone had mentioned through carelessness, or foolish zeal, a book whose difficulty had offended indolence, or a man who had not forgotten that beauty is an accusation. Those formulas and generalizations, in which a hidden sergeant has drilled the ideas of journalists and through them the ideas of all but all the modern world, have created in their turn a forgetfulness like that of soldiers in battle, so that journalists and their readers have forgotten, among many like events, that Wagner spent seven years arranging and explaining his ideas before he began his most characteristic music; that opera, and with it modern music, arose from certain talks at the house of one Giovanni Bardi of Florence; and that the Pléiade laid the foundations of modern French literature with a pamphlet. Goethe has said, 'a poet needs all philosophy, but he must keep it out of his work', though that is not always necessary; and almost certainly no great art, outside England, where journalists are more powerful and ideas less plentiful than elsewhere, has arisen without a great criticism, for its herald or its interpreter and protector, and it may be for this reason that great art, now that vulgarity has armed itself and multiplied itself, is perhaps dead in England.

All writers, all artists of any kind, in so far as they have had any philosophical or critical power, perhaps just in so far as they have been delicate artists at all, have had some philosophy, some criticism of their art; and it has often been this philosophy, or this criticism, that has evoked their most startling inspiration, calling into outer life some portion of the divine life, or of the buried reality, which could alone extinguish in the emotions what their philosophy or their criticism would extinguish in the intellect. They had sought for no new thing it may be, but only to understand and to copy the pure inspiration of early times, but because the divine life wars upon our outer life, and must needs change its weapons and its movements as we change ours, inspiration has come to them in beautiful startling shapes. The scientific movement brought with it a literature which was always tending to lose itself in externalities of all kinds, in opinion, in declamation, in picturesque writing, in word-painting, or in what Mr Symons has called an attempt 'to build in brick and mortar inside the covers of a book'; and now writers have begun to dwell upon the element of evocation, of suggestion, upon what we call the symbolism in great writers.

II

In 'Symbolism in Painting', I tried to describe the element of symbolism that is in pictures and sculpture, and described a little the symbolism in poetry, but did not describe at all the continuous indefinable symbolism which is the substance of all style.

There are no lines with more melancholy beauty than these by Burns :

> The white moon is setting behind the white wave,*
> And Time is setting with me, O !

*[Burns actually wrote:

> 'The wan moon is setting ayont the white wave,'

but Yeats's version has been retained for the sake of his comments.]

and these lines are perfectly symbolical. Take from them the white-ness of the moon and of the wave, whose relation to the setting of Time is too subtle for the intellect, and you take from them their beauty. But, when all are together, moon and wave and whiteness and setting Time and the last melancholy cry, they evoke an emotion which cannot be evoked by any other arrangement of colours and sounds and forms. We may call this metaphorical writing, but it is better to call it symbolical writing, because metaphors are not profound enough to be moving, when they are not symbols, and when they are symbols they are the most perfect of all, because the most subtle, outside of pure sound, and through them one can best find out what symbols are. If one begins the reverie with any beautiful lines that one can remember, one finds they are like those by Burns. Begin with this line by Blake :

> The gay fishes on the wave when the moon sucks up the dew;

or these lines by Nash :

> Brightness falls from the air,
> Queens have died young and fair,
> Dust hath closed Helen's eye;

or these lines by Shakespeare :

> Timon hath made his everlasting mansion
> Upon the beached verge of the salt flood;
> Who once a day with his embossed froth
> The turbulent surge shall cover;

or take some line that is quite simple, that gets its beauty from its place in a story, and see how it flickers with the light of the many symbols that have given the story its beauty, as a sword-blade may flicker with the light of burning towers.

All sounds, all colours, all forms, either because of their preordained energies or because of long association, evoke indefinable and yet precise emotions, or, as I prefer to think, call down among us certain disembodied powers, whose footsteps over our hearts we call emotions; and when sound, and colour, and form are in a musical relation, a beautiful relation to one another, they become, as it were, one sound, one colour, one form, and evoke an emotion that is made out of their distinct evocations and yet is one emotion. The same relation exists between all portions of every work of art, whether it be an epic or a song, and the more perfect it is, and the more various and numerous the elements that have flowed into its perfection, the more powerful will be the emotion, the power, the god it calls among us. Because an emotion does not exist, or does not become perceptible and active among us, till it has found its expression, in colour or in sound or in form, or in all of these, and because no two modulations or arrangements of these evoke the same emotion, poets and painters and musicians, and in a less degree because their effects are momentary, day and night and cloud and shadow, are continually making and unmaking mankind. It is indeed only those things which seem useless or very feeble that have any power, and all those things that seem useful or strong, armies, moving wheels, modes of architecture, modes of government, speculations of the reason, would have been a little different if some mind long ago had not given itself to some emotion, as a woman gives herself to her lover, and shaped sounds or colours or forms, or all of these, into a musical relation, that their emotion might live in other minds. A little lyric evokes an emotion, and this emotion gathers others about it and melts into their being in the making of some great epic; and at last, needing an always less delicate body, or symbol, as it grows more powerful, it flows out, with all it has gathered, among the blind instincts of daily life, where it moves a power within powers, as one sees ring within ring in the stem of an old tree. This is maybe what Arthur O'Shaughnessy meant when he made his poets say they had built Nineveh with their sighing; and I am certainly never sure, when I hear of some war, or of some religious excitement, or of some new manufacture, or of anything else that fills the ears of the world, that it has not all happened because of something that a boy piped in Thessaly. I remember once telling a seeress to ask one among the gods who, as she believed, were standing about her in their symbolic bodies, what would come of a charming but seeming trivial labour of a friend, and the form answering, 'the devastation of peoples and the overwhelming of cities'. I doubt indeed if the crude circumstance of the world, which seems to create all our emotions, does more than reflect, as in multiplying mirrors, the emotions that have come to solitary men in moments of poetical contemplation; or that love itself would be more than an animal hunger but for the poet and his shadow the priest, for unless we believe that outer things are the reality, we must believe that the gross is the shadow of the subtle, that things are wise before they become foolish, and secret before they cry out in the market-place. Solitary men in moments of contemplation receive, as I think, the creative impulse from the lowest of the Nine Hierarchies, and so make and unmake mankind, and even the world itself, for does not 'the eye altering alter all'?

> Our towns are copied fragments from our breast;
> And all man's Babylons strive but to impart
> The grandeurs of his Babylonian heart.

III

The purpose of rhythm, it has always seemed to me, is to prolong the moment of contemplation, the moment when we are both asleep and awake, which is the one moment of creation, by hushing us with an alluring monotony, while it holds us waking by variety, to keep us in that state of perhaps real trance, in which the mind liberated from the pressure of the will is unfolded in symbols. If certain sensitive persons listen persistently to the ticking of a watch, or gaze persistently on the monotonous flashing of a light, they fall into the hypnotic trance; and rhythm is but the ticking of a watch made softer, that one must needs listen, and various, that one may not be swept beyond memory or grow weary of listening; while the patterns of the artist are but the monotonous flash woven to take the eyes in a subtler enchantment. I have heard in meditation voices that were forgotten the moment they had spoken; and I have been swept, when in more profound meditation, beyond all memory but of those things that came from beyond the threshold of waking life. I was writing once at a very symbolical and abstract poem, when my pen fell on the ground; and as I stooped to pick it up, I remembered some fantastic adventure that yet did not seem fantastic, and then another like adventure, and when I asked myself when these things had happened, I found that I was remembering my dreams for many nights. I tried to remember what I had done the day before, and then what I had done that morning; but all my waking life had perished from me, and it was only after a struggle that I came to remember it again, and as I did so that more powerful and startling life perished in its turn. Had my pen not fallen on the ground and so made me turn from the images that I was weaving into verse, I would never have known that meditation had become trance, for I would have been like one who does not know that he is passing through a wood because his eyes are on the pathway. So I think that in the making and in the understanding of a work of art, and the more easily if it is full of patterns and symbols and music, we are lured to the threshold of sleep, and it may be far beyond it, without knowing that we have ever set our feet upon the steps of horn or of ivory.

IV

Besides emotional symbols, symbols that evoke emotions alone – and in this sense all alluring or hateful things are symbols, although their relations with one another are too subtle to delight us fully, away from rhythm and pattern – there are intellectual symbols, symbols that evoke ideas alone, or ideas mingled with emotions; and outside the very definite traditions of mysticism and the less definite criticism of certain modern poets, these alone are called symbols. Most things belong to one or another kind, according to the way we speak of them and the companions we give them, for symbols, associated with ideas that are more than fragments of the shadows thrown upon the intellect by the emotions they evoke, are the playthings of the allegorist or the pedant, and soon pass away. If I say 'white' or 'purple' in an ordinary line of poetry, they evoke emotions so exclusively that I cannot say why they move me; but if I bring them into the same sentence with such obvious intellectual symbols as a cross or a crown of thorns, I think of purity and sovereignty. Furthermore, innumerable meanings, which are held to 'white' or to 'purple' by bonds of subtle suggestion, and alike in the emotions and in the intellect, move visibly through my mind, and move invisibly beyond the threshold of sleep, casting lights and shadows of an indefinable wisdom on what had seemed before, it may be, but sterility and noisy violence. It is the intellect that decides where the reader shall ponder over the procession of the symbols, and if the symbols are merely emotional, he gazes from amid the accidents and destinies of the world; but if the symbols are intellectual too, he becomes himself a part of pure intellect, and he is himself mingled with the procession. If I watch a rushy pool in the moonlight, my emotion at its beauty is mixed with memories of the man that I have seen ploughing by its margin, or of the lovers I saw there a night ago; but if I look at the moon herself and remember any of her ancient names and meanings, I move among divine people, and things that have shaken off our mortality, the tower of ivory, the queen of waters, the shining stag among enchanted woods, the white hare sitting upon the hilltop, the fool of Faery with his shining cup full of dreams, and it may be 'make a friend of one of these images of wonder', and 'meet the Lord in the air'. So, too, if one is moved by Shakespeare, who is content with emotional symbols that he may come the nearer to our sympathy, one is mixed with the whole spectacle of the world; while if one is moved by Dante, or by the myth of Demeter, one is mixed into the shadow of God or of a goddess. So, too, one is furthest from symbols when one is busy doing this or that, but the soul moves among symbols and unfolds in symbols when trance, or madness, or deep meditation has withdrawn it from every impulse but its own. 'I then saw,' wrote Gérard de Nerval of his madness, 'vaguely drifting into form, plastic images of antiquity, which outlined themselves, became definite, and seemed to represent symbols of which I only seized the idea with difficulty.' In an earlier time he would have been of that multitude whose souls austerity withdrew, even more perfectly than madness could withdraw his soul, from hope and memory, from desire and regret, that they might reveal those processions of symbols that men bow to before altars, and woo with incense and offerings. But being of our time, he has been like Maeterlinck, like Villiers de l'Isle-Adam in *Axël*, like all who are preoccupied with intellectual symbols in our time, a foreshadower of the new sacred book, of which all the arts, as somebody has said, are beginning to dream. How can the arts overcome the slow dying of men's hearts that we call the progress of the world, and lay their hands upon men's heartstrings again, without becoming the garment of religion as in old times?

V

If people were to accept the theory that poetry moves us because of its symbolism, what change should one look for in the manner of our poetry? A return to the way of our fathers, a casting out of descriptions of nature for the sake of nature, of the moral law for the sake of the moral law, a casting out of all anecdotes and of that brooding over scientific opinion that so often extinguished the central flame in Tennyson, and of that vehemence that would make us do or not do certain things; or, in other words, we should come to understand that the beryl stone was enchanted by our fathers that it might unfold the pictures in its heart, and not to mirror our own excited faces, or the boughs waving outside the window. With this change of substance, this return to imagination, this understanding that the laws of art, which are the hidden laws of the world, can alone bind the imagination, would come a change of style, and we would cast out of serious poetry those energetic rhythms, as of a man running, which are the invention of the will with its eyes always on something to be done or undone; and we would seek out those wavering, meditative, organic rhythms, which are the embodiment of the imagination, that neither desires nor hates, because it has done with time, and only wishes to gaze upon some reality; some beauty; nor would it be any longer possible for any-body to deny the importance of form, in all its kinds, for although you can expound an opinion, or describe a thing, when your words are not quite well chosen, you cannot give a body to something that moves beyond the senses, unless your words are as subtle, as complex, as full of mysterious life, as the body of a flower or of a woman. The form of sincere poetry, unlike the form of the 'popular poetry', may indeed be sometimes obscure, or ungrammatical as in some of the best of the *Songs of Innocence and Experience*, but it must have the perfections that escape analysis, the subtleties that have a new meaning every day, and it must have all this whether it be but a little song made out of a moment of dreamy indolence, or some great epic made out of the dreams of one poet and of a hundred generations whose hands were never weary of the sword.

1900 [date of magazine publication]

(FROM 'IDEAS OF GOOD AND EVIL', 1903)

HAVELOCK ELLIS

1859-1939

Henry Havelock Ellis, the future pioneer, sage and prophet of the permissive society, was born on 2 February 1859 at Croydon in Surrey. His mother – related to Sir Henry Havelock, hero of the Indian Mutiny, after whom her son was named – was a woman of unusual strength of character, not to say obstinacy. His father, a sea captain with whom the boy sailed round the world when he was only seven years old, was a gentle being dominated by his wife. At the age of sixteen Havelock Ellis travelled to Australia, remaining there as an assistant teacher till 1879. Returned to England, he studied medicine at St Thomas's Hospital and in 1889 obtained the Licentiate in Medicine, Surgery and Midwifery of the Society of Apothecaries, though he practised medicine only as an assistant during certain of his student days.

The essential biographical documents in the case are Havelock Ellis's own account, published posthumously, *My Life* (1940) – a long painstaking attempt at honesty which, none the less, needs to be supplemented by the records and examinations of others. Chief of these are the two-volumes of autobiography (*Françoise: In Love with Life*, 1962, and *Friendship's Odyssey: In Love with Life*, 1964) by Françoise Delisle, who was Ellis's mistress and friend during the last twenty-three years of his life. Two-thirds of Françoise's story (her name is really an anagram of Ellis: 'Delisle' – 'de Ellis') is taken up with the years in which she knew Havelock. Other documents which offer intimate material for a full as yet uncompounded picture of the man are *Kanga Creek – an Australian Idyll* (1922), a short novel by Havelock Ellis, which treats of the loneliness of youth and is largely autobiographical; *Sonnets, with Folk Songs from the Spanish* by Havelock Ellis (1925), and Ellis's *Poems*, selected by John Gawsworth, with a preface by the author (1937); *Notes on the Letters of Havelock Ellis to Bernard Sleigh 1916 to 1939*, with a foreword by Laurence Houseman (1940); and *Fragments of an Analysis with Freud* by Joseph Wartis, M.D. (N.Y., 1954). The two leading critical biographical studies are *An Artist of Life* by John Stewart Collis (1959), and *Havelock Ellis: A Study* (1959) by Arthur Calder Marshall, the first sympathetic, the second denigrative.

Havelock Ellis is known first and foremost as a sexological author but he was indeed a writer on many subjects, and has good claim to be remembered as a literary critic of distinction.

In the ambience of the 'nineties, he is of importance because of his double hold on the intellectual life of his time. Ellis, in fact, was the only man of that decade who easily and earnestly bestrode what Sir Charles Snow has called 'The Two Cultures' – a knowledge of the arts and knowledge of science. His career as an author may be thought to commence with his editorial work for the Mermaid series of British dramatists during the years 1887–8. In 1889, when he became a Fellow of the Anthropological Institute, he launched, with himself as editor, the Contemporary Science Series which the Walter Scott Company undertook to publish. Ellis's individual début came with two books in 1890 : one a literary title *The New Spirit* ('Small beer,' wrote Wilde in a review of it under the caption 'The New Spirit – Not Intoxicating'[1]), the other scientific, *The Criminal*, being the second publication in Ellis's Contemporary Science Series.

The alternating pattern of Ellis's production was confirmed by his next two books : *Man and Woman: A Study of Human Secondary Characteristics* (1894) – a study of Casanova, Nietzsche, Zola and others. 'In this book,' wrote Ellis in the preface, 'I deal with the questions of life as they are expressed in literature, or as they are suggested by literature. Throughout I am discussing morality as revealed or disguised by literature.' Just how much this opinion flouted the current aestheticism of the epoch may be seen by placing it beside that of his friend Arthur Symons – 'Criticism is not an examination with marks and prizes. It is a valuation of forces, and it is indifferent to their direction.'[2] Or Wilde's more

[1] Quoted by Ernest Rhys: *Everyman Remembers* (1931)
[2] Arthur Symons: *Studies in Prose and Verse* (1904)

arrogant paradox : 'There is no such thing as a moral or an immoral book. Books are well written, or badly written. That is all.'[3]

Talk of morality may be thought to imply the doctrinaire, which was not the case with Ellis. As a prophet of the permissive outlook, he sought to replace the accepted dogmas of common morality, or the more learned dogmas of the philosophers with intellectual attitudes or dispositions, states-of-mind and even states-of-heart. Then, too, as his title suggests, there is a frankly personal concern with the subjects of his study and the conclusion he reaches through them. 'The final value of any book,' he wrote in his preface to *Affirmations*, 'is not the beliefs which it may give us or take away from us, but its power to reveal to us our own true selves. If I can stimulate any one in the search for his own proper affirmation, he and I may well rest content. He is welcome to cast aside mine as the idle conclusions of a dreamer lying in the sunshine. Our own affirmations are always the best. Let us but be sure that they are our own, that they have grown up slowly and quietly, fed with the strength of our own blood and brains.' There is, in this passage, a strong echo of Pater's subjectivist 'Conclusion' to his *Studies in the History of the Renaissance* or of Arthur Symons's equally personal verse-interpretation of it in his poem 'Credo'.[4]

There is, however, something else as well – something which may be spoken of as the organic or physiological interest, as manifest by Ellis's reference to 'our own blood and brains'. The principle behind this concern was formulated clearly by him in 'An Open Letter to Biographers' : 'In every man of genius,' he declares, 'a new strange force is brought into the world. The biographer is the biologist of this new life. . . . We desire to know the influences, physical and moral, which surrounded the period of his conception, the welfare of his pre-natal life, whether he was born naturally and in due season.'[5] Alone among 'the men of the 'nineties' (with the exception of the critic, economist and politician J. M. Robertson), Ellis looked to science and scientific method for all truths not of an imaginative order. 'Biography,' he wrote, 'is strictly analogous to ethnography, the one being the picture of the life of a race, the

---

[3] 'A Preface to Dorian Gray' (*Fortnightly*, March 1890)

[4] *London Nights*, 1895

[5] 'An Open Letter to Biographers' (*Views and Reviews – First Series 1884–1919*, 1932)

other the intimate picture of the life of a man. Now both the one, and the other are branches of applied psychology, a strict method of scientific research.'[6]

Ellis's first essays in literary criticism had been written and published while he was still a medical student, and the trend and regimen of thought which his training accustomed him to was carried over into the field of literary examination. Appreciative as he was of the style and content of a book, it is always the man he seeks beyond the image of the author. Nor is his interest here focused solely on the *intellectual* aspect of the person. Instead, he seeks to trace his features in the records of childhood, youth, and adulthood; in his conduct as son, lover, husband and father. Can one locate some temperamental essence? – it is this which Ellis wishes to know.

Perhaps, then, we may describe him as a critic whose twin keys are those of heredity and environment; and where Sainte-Beuve might resort to the diaries and letters of the author and his circle, the gossip of cliques and *salons*, Ellis would more likely turn to the ramifications of a family tree and to every scrap of knowledge concerning his forebears. In Ellis's criticism, physical and tempera-mental traits, ancestral details and place of birth with conditions and locations of up-bringing abound. The head of Verlaine (half cenobite, half satyr), the gray Ardennes countryside where he was reared; the Norman-Norse inheritance in Remy de Gourmont; Zola's explosive energy derived from the racial compound of French, Greek and Italian blood; Casanova's freak exuberance, product of his Hispanic-Venetian parentage – these are but a few of the guiding images which we encounter in Ellis's criticism.

Unlike so many writers of the 'nineties, these of Ellis make for naturalness and health. The notion of masks, which Wilde and Yeats sponsored, offered a good argument for artificiality and affectation. Ellis distinguished between two types of literary expression : 'the literature that is all art' and 'the literature of life', choosing only to write, at any length, upon the latter. From this one might guess rightly that it was contents and outlook which called forth his focussing attention. Literature he saw as something contributing to sanity – something which strengthened what was authentic. In the preface to his book *The New Spirit*, he spoke of

[6] *Ibid*

the constituent essays as 'a bundle of sphygmographic tracings' – apt metaphor for one concerned with cultural health! – and spoke of the critic's engagement with the author of power or talent in terms which suggested those later employed in 'An Open Letter to Biographers'. 'Whenever,' he declared, 'a great literary personality comes before us . . . it is our business to discover or divine its fundamental instincts; we ought to do this with the same austerity and keen-eyed penetration as, if we were wise, we should exercise in choosing the comrades of our daily life. He poses well in public; he has said these brave words on the platform; he has written those rows of eloquent books – but what (one asks oneself) is all that to me? I went to get at the motive forces at work in the man; to know what his intimate companions thought of him; how he acted in the affairs of everyday, and in the great crises of his life; the fashion of his face and form, the tone of his voice. How he desired to appear is of little importance. I can perhaps learn all that is important from a single involuntary glance, or one glance into his eyes.'[7]

This is a model *declaration of intention* and serves to distinguish Ellis as a critic from those of both his decade and the present. Unlike him, the aesthete of the day was concerned with his author in terms of that author's literary pose. Whether he posed ill or well was the question that interested the aesthetic critic most (as one sees from such books as Wilde's *Intentions* and Ross's *Masques and Phrases*). To this position Ellis made reply that 'how he [the author] desired to appear is of little importance'. In distinction to those aesthetic critics who took art to be the *precious surface* of an author, Ellis proclaimed his desire to 'get at the motive forces at work in the man'.

This declaration sets Ellis apart from the American New Critics of the 'thirties, or our own Dr Leavis today, whose motto might well be 'not the singer but the song', 'The text's the thing' is what they both affirm; but for Ellis the text may be a starting point, a shaft down into the essential man. Ellis's concern with this 'essential man' determines his slant as a critic, which is that of the biographer. And the biographical angle which fascinates him most pertains to a physiological and psychological assessment of his subject.

[7] Preface to *The New Spirit* (1890)

Aristotle tells us that if we wish to understand the nature of a thing we shall attain this information best by looking at its origins; and no critic of the 'nineties, within essay-length limits, has better practised this procedure.

Ellis's concern as a biographer with 'the influences, physical and moral, which surround the period of [his subject's] conception, the welfare of his pre-natal life, whether he was born naturally and in due season'[8] and his belief that 'the fate of all of us is in large measure sealed at the moment we leave the womb',[9] naturally establishes a link between sexology and criticism. It is a connection we find maintained, with liberal unpedantic application, in most of the essays in *The New Spirit* and *Affirmations* and even more so in those papers (many written much earlier) which were finally gathered together in his chief book on French literature *From Rousseau to Proust* (1936).

The relationship between sexology and criticism posited by Ellis leads him to espouse what we today should term 'the new morality'. In his essay 'Concerning Jude the Obscure' (first published in *The Savoy*, no. 6, October 1896) he remarks that 'the great novelists of the present century who have chiefly occupied themselves with the problem of passion and the movements of women's hearts . . . have all shown a reverent faith in what we call Nature as opposed to Society; they have all regarded the impulses and the duties of love in women as independent of social regulation, which may or may not impede the free play of passion and natural morality'.

The basis of our new permissive morality, Ellis sees as rooted in a concept of Nature as distinct from Society. This is how he states the opposition between these two ideas. 'On the one side . . . we have Nature and her unconsciousness of all but essential law, on the other the laws framed merely as social expedients without a base in the heart of things, and merely expressing the triumph of the majority over the individual. . . . This conflict reaches its highest point around women.'[10] 'True or falsely,' Ellis continues, 'woman has always been for man the supreme priestess . . . of Nature' – a statement which, in the context of the debate, carries forward the

[8] *Ibid*
[9] 'An Open Letter to Biographers'
[10] 'Concerning Jude the Obscure'

'nineties Cult of Woman to the point where it gives rise to 'the new morality' we have with us today.

Considering Ellis's close connection, through his friend Arthur Symons, with the *literati* of the 'nineties, it is in fact surprising that his vast sexological knowledge did not make a deeper impression on them. Ellis has spoken of his association with Symons – of how he shared chambers with him in Fountain Court, Middle Temple ('Coin exquis de ce coin délicat,' as Verlaine once termed it after a visit), and how they travelled abroad together in France, Italy, Russia and Spain – in his autobiography *My Life*. His essay 'Early Impressions of Paris' gives far fuller details of the joint pilgrimage made by him and Symons in 1889 and 1890 to Paris, the capital of Symbolist culture.

It is particularly in the field of literary symbolism that one might expect to find the influence of Ellis's sexological thought. In the field of sex Ellis had early realized that 'every fetish is a symbol'[11] and that 'the number of objects . . . which may acquire special erotic significance is practically infinite'.[12] Ellis had dealt comprehensively with the factor of 'Erotic Symbolism' in volume V of his *Studies in the Psychology of Sex* (1906) and with 'Symbolism in Dreams' in his book *The World of Dreams* (1911). The ideas he expounded in these volumes were most likely present to him, embryonically, in earlier years; but no reflection of them seems apparent in either Symons or Yeats – the two British authors of the 'nineties consciously concerned with Symbolist theory. How different, for example, might Yeats' collection *The Rose* have been had the poem considered the sexological symbolism of that flower! Indeed, it is not perhaps too great a claim to suggest that the weakness of the Symbolist Movement was related to its exponents' all but total lack of scientific knowledge. Alone of the men of the 'nineties, Ellis possessed, to a high degree, the anthropological intelligence. Those amateur dabblings in alchemy, astrology, and the occult – which certain partisans of Symbolism professed – were no efficient substitute for his. The Irish contingent could possibly claim some folk-lore studies to bear out their arcane logic; but, for the most part, the Symbolists in Britain were subjective doodling obscurantists, idly indulging in weak dreams of escape.

[11] *Psychology of Sex: A Manual for Students* (1933)
[12] *Ibid*

Havelock Ellis

If Ellis's influence on the sphere of contemporary poetry was nil, in the field of fiction it was not much larger. Two volumes of his *Studies in the Psychology of Sex* had appeared by 1899. This was preceded by *Man and Woman: A Study of Human Secondary Sexual Characteristics* (1894), intended, Ellis tells us, 'as an introduction to my later and more extensive work'. 'Before entering on that great task,' he continues, 'dealing with the primary sexual functions on their psychic side, it was necessary to clear the ground – entangled and over-grown by many weeds – for the presentation of the secondary and, as I term them, tertiary sexual characters. That had never been undertaken before on a comprehensive basis and in a critical spirit.'[13] The image of woman in the fiction of the 'nineties is less sentimental, more objectively observed than in that of the six, say, previous decades; yet, even so, one feels, time and time again, a defective knowledge on the author's part. Just how widely Ellis's ideas and information were defused among the *literati* of the 'nineties it would be hard to say. One can only conjecture : not enough.

More of a realist than Wells or Shaw, Havelock Ellis suffered much the same eclipse as these two veteran Utopians with the coming of the Second World War. Nursed by his mistress Françoise Delisle, he died on 8 July 1939 at Cherry Ground, Hintlesham in the parish of Washbrook, Suffolk, his favourite county and one from which many of his ancestors had come. Reviewing his autobiography, published the next year, Herbert Read's words reflect the diminution overtaking Ellis's reputation. His life, writes Read, was that of 'a natural historian of the old school – not essentially different from that of a village botanist collecting his specimens on his solitary walks and patiently classifying them in a 'home-made herbarium'.[14] It is the tone of gentle patronage which one notices about this passage, a tone which has persisted, with some exceptions, until quite recently. The expanding element of permissiveness in our society within the last few years, however, has led to a renewed interest in the sage and his writings, and the foundation of the Havelock Ellis Society in 1967 should guarantee his reviving status.

[13] Preface to the sixth edition of *Man and Woman* (1926)
[14] 'Havelock Ellis' (*A Coat of Many Colours*, 1945)

HUYSMANS

I

In trying to represent the man who wrote the extraordinary books grouped around *A Rebours* and *En Route*, I find myself carried back to the decline of the Latin world. I recall those restless Africans who were drawn into the vortex of decadent Rome, who absorbed its corruptions with all the barbaric fervour of their race, and then with a more natural impetus of that youthful fervour threw themselves into the young current of Christianity, yet retaining in their flesh the brand of an exotic culture. Tertullian, Augustine, and the rest gained much of their power, as well as their charm, because they incarnated a fantastic mingling of youth and age, of decayed Latinity, of tumultuously youthful Christianity. Huysmans, too, incarnates the old and the new, but with a curious, a very vital difference. To-day the *rôles* are reversed; it is another culture that is now young, with its aspirations after human perfection and social solidarity, while Christianity has exchanged the robust beauty of youth for the subtler beauty of age. 'The most perfect analogy to our time which I can find,' wrote Renan to his sister amid the tumults of Paris in 1848, a few weeks after Huysmans had been born in the same city, 'is the moment when Christianity and paganism stood face to face.' Huysmans had wandered from ancestral haunts of mediæval peace into the forefront of the struggles of our day, bringing the clear, refined perceptions of old culture to the intensest vision of the modern world yet attained, but never at rest, never once grasping except on the purely aesthetic side the significance of the new age, always haunted by the memory of the past and perpetually feeling his way back to what seems to him the home of his soul. The fervent seeker of those early days, indeed, but *à rebours!*

This is scarcely a mere impression; one might be tempted to say that it is strictly the formula of this complex and interesting personality. Coming on the maternal side from an ordinary Parisian bourgeois stock, though there chanced to be a sculptor even along this line, on the paternal side he belongs to an alien aristocracy of art. From father to son his ancestors were painters, of whom at least one, Cornelius Huysmans, still figures honourably in our public galleries, while the last of them left Breda to take up his domicile in Paris. Here his son, Joris Karl, has been the first of the race to use the pen instead of the brush, yet retaining precisely those characters of 'veracity of imitation, jewel-like richness of colour, perfection of finish, emphasis of character', which their historian finds in the painters of his land from the fourteenth century onwards. Where the Meuse approaches the Rhine valley we find the home of the men who, almost alone in the north, created painting and the arts that are grouped around painting, and evolved religious music. On the side of art the Church had found its chief builders in the men of these valleys, and even on the spiritual side also, for here is the northern home of mysticism. Their latest child has fixed his attention on the feverish activities of Paris with the concentrated gaze of a stranger in a strange land, held by a fascination which is more than half repulsion, always missing something, he scarcely knows what. He has ever been seeking the satisfaction he had missed, sometimes in the aesthetic vision of common things, sometimes in the refined Thebaid of his own visions, at length more joyfully in the survivals of mediæval mysticism. Yet as those early Africans still retained their acquired Roman instincts, and that fantastic style which could not be shaken off, so Huysmans will surely retain to the last the tincture of Parisian modernity.

Yet we can by no means altogether account for Huysmans by race and environment. Every man of genius is a stranger and a pilgrim on the earth, unlike other men, seeing everything as it were at a different angle, mirroring the world in his mind as in those concave or convex mirrors which elongate or abbreviate absurdly all who approach them. No one ever had a keener sense of the distressing absurdity of human affairs than M. Huysmans. The Trocadero is not a beautiful building, but to no one else probably has it appeared as an old hag lying on her back and elevating her spindle shanks towards the sky. Such images of men's works and ways abound in Huysmans' books, and they express his unaffected vision of life, his disgust for men and things, a shuddering disgust, yet patient, half-amused. I can well recall an evening spent some years ago in M. Huysmans' company. His face, with the sensitive, luminous eyes, reminded one of Baudelaire's portraits, the face of a resigned and benevolent Mephistopheles who has discovered the absurdity of the Divine order but has no wish to make any improper use of his discovery. He talked in low and even tones, never eagerly, without any emphasis or gesture, not addressing any special person; human imbecility was the burden of nearly all that he said, while a faint twinkle of amused wonderment lit up his eyes. And throughout all his books until almost the last 'l'éternelle bêtise de l'humanité' is the ever-recurring refrain.

Always leading a retired life, and specially abhorring the society and conversation of the average literary man, M. Huysmans has for many years been a government servant – a model official, it is said – at the Ministry of Foreign Affairs. Here, like our own officials at Whitehall, he serves his country in dignified leisure – on the only occasion on which I have seen him in his large and pleasant *bureau*, he was gazing affectionately at Chéret's latest *affiche*, which a lady of his acquaintance had just brought to show him – and such duties of routine, with the close contact with practical affairs they involve, must always be beneficial in preserving the sane equipoise of an imaginative temperament. In this matter Huysmans has been more fortunate than his intimate friend Villiers de l'Isle-Adam, who had wandered so far into the world of dreams that he lost touch with the external world and ceased to distinguish them clearly. One is at first a little surprised to hear of the patient tact and diplomacy which the author of *A Rebours* spent round the death-bed of the author of *Contes Cruels* to obtain the dying dreamer's consent to a ceremony of marriage which would legitimate his child. But Huysman's sensitive nervous system and extravagant imagination have ever been under the control of a sane and forceful intellect; his very idealism has been nourished by the contemplation of a world which he has seen too vividly ever to ignore. We may read that in the reflective deliberation of his grave and courteous bearing, somewhat recalling, as more than one observer has noted, his own favourite animal, the cat, whose outward repose of Buddhistic contemplation envelops a highly-strung nervous system, while its capacity to enjoy the refinements of human civilization comports a large measure of spiritual freedom and ferocity. Like many another man of letters, Huysmans suffers from neuralgia and dyspepsia; but no novelist has described so persistently and so poignantly the pangs of toothache or the miseries of *maux d'estomac*, a curious proof of the peculiarly personal character of Huysmans' work throughout. His sole pre-occupation has been with his own impressions. He possessed no native genius for the novel. But with a very sound instinct he set himself, almost at the outset of his career, to describe intimately and faithfully the crudest things of life, the things most remote from his own esoteric tastes but at that time counted peculiarly 'real'. There could be no better discipline for an idealist. Step by step he has left the region of vulgar actualities to attain his proper sphere, but the marvellous and slowly won power of expressing the spiritually impalpable in concrete imagery is the fruit of that laborious apprenticeship. He was influenced in his novels at first by Goncourt, afterwards a little by Zola, as he sought to reproduce his own vivid and personal vision of the world. This vision is like that of a man with an intense exaltation of the senses, especially the senses of sight and smell. Essentially Huysmans is less a novelist than a poet, with an instinct to use not verse but prose as his medium. Thus he early fell under the influence of Baudelaire's prose-poems. His small and slight first volume, *Le Drageoir à Epices*, bears witness to this influence, while yet revealing a personality clearly distinct from Baudelaire's. This personality is already wholly revealed in the quaint audacity of the little prose-poem entitled 'L'Extase'. Here, at the very outset of Huysmans' career, we catch an unconscious echo of mediæval asceticism, the voice, it might be, of Odo of Cluny, who nearly a thousand years before had shrunk with horror from embracing a 'sack of dung'; 'quomodo ipsum stercoris saccum amplecti desideramus!' 'L'Extase' describes how the lover lies in the wood clasping the hand of the beloved and bathed in a rapture of blissful emotion; 'suddenly she rose, disengaged her hand, disappeared in the bushes, and I heard as it were the rustling of rain on the leaves'; at once the delicious dream fled and the lover awakes to the reality of commonplace human things. That is a parable of the high-strung idealism, having only contempt for whatever breaks in on its ideal, which has ever been the mark of Huysmans. His sensitive ear is alive to the gentlest ripple of nature, and it jars on him; it becomes the deafening Niagara of 'the incessant deluge of human foolishness'; all his art is the research for a Heaven where the voice of Nature shall no more be heard. Baudelaire was also such a hyperaesthetic idealist, but the human tenderness which vibrates beneath the surface of

Baudelaire's work has been the last quality to make itself more than casually felt in Huysmans. It is the defect which vitiated his early work in the novel, when he was still oscillating between the prose-poem and the novel, clearly conscious that while the first suited him best only in the second could mastery be won. His early novels are sometimes portentously dull, with a lack of interest, or even attempt to interest, which itself almost makes them interesting, as frank ugliness is. They are realistic with a veracious and courageously abject realism, never, like Zola's, carefully calculated for its pictorial effectiveness, but dealing simply with the trivialest and sordidest human miseries. His first novel *Marthe* – which inaugurated the long series of novels devoted to state-regulated prostitution in those slaughter-houses of love, as Huysmans later described them, where Desire is slain at a single stroke, sufficiently repulsive on the whole, is not without flashes of insight which reveal the future artist, and to some readers indeed make it more interesting than *La Fille Elisa*, which the Goncourts published shortly afterwards. Unlike the crude and awkward *Marthe* – though that book reveals the influence of the Goncourts – *La Fille Elisa* shows the hand of an accomplished artist, but it is also the work of a philanthropist writing with an avowed object, and of a fine gentleman ostentatiously anxious not to touch pitch with more than a finger-tip. The Preface to *Marthe* contains a declaration which remains true for the whole of Huysmans' work : 'I set down what I see, what I feel, what I have lived, writing it as well as I am able, *et voilà tout!*' But it has ever been a dangerous task to set down what one sees and feels and has lived; for no obvious reason, except the subject, *Marthe* was immediately suppressed by the police. This first novel remains the least personal of Huysmans' books; in his next novel, *Les Sœurs Vatard* – a study of Parisian work-girls and their lovers – a more characteristic vision of the world begins to be revealed, and from that time forward there is a continuous though irregular development both in intellectual grip and artistic mastery. 'Sac au Dos', which appeared in the *Soirées de Medan*, represents a notable stage in this development, for here, as he has since acknowledged, Huysmans' hero is himself. It is the story of a young student who serves during the great war in the Garde Mobile of the Seine, and is invalided with dysentery before reaching the front. There is no story, no striking impression to record – nothing to compare with

Guy de Maupassant's incomparably more brilliant 'Boule-de-Suif', also dealing with the fringe of war, which appears in the same volume – no opportunity for literary display, nothing but a record of individual feelings with which the writer seems satisfied because they are interesting to himself. It is, in fact, the germ of that method which Huysmans has since carried to so brilliant a climax in *En Route*. All the glamour of war and the enthusiasm of patriotism are here – long before *Zola* wrote his *Débâcle* – reduced to their simplest terms in the miseries of the individual soldier whose chief aspiration it becomes at last to return to a home where the necessities of nature may be satisfied in comfort and peace. At that time Huysmans' lack of patriotic enthusiasm seemed almost scandalous; but when we bear in mind his racial affinities it is natural that he should, as he once remarked to an interviewer, 'prefer a Leipzig man to a Marseilles man', 'the big, phlegmatic, taciturn Germans' to the gesticulating and rhetorical people of the French south. In *Là-Bas*, at a later date, through the mouth of one of his characters, Huysmans goes so far as to regret the intervention of Joan of Arc in French history, for had it not been for Joan France and England would have been restored to their racial and prehistoric unity, consolidated into one great kingdom under Norman Plantagenets, instead of being given up to the southerners of Latin race who surrounded Charles VII.

The best of Huysmans' early novels is undoubtedly *En Ménage*. It is the intimate history of a young literary man who, having married a wife whom he shortly afterwards finds unfaithful, leaves her, returns to his bachelor life, and in the end becomes reconciled to her. This picture of a studious man who goes away with his books to fight over again the petty battles of bachelorhood with the *bonne* and the *concierge* and his own cravings for womanly love and companionship, reveals clearly for the first time Huysmans' power of analysing states of mind that are at once simple and subtle. Perhaps no writer surprises us more by his revealing insight into the commonplace experiences which all a novelist's traditions lead him to idealize or ignore. As a whole, however, *En Ménage* is scarcely yet a master's work, a little laboured, with labour which cannot yet achieve splendour of effect. Nor can a much slighter story, *A Vau l'Eau*, which appeared a little later, be said to mark a further stage in development, though it is a characteristic study, this sordid history of Folantin, the poor, lame, discontented, middle-aged clerk. Cheated and bullied on every side, falling a prey to the vulgar woman of the street who boisterously takes possession of him in the climax of the story, all the time feeling poignantly the whole absurdity of the situation, there is yet one spot where hope seems possible. He has no religious faith; 'and yet,' he reflects, 'yet mysticism alone could heal the wound that tortures me.' Thus Folantin, though like André in *En Ménage* he resigns himself to the inevitable stupidity of life, yet stretches out his hands towards the Durtal of Huysmans' latest work.

In all these novels we feel that Huysmans has not attained to full self-expression. Intellectual mastery, indeed, he is attaining, but scarcely yet the expression of his own personal ideals. The poet in Huysmans, the painter enamoured of beauty and seeking it in unfamiliar places, has little scope in these detailed pictures of sordid or commonplace life. At this early period it is still in prose-poems, especially in *Croquis Parisiens*, that this craving finds satisfaction. Des Esseintes, the hero of *A Rebours*, who on so many matters is Huysmans' mouthpiece, of all forms of literature preferred the prose-poem when, in the hands of an alchemist of genius, it reveals a novel concentrated into a few pages or a few lines, the concrete juice, the essential oil of art. It was 'a communion of thought between a magical writer and an ideal reader, a spiritual collaboration among a dozen superior persons scattered throughout the world, a delectation offered to the finest wits, and to them alone accessible'. Huysmans took up this form where Baudelaire and Mallarmé had left it, and sought to carry it yet further. In that he was scarcely successful. The excess of tension in the tortured language with which he elaborates his effects too often holds him back from the goal of perfection. We must yet value in *Croquis Parisiens* its highly wrought and individual effects of rhythm and colour and form. In France, at all events, Huysmans is held to inaugurate the poetic treatment of modern things – a characteristic already traceable in *Les Sœurs Vatard* – and this book deals with the aesthetic aspects of latter-day Paris, with the things that are 'ugly and superb, outrageous and yet exquisite', as a type of which he selects the Folies-Bergère, at that time the most characteristic of Parisian music-halls, and he was thus the first to discuss the aesthetic value of the variety stage which has been made cheaper since. For the most part, however, these *Croquis* are of the simplest and most commonplace things – the forlorn Bièvre district, the poor man's *café*, the roast-chestnut seller – extracting the beauty or pathos or strangeness of all these things. 'Thy garment is the palette of setting suns, the rust of old copper, the brown gilt of Cordovan leather, the sandal and saffron tints of the autumn foliage. . . . When I contemplate thy coat of mail I think of Rembrandt's pictures, I see again his superb heads, his sunny flesh, his gleaming jewels on black velvet. I see again his rays of light in the night, his trailing gold in the shade, the dawning of suns through dark arches.' The humble bloater has surely never before been sung in language which recalls the Beloved of the 'Song of Songs'. Huysmans has carried to an even extravagant degree that re-valuation of the world's good in which genius has ever found its chief function. To abase the mighty and exalt the humble seems to man the divinest of prerogatives, for it is that which he himself exercises in his moments of finest inspiration. To find a new vision of the world, a new path to truth, is the instinct of the artist or the thinker. He changes the whole system of our organized perceptions. That is why he seems to us at first an incarnate paradox, a scoffer at our most sacred verities, making mountains of our mole-hills and counting as mere mole-hills our everlasting mountains, always keeping time to a music that clashes with ours, at our hilarity *tristis, in tristitia hilaris.*

In 1889 *A Rebours* appeared. Not perhaps his greatest achieve-ment, it must ever remain the central work in which he has most powerfully concentrated his whole vision of life. It sums up the progress he had already made, foretells the progress he was afterwards to make, in a style that is always individual, always masterly in its individuality. Technically, it may be said that the power of *A Rebours* lies in the fact that here for the first time Huysmans has succeeded in uniting the two lines of his literary development : the austere analysis in the novels of common-place things mostly alien to the writer, and the freer elaboration in the prose-poems of his own more intimate personal impressions. In their union the two streams attain a new power and a more intimately personal note. Des Esseintes, the hero of this book, may possibly have been at a few points suggested by a much less interest-ing real personage in contemporary Paris, the Comte de Montesquiou-Fezensac, but in the main he was certainly created by

Huysmans' own brain, as the representative of his author's hyper-aesthetic experience of the world and the mouthpiece of his most personal judgments. The victim of over-wrought nerves, of neuralgia and dyspepsia, Des Esseintes retires for a season from Paris to the solitude of his country house at Fontenay, which he has fitted up, on almost cloistral methods, to soothe his fantasy and to gratify his complex aesthetic sensations, his love of reading and contemplation. The finest pictures of Gustave Moreau hang on the walls, with the fantastic engravings of Luyken, and the strange visions of Odilon Redon. He has a tortoise curiously inlaid with precious stones; he delights in all those exotic plants which reveal Nature's most un-natural freaks; he is a sensitive amateur of perfumes, and considers that the pleasures of smell are equal to those of sight or sound; he possesses a row of little barrels of liqueurs so arranged that he can blend in infinite variety the contents of this instrument, his 'mouth-organ' he calls it, and produce harmonies which seem to him comparable to those yielded by a musical orchestra. But the solitary pleasures of this palace of art only increase the nervous strain he is suffering from; and at the urgent bidding of his doctor Des Esseintes returns to the society of his abhorred fellow-beings in Paris, himself opening the dyke that admitted the 'waves of human mediocrity' to engulf his refuge. And this wonderful confession of aesthetic faith – with its long series of deliberately searching and decisive affirmations on life, religion, literature, art – ends with a sudden solemn invocation that is surprisingly tremulous : 'Take pity, O Lord, on the Christian who doubts, on the sceptic who desires to believe, on the convict of life who embarks alone, in the night, beneath a sky no longer lit by the consoling beacons of ancient faith.'

'He who carries his own most intimate emotions to their highest point becomes the first in file of a long series of men'; that saying is peculiarly true of Huysmans. But to be a leader of men one must turn one's back on men. Huysmans' attitude towards his readers was somewhat like that of Thoreau, who spoke with lofty disdain of such writers as 'would fain have one reader before they die'. As he has since remarked, Huysmans wrote *A Rebours* for a dozen persons, and was himself more surprised than any one at the wide interest it evoked. Yet that interest was no accident. Certain aesthetic ideals of the latter half of the nineteenth century are more quintessentially expressed in *A Rebours* than in any other book. Intensely personal, audaciously independent, it yet sums up a movement which has scarcely now worked itself out. We may read it and re-read, not only for the light which it casts on that movement, but upon every similar period of acute aesthetic perception in the past.

II

The aesthetic attitude towards art which *A Rebours* illuminates is that commonly called decadent. Decadence in art, though a fairly simple phenomenon, and world-wide as art itself, is still so ill understood that it may be worth while to discuss briefly its precise nature, more especially as manifested in literature.

Technically, a decadent style is only such in relation to a classic style. It is simply a further development of a classic style, a further specialization, the homogeneous, in Spencerian phraseology, having become heterogeneous. The first is beautiful because the parts are subordinated to the whole; the second is beautiful because the whole is subordinated to the parts. Among our own early prose-writers Sir Thomas Browne represents the type of decadence in style. Swift's prose is classic, Pater's decadent. Hume and Gibbon are classic, Emerson and Carlyle decadent. In architecture, which is the key to all the arts, we see the distinction between the classic and the decadent visibly demonstrated; Roman architecture is classic, to become in its Byzantine developments completely decadent, and St Mark's is the perfected type of decadence in art; pure early Gothic, again, is strictly classic in the highest degree because it shows an absolute subordination of detail to the bold harmonies of structure, while later Gothic, grown weary of the commonplaces of structure and predominantly interested in beauty of detail, is again decadent. In each case the earlier and classic manner – for the classic manner, being more closely related to the ends of utility, must always be earlier – subordinates the parts to the whole, and strives after those virtues which the whole may best express; the later manner depreciates the importance of the whole for the benefit of its parts, and strives after the virtues of individualism. All art is the rising and falling of the slopes of a rhythmic curve between these two classic and decadent extremes.

Decadence suggests to us going down, falling, decay. If we walk down a real hill we do not feel that we commit a more wicked act than when we walked up it. But if it is a figurative hill then we view Hell at the bottom. The word 'corruption' – used in a precise and technical sense to indicate the breaking up of the whole for the benefit of its parts – serves also to indicate a period or manner of decadence in art. This makes confusion worse, for here the moralist feels that surely he is on safe ground. But as Nietzsche, with his usual acuteness in cutting at the root of vulgar prejudice, has well remarked (in *Die Fröhliche Wissenschaft*), even as regards what is called the period of 'corruption' in the evolution of societies, we are apt to overlook the fact that the energy which in more primitive times marked the operations of the community as a whole has now simply been transferred to the individuals themselves, and this aggrandisement of the individual really produces an even greater amount of energy. The individual has gained more than the community has lost. An age of social decadence is not only the age of sinners and degenerates, but of saints and martyrs, and decadent Rome produced an Autoninus as well as a Heliogabalus. No doubt social 'corruption' and literary 'corruption' tend to go together; an age of individualism is usually an age of artistic decadence, and we may note that the chief literary artists of America – Poe, Hawthorne, Whitman – are for the most part in the technical sense decadents.

Rome supplies the first clear types of classic and decadent literature, and the small group of recent French writers to whom the term has been more specifically applied were for the most part peculiarly attracted by later Latin literature. So far as I can make out, it is to the profound and penetrating genius of Baudelaire that we owe the first clear apprehension of the legitimate part which decadence plays in literature. We may trace it, indeed, in his own style, clear, pure, and correct as that style always remains, as well as in his literary preferences. He was a good Latinist, and his favourite Latin authors were Apuleius, Juvenal, Petronius, Saint Augustine, Tertullian, and other writers in prose and verse of the early Christian Church. He himself wrote a love-poem in rhymed Latin verse, adding to it a note concerning the late Latin decadence regarded as 'the supreme sigh of a vigorous person already transformed and prepared for the spiritual life', and specially apt to express passion as the modern world feels it, one pole of the magnet at the opposite end of which are Catullus and his band. 'In this marvellous tongue,' he added, 'solecism and barbarism seem to me to render the forced negligences of a passion which forgets itself and mocks at rules. Words taken in a new meaning reveal the charming awkwardness of the northern barbarian kneeling before the Roman beauty.' But the best early statement of the meaning of decadence in style – though doubtless inspired by Baudelaire – was furnished by Gautier in 1868 in the course of the essay on Baudelaire which is probably the most interesting piece of criticism he ever achieved. The passage is long, but so precise and accurate that it must here in part be quoted : 'The poet of the *Fleurs du Mal* loved what is improperly called the style of decadence, and which is is nothing else but art arrived at that point of extreme maturity yielded by the slanting suns of aged civilizations : an ingenious complicated style, full of shades and of research, constantly pushing back the boundaries of speech, borrowing from all the technical vocabularies, taking colour from all palettes and notes from all keyboards, struggling to render what is most inexpressible in thought, what is vague and most elusive in the outlines of form, listening to translate the subtle confidences of neurosis, the dying confessions of passion grown depraved, and the strange hallucinations of the obsession which is turning to madness. The style of decadence is the ultimate utterance of the Word, summoned to final expression and driven to its last hiding-place. One may recall in this connection the language of the later Roman Empire, already marbled with the greenness of decomposition, and, so to speak, gamy, and the complicated refinements of the Byzantine school, the last forms of Greek art falling into deliquescence. Such indeed is the necessary and inevitable idiom of peoples and civilizations in which factitious life has replaced natural life, and developed unknown wants in men. It is, besides, no easy thing, this style disdained of pedants, for it expresses new ideas in new forms, and in words which have not yet been heard. Unlike the classic style it admits shadow. . . . One may well imagine that the fourteen hundred words of the Racinian vocabulary scarcely suffice the author who has undertaken the laborious task of rendering modern ideas and things in their infinite complexity and multiple colouration.'

Some fifteen years later, Bourget, again in an essay on Baudelaire *(Essais de Psychologie Contemporaine),* continued the exposition of the theory of decadence, elaborating the analogy to the social organism which enters the state of decadence as soon as the individual life of the parts is no longer subordinated to the whole. 'A similar law governs the development and decadence of that other organism which we call language. A style of decadence is one in which the unity of the book is decomposed to give place to the independence of the page, in which the page is decomposed to give place to the independence of the phrase, and the phrase to give place to the independence of the word.' It was at this time (about 1884) that the term 'decadent' seems first to have been applied by Barrès and others to the group of which Verlaine, Huysmans, Mallarmé were the most distinguished members, and in so far as it signified an ardent and elaborate search for perfection of detail beyond that attained by Parnassian classicality it was tolerated or accepted. Verlaine, indeed, was for the most part indifferent to labels, neither accepting nor rejecting them, and his work was not bound up with any theory. But Huysmans, with the intellectual passion of the pioneer in art, deliberate and relentless, has carried both the theory and the practice of decadence in style to the farthest point. In practice he goes beyond Baudelaire, who, however enamoured he may have been of what he called the phosphorescence of putrescence, always retained in his own style much of what is best in the classic manner. Huysmans' vocabulary is vast, his images, whether remote or familiar, always daring – 'dragged,' in the words of one critic, 'by the hair or by the feet, down the worm-eaten staircase of terrified Syntax,' – but a heart-felt pulse of emotion is restrained beneath the sombre and extravagant magnificence of this style, and imparts at the best that modulated surge of life which only the great masters can control.

Des Esseintes's predilections in literature are elaborated through several chapters, and without question he faithfully reflects his creator's impressions. He was indifferent or contemptuous towards the writers of the Latin Augustan age; Virgil seemed to him thin and mechanical, Horace a detestable clown; the fat redundancy of Cicero, we are told, and the dry constipation of Cæsar alike disgusted him; Sallust, Livy, Juvenal, even Tacitus and Plautus, though for these he had words of praise, seemed to him for the most part merely the delights of pseudo-literary readers. Latin only began to be interesting to Des Esseintes in Lucan, for here at least, in spite of the underlying hollowness, it became expressive and studded with brilliant jewels. The author whom above all he delighted in was Petronius – who reminded Des Esseintes of the modern French novelists he most admired – and several eloquent pages are devoted to that profound observer, delicate analyst, and marvellous painter who modelled his own vivid and precise style out of all the idioms and slang of his day. After Petronius there was a gap in his collection of Latin authors until the second century of our own era is reached with Apuleius and the sterner Christian contemporaries of that jovial pagan, Tertullian and the rest, in whose hands the tongue that in Petronius had reached supreme maturity now began to dissolve. For Tertullian he had little admiration, and none for Augustine, though sympathizing with his *City of God* and his general disgust for the world. But the special odour which the Christians had by the fourth century imparted to decomposing pagan Latin was delightful to him in such authors as Commodian of Gaza, whose tawny, sombre, and tortuous style he even preferred to Claudian's sonorous blasts, in which the trumpet of paganism was last heard in the world. He was also able to maintain interest in Prudentius, Sedulius, and a host of unknown Christians who combined Catholic fervour with a Latinity which had become, as it were, completely putrid, leaving but a few shreds of torn flesh for the Christians to 'marinate in the brine of their new tongue'. His shelves continued to show Latin books of the sixth, seventh, and eighth centuries, among which he found special pleasure in the Anglo-Saxon writers, and only finally ceased at the beginning of the tenth century, when 'the curiosity, the complicated *naïveté*' of the earlier tongue were finally lost in scholastic philosophy and mere cartalaries and chronicles.* Then, with a formidable leap of ten centuries, his Latin books gave place to nineteenth-century French books.

Des Esseintes is no admirer of Rabelais or Molière, of Voltaire or Rousseau. Among the older French writers he read only Villon, D'Aubigné, Bossuet, Bourdaloue, Nicole, and especially Pascal.

---

* It may be gathered from the Preface he wrote at a later date for M. Remy de Gourmont's delightful volume, *Le Latin Mystique*, that Huysmans would no longer draw a line at this point; for he here speaks with enthusiasm of the styles of St Bernard, St Bonaventure, and St Thomas d'Aquinas.

Putting these aside, his French library began with Baudelaire, whose works he had printed in an edition of one copy, in episcopal letters, in large missal *format*, bound in flesh-coloured pig-skin; he found an unspeakable delight in reading this poet who, 'in an age when verse only served to express the external aspects of things, has succeeded in expressing the inexpressible, by virtue of a muscular and sinewy speech which more than any other possessed the marvellous power of fixing with strange sanity of expression the most morbid, fleeting, tremulous states of weary brains and sorrowful souls.' After Baudelaire the few French books on Des Esseintes's shelves fall into two groups, one religious, one secular. Most of the French clerical writers he disregarded, for they yield a pale flux of words which seemed to him to come from a school-girl in a convent. Lacordaire he regarded as an exception, for his language had been fused and moulded by ardent eloquence, but for the most part the Catholic writers he preferred were outside the Church. For Hello's *Homme*, especially, he cherished profound admiration, and an inevitable sympathy for its author, who seemed to him 'a cunning engineer of the soul, a skilful watchmaker of the brain, delighting to examine the mechanism of a passion and to explain the play of the wheel-work', and yet united to this power of analysis all the fanaticism of a Biblical prophet, and the tortured ingenuity of a master of style – an ill-balanced, incoherent, yet subtle personality. But above all he delighted in Barbey d'Aurevilly, shut out from the Church as an unclean and pestiferous heretic, yet glorying to sing her praises, insinuating into that praise a note of almost sadistic sacrilege, a writer at once devout and impious, altogether after Des Esseintes's own heart, so that a special copy of the *Diaboliques*, in episcopal violet and cardinal purple, printed on sanctified vellum with initials adorned by satanic tails, formed one of his most cherished possessions. In D'Aurevilly's style alone he truly recognized the same gaminess, the speckled morbidity, the flavour as of a sleepy pear which he loved in decadent Latin and the monastic writers of old time. Of contemporary secular books he possessed not many; by force of passing them through the screw-press of his brain few were finally found solid enough to emerge intact and bear re-reading, and in this process he had accelerated 'the incurable conflict which existed between his ideas and those of the world into which by chance he had been born'. Certain selected works of the three great

French novelists of his time – Flaubert, Goncourt, and Zola – still remained, for in all three he found in various forms that 'nostalgie des au-delà' by which he was himself haunted; and with Baudelaire, these three were, in modern profane literature, the authors by whom he had chiefly been moulded. The scanty collection also included Verlaine, Mallarmé, Poe, and Villiers de l'Isle-Adam, whose firm fantastic style and poignantly ironic attitude towards the utilitarian modern world he found entirely to his taste. Finally, there only remained the little anthology of prose-poems. Des Esseintes thought it improbable that he would ever make any additions to his library; it seemed impossible to him that a decadent language – 'struggling on its death-bed to repair all the omissions of joy and bequeath the subtlest memories of pain' – would ever go beyond Mallarmé. This brief summary of the three chapters, all full of keen if wayward critical insight, which describe Des Esseintes's library, may serve at once both to indicate the chief moulding influences on Huysmans' own style and to illustrate the precise nature of decadence in art and the fundamental part it plays.

We have to recognize that decadence is an aesthetic and not a moral conception. The power of words is great, but they need not befool us. The classic herring should suggest no moral superiority over the decadent bloater. We are not called upon to air our moral indignation over the bass end of the musical clef. All confusion of intellectual substances is foolish, and one may well sympathize with that fervid unknown metaphysician to whom we owe the Athanasian creed when he went so far as to assert that it is damnable. It is not least so in the weak-headed decadent who falls into the moralist's snare and complacently admits his own exceeding wickedness. We may well reserve our finest admiration for the classic in art, for therein are included the largest and most imposing works of human skill; but our admiration is of little worth if it is founded on incapacity to appreciate the decadent. Each has its virtues, each is equally right and necessary. One ignorant of plants might well say, on gazing at a seed-capsule with its seeds disposed in harmonious rows, that there was the eternally natural and wholesome order of things, and on seeing the same capsule wither and cast abroad its seeds to germinate at random in the earth, that here was an unwholesome and deplorable period of decay. But he would know little of the transmutations of life. And we have to recognize that those persons who bring the same crude notions into the field of art know as little of the life of the spirit.

III

For some years after the appearance of *A Rebours* Huysmans produced nothing of any magnitude. *En Rade*, his next novel, the experience of a Parisian married couple who, under the stress of temporary pecuniary difficulties, go into the country to stay at an uncle's farm, dwells in the memory chiefly by virtue of two vividly naturalistic episodes, the birth of a calf and the death of a cat. More interesting, more intimately personal, are the two volumes of art criticism, *L'Art Moderne* and *Gertains*, which Huysmans published at about this period. Degas, Rops, Raffaelli, Odilon Redon are among the artists of very various temperament whom Huysmans either discovered, or at all events first appreciated in their full significance, and when he writes of them it is not alone critical insight which he reveals, but his own personal vision of the world.

To Huysmans the world has ever been above all a vision; it was no accident that the art that appeals most purely to the eyes is that of which he has been the finest critic. One is tempted, indeed, to suggest that this aptitude is the outcome of heredity, of long generations devoted to laborious watchfulness of the desire of the eye in the external world, not indeed by actual accumulation of acquired qualities, but by the passing on of a nervous organism long found so apt for this task. He has ever been intensely preoccupied with the effort to express those visible aspects of things which the arts of design were made to express, which the art of speech can perhaps never express. The tortured elaboration of his style is chiefly due to this perpetual effort to squeeze tones and colours out of this foreign medium. The painter's brain holds only a pen and cannot rest until it has wrung from it a brush's work. But not only is the sense of vision marked in Huysmans. We are conscious of a general hyperaesthesia, an intense alertness to the inrush of sensations, which we might well term morbid if it were not so completely intellectualized and controlled. Hearing, indeed, appears to be less acutely sensitive than sight, the poet is subordinated to the painter, though that sense still makes itself felt, and the heavy multicoloured paragraphs often fall at the close into a melancholy and poignant

rhythm laden with sighs. It is the sense of smell which Huysmans'
work would lead us to regard as most highly developed after that
of sight. The serious way in which Des Esseintes treats perfumes is
characteristic, and one of the most curious and elaborate of the
Croquis Parisiens is 'Le Gousset', in which the capacities of language
are strained to define and differentiate the odours of feminine arm-
pits. Again, earlier, in a preface written for Hannon's *Rimes de Joie*,
Huysmans points out that that writer – who failed to fulfil his early
promise – alone of contemporary poets possessed 'la curiosité des
parfums', and that his chief poem was written in honour of what
Huysmans called 'the libertine virtues of that glorious perfume',
opopanax. This sensitiveness to odour is less marked in Huysmans'
later work, but the dominance of vision remains.

The two volumes of essays on art incidentally serve to throw
considerable light on Huysmans' conception of life. For special
illustration we may take his attitude towards women, whom in
his novels he usually treats, from a rather conventionally sexual
point of view, as a fact in man's life rather than as a subject for
independent analysis. In these essays we may trace the development
of his own personal point of view, and in comparing the earlier
with the later volume we find a change which is significant of the
general evolution of Huysmans' attitude towards life. He is at once
the ultra-modern child of a refined civilization and the victim of
nostalgia for an ascetic mediævalism; his originality lies in the fact
that in him these two tendencies are not opposed but harmonious,
although the second has only of late reached full development. In a
notable passage in *En Rade*, Jacques, the hero, confesses that he
can see nothing really great or beautiful in a harvest field, with
its anodyne toil, as compared with a workshop or a steamboat, 'the
horrible magnificence of machines, that one beauty which the
modern world has been able to create'. It is so that Huysmans views
women also; he is as indifferent to the feminine ideals of classical
art as to its literary ideals. In *L'Art Moderne*, speaking with admiration of a study of the nude by Gauguin, he proceeds to lament that
no one has painted the unclothed modern woman without falsifica-
tion or premeditated arrangement, real, alive in her own intimate
personality, with her own joys and pains incarnated in the curves
of her flesh, and the lash of child-birth traceable on her flanks. We
go to the Louvre to learn how to paint, he remarks, forgetting that

'beauty is not uniform and invariable, but changes with the age and the climate, that the Venus of Milo, for instance, is now not more beautiful and interesting than those ancient statues of the New World, streaked and tattooed and adorned with feathers; that both are but diverse manifestations of the same ideal of beauty pursued by different races; that at the present date there can be no question of reaching the beautiful by Venetian, Greek, Dutch, or Flemish rites; but only by striving to disengage it from contemporary life, from the world that surrounds us'. 'Un nu fatigué, délicat, affiné, vibrant' can alone conform to our own time; and he adds that no one has truly painted the nude since Rembrandt. It is instructive to turn from this essay to that on Degas, written some six years later. It may fairly be said that to Degas belongs the honour of taking up the study of the nude at the point where Rembrandt left it; and like Rembrandt, he had realized that the nude can only be rightly represented in those movements, postures, and avocations by which it is naturally and habitually exposed. It is scarcely surprising, therefore, that Huysmans at once grasped the full significance of the painter's achievement. But he has nothing now to say of the beauty that lies beneath the confinement of modern garments, 'the delicious charm of youth, grown languid, rendered as it were divine by the debilitating air of cities'. On the contrary, he emphasizes the vision which Degas presents of women at the bath-tub revealing in every 'frog-like and simian attitude' their pitiful homeliness, 'the humid horror of a body which no washing can purify'. Such a glorified contempt of the flesh, he adds, has never been achieved since the Middle Ages. There we catch what had now become the dominant tone in Huysmans' vision; the most modern things in art now suggest to him, they seem to merge into, the most mediæval and ascetic. And if we turn to the essay on Félicien Rops in the same volume – the most masterly of his essays – we find the same point developed to the utmost. Rops in his own way is as modern and as daring an artist of the nude as Degas. But, as Huysmans perceives, in delineating the essentially modern he is scarcely a supreme artist, is even inferior to Forain, who in his own circumscribed region is insurpassable. Rops, as Huysmans points out, is the great artist of the symbolical rather than the naturalistic modern, a great artist who furnishes the counterpart to Memlinc and Fra Angelico. All art, Huysmans proceeds, 'must gravitate, like humanity which has given birth to it and the earth which carries it, between the two poles of Purity and Wantonness, the Heaven and the Hell of art'. Rops has taken the latter pole, in no vulgar nymphomaniacal shapes, but 'to divulge its causes, to summarize it Catholically, if one may say so, in ardent and sorrowful images'; he has drawn women who are 'diabolical Theresas, satanized saints'. Following in the path initiated by Baudelaire and Barbey D'Aurevilly, Huysmans concludes, Rops has restored Wantonness to her ancient and Catholic dignity. Thus is Huysmans almost imperceptibly led back to the old standpoint from which woman and the Devil are one.

Certains was immediately followed by *Làbas*. This novel is mainly a study of Satanism, in which Huysmans interested himself long before it attracted the general attention it has since received in France. There are, however, three lines of interest in the book, the story of Gilles de Rais and his Sadism, the discussion of Satanism culminating in an extraordinary description of a modern celebration of the Black Mass, and the narration of Durtal's *liaison* with Madame Chantelouve, wherein Huysmans reaches, by firm precision and triumphant audacity, the highest point he has attained in the analysis of the secrets of passion. But though full of excellent matter, the book loses in impressiveness from the multiplicity of these insufficiently compacted elements of interest.

While not among his finest achievements, however, it serves to mark the definite attainment of a new stage in both the spirit and the method of his work. Hitherto he had been a realist, in method if not in spirit, and had conquered the finest secrets of naturalistic art; by the help of *En Ménage* alone, as Hennequin, one of his earliest and best critics has said, 'it will always be possible to restore the exact physiognomy of Paris to-day'. At the outset of *Là-bas* there is a discussion concerning the naturalistic novel and its functions which makes plain the standpoint to which Huysmans had now attained. Pondering the matter, Durtal, the hero of the book, considers that we need, on the one hand, the veracity of document, the precision of detail, the nervous strength of language, which realism has supplied; but also, on the other hand, we must draw water from the wells of the soul. We cannot explain everything by sexuality and insanity; we need the soul and the body in their natural reactions, their conflict and their union. 'We must, in short, follow the great high-way so deeply dug out by Zola, but it is also necessary to trace a parallel path in the air, another road by which we may reach the Beyond and the Afterward, to achieve thus, in one word, a spiritualistic naturalism.' Dostoievsky comes nearest to this achievement, he remarks, and the real psychologist of the century is not Stendhal but Hello. In another form of art the early painters – Italian, German, especially Flemish – realized this ideal. Durtal sees a consummate revelation of such spiritual naturalism in Matthæus Grünewald's crucifixion at Cassel – the Christ who was at once a putrid and unaureoled corpse and yet a manifest god bathed in invisible light, the union of outrageous realism and outrageous idealism. 'Thus from triumphal ordure Grünewald extracted the finest mints of dilection, the sharpest essences of tears.' One may say that the tendency Huysmans here so clearly asserts had ever been present in his work. But in his previous novels his own native impulse was always a little unduly oppressed by the naturalistic formulas of Goncourt and Zola. The methods of these great masters had laid a burden on his work, and although the work developed beneath, and because of, that burden, a sense of laborious pain and obscurity too often resulted. Henceforth this disappears. Huysmans retains his own complexity of style, but he has won a certain measure of simplicity and lucidity. It was a natural development, no doubt furthered also by the position which Huysmans had now won in the world of letters. *A Rebours*, which he had written for his own pleasure, had found an echo in thousands of readers, and the consciousness of an audience inspired a certain clarity of speech. From this time we miss the insults directed at the *bêtise* of humanity. These characteristics clearly mark Huysmans' next and perhaps greatest book, in which the writer who had conquered all the secrets of decadent art now sets his face towards the ideals of classic art.

In *En Route*, indeed, these new qualities of simplicity, lucidity, humanity, and intensity of interest attain so high a degree that the book has reached a vast number of readers who could not realize the marvellous liberation from slavery to its material which the slow elaboration of art has here reached. In *A Rebours* Huysmans succeeded in taking up the prose-poem into his novel form, while at the same time certainly sacrificing something of the fine analysis of familiar things which he had developed in *En Ménage*. In *En*

Route he takes the novel from the point he had reached in *A Rebours*, incorporates into it that power of analysis which has now reached incomparable simplicity and acuity, and thus wields the whole of the artistic means which he has acquired during a quarter of a century to one end, the presentation of a spiritual state which has become of absorbing personal interest to himself.

I well remember hearing M. Huysmans, many years ago, tell how a muddle-headed person had wished to commission him to paint a head of Christ. It seemed then a deliciously absurd request to make of the author of *A Rebours*, and his face wore the patient smile which the spectacle of human stupidity was wont to evoke, but I have since thought that that muddle-headed person was wiser than he knew. As we look back on Huysmans' earlier work it is now easy to see how he has steadily progressed towards his present standpoint. *En Route* does not represent, as some might imagine, the reaction of an exhausted debauchee or even the self-deception of a disappointed man of the world. The temperament of Durtal is that of André and Folantin and Des Esseintes; from the first, in the *Drageoir à Epices*, Huysmans has been an idealist and a seeker, by no means an ascetic, rather a man whose inquisitive senses and restless imagination had led him to taste of every forbidden fruit, but never one to whom the vulgar pleasures of life could offer any abiding satisfaction. The more precise record of Des Esseintes's early sexual life may help us here; while for the penultimate stage Durtal's relations with Madame Chantelouve in *Là-bas*, and the mingled attraction and repulsion which he felt for her, are certainly significant. In *En Route* Durtal magnifies his own wickedness, as Bunyan did in his *Grace Abounding*; the saints have always striven to magnify their wickedness, leaving to the sinners the congenial function of playing at righteousness. To trace the real permanence of Huysmans' attitude towards religion it is enough to turn back to *A Rebours*. Des Esseintes had been educated by the Jesuits, and it sometimes seemed to him that that education had put into him some extra-terrestrial ferment which never after ceased to work, driving him in search of a new world and impossible ideals. He could find no earthly place of rest; he sought to build for himself a 'refined Thebaid' as a warm and comfortable ark wherein to find shelter from the flood of human imbecility. He was already drawn towards the Church by many bonds, by his predilection for early Christian

Latinity, by the exquisite beauty of the ecclesiastical art of the Middle Ages, by his love for monastic mediæval music, 'that emaciated music which acted instinctively on his nerves' and seemed to him precious beyond all other. Just as Nietzsche was always haunted by the desire for a monastery for freethinkers, so Des Esseintes dreamed of a hermitage, of the advantages of the cloistered life of convents, wherein men are persecuted by the world for meting out to it the just contempt of silence.

Des Esseintes, and even the Durtal of *Là-bas*, always put aside these thoughts with the reflection that, after all, the Church is only an out-worn legend, a magnificent imposture. In *En Route* Durtal has taken a decisive step. He has undergone that psychological experience commonly called 'conversion'. It is only of recent years that the phenomena of conversion have been seriously studied, but we know at all events that it is not intellectual, not even necessarily moral transformation, though it may react in either direction, but primarily an emotional phenomenon; and that it occurs especially in those who have undergone long and torturing disquietude, coming at last as the spontaneous resolution of all their doubts, the eruption of a soothing flood of peace, the silent explosion of inner light. The insight with which this state is described in *En Route* seems to testify to a real knowledge of it. No obvious moral or intellectual change is effected in Durtal, but he receives a new experience of reposeful faith, a conviction deeper than all argument. It is really the sudden emergence into consciousness of a very gradual process, and the concrete artistic temperament which had been subjected to the process reacts in its own way. A more abstract intelligence would have asked : 'But, after all, is my faith true?' Durtal, in the presence of the growing structure of sensory and imaginative forms within him, which has become as it were a home, feels that the question of its truth has fallen into the background. Its perfect fitness has become the affirmation of its truth. Henceforth it is the task of his life to learn how best to adapt himself to what he recognizes as his eternal home. *En Route* represents a stage in this adaptation.

By a rare chance – a happier chance than befell Tolstoï under somewhat similar circumstances – a new development in artistic achievement has here run parallel, and in exquisite harmony, with the new spiritual development. The growing simplicity of Huys-

mans' work has reached a point beyond which it could not perhaps
be carried without injury to his vivid and concrete style. And the
new simplicity of spirit, of which it is the reflection, marks the final
retreat into the background of that unreasonable contempt for
humanity which ran through nearly all the previous books, and
now at last passes even into an ecstasy of adoration in the passages
concerning old Simon, the monastery swine-herd. Huysmans has
chiefly shown his art, however, by relying almost solely for the
interest of his book on his now consummate power of analysis. This
power, which we may perhaps first clearly trace in 'Sac au Dos',
had developed in *En Ménage* into a wonderful skill to light up the
unexplored corners of the soul and to lay bare those terrible thoughts
which are, as he has somewhere said, the lamentable incarnation
of 'the unconscious ignominy of pure souls'. In his earlier masterpiece, *A Rebours*, however, it is little seen, having mostly passed
into aesthetic criticism. The finest episode of emotional analysis here
is the admirable chapter in which Des Esseintes's attempt to visit
London is narrated. All his life he had wished to see two countries,
Holland and England. (And here we may recall that the former is
Huysmans' own ancestral land, and that his French critics find in
his work a distinct flavour of English humour.) He had actually
been to Holland, and with visions won from the pictures of
Rembrandt, Steen, and Teniers he had returned disillusioned. Now
he went to Galignani's, bought an English Baedeker, entered the
bodega in the Rue de Rivoli to drink of that port which the English
love, and then proceeded to a tavern opposite the Gare St Lazare to
eat what he imagined to be a characteristic English meal, surrounded
by English people, and haunted by memories of Dickens. And as
time went by he continued to sit still, while all the sensations of
England seemed to pass along his nerves, still sat until at last the
London mail had started. 'Why stir,' he asked himself, 'when one can
travel so magnificently in a chair? . . . Besides, what can one expect
save fresh disillusionment, as in Holland? . . . And then I have
experienced and seen what I wanted to experience and see
I have saturated myself with English life; it would be madness to lose by an awkward change of place these imperishable sensations. . . . He called a cab and returned with his
portmanteaus, parcels, valises, rugs, umbrellas, and sticks to
Fontenay, feeling the physical and mental fatigue of a man who

returns home after a long and perilous journey.' There could be
no happier picture of the imaginative life of the artistic temperament. But in *En Route* analysis is the prime element of interest;
from first to last there is nothing to hold us but this searching and
poignant analysis of the fluctuations of Durtal's soul through the
small section which he here travels in the road towards spiritual
peace. And on the way, lightly, as by chance, the author drops
the finest appreciations of liturgical aesthetics, of plain-chant, of
the way of the Church with the soul, of the everlasting struggle
with the Evil One. There could, for instance, be no better statement
than this of one of the mystic's secrets : 'There are two ways of
ridding ourselves of a thing which burdens us, casting it away or
letting it fall. To cast away requires an effort of which we may not
be capable, to let fall imposes no labour, is simpler, without peril,
within reach of all. To cast away, again, implies a certain interest,
a certain animation, even a certain fear; to let fall is absolute
indifference, absolute contempt; believe me, use this method, and
Satan will flee.' How many forms of Satan there are in the world
before which we may profitably meditate on these words ! To strive
or cry in the face of human stupidity is not the way to set it to
flight; that is the lesson which Des Esseintes would never listen to,
which Durtal has at last learnt.*

En Route is the first of a trilogy, and the names of the succeeding
volumes, *La Cathédrale* and *L'Oblat*, sufficiently indicate the end
of the path on which Durtal, if not indeed his creator, has started.
But however that may prove, whatever Huysmans' own final stage
may be, there can be little doubt that he is the greatest master of
style, and within his own limits the subtlest thinker and the acutest
psychologist who in France to-day uses the medium of the novel.
Only Zola can be compared with him, and between them there
can be no kind of rivalry. Zola, with his immense and exuberant
temperament, his sanity and width of view, his robust and plebeian
art, has his own place on the high-road of modern literature.

---

* In the seventeenth century a great English man of science, Stephen
Hales, had discovered the same truth, for we are told that 'he could look
even upon wicked men, and those who did him unkind offices, without any
emotion of particular indignation, not from want of discernment or
sensibility; but he used to consider them only like those experiments which,
upon trial, he found could never be applied to any useful purpose, and
which he therefore calmly and dispassionately laid aside'.

Huysmans, an intellectual and aesthetic aristocrat, has followed with unflinching sincerity the by-path along which his own more high-strung and exceptional temperament has led him, and his place, if seemingly a smaller one, is at least as sure; wherever men occupy themselves with the literature of the late nineteenth century they will certainly sometimes talk about Zola, sometimes read Huysmans. Zola's cyclopean architecture can only be seen as a whole when we have completed the weary task of investigating it in detail; in Huysmans we seek the expressiveness of the page, the sentence, the word. Strange as it may seem to some, it is the so-called realist who has given us the more idealized rendering of life; the concentrated vision of the idealist in his own smaller sphere has revealed not alone mysteries of the soul, but even the exterior secrets of life. True it is that Huysmans has passed by with serene indifference, or else with contempt, the things which through the ages we have slowly learnt to count beautiful. But on the other hand, he has helped to enlarge the sphere of our delight by a new vision of beauty where before to our eyes there was no beauty, exercising the proper function of the artist who ever chooses the base and despised things of the world, even the things that are not, to put to nought the things that are. Therein the decadent has his justification. And while we may accept the pioneer's new vision of beauty, we are not called upon to reject those old familiar visions for which he has no eyes, only because his gaze must be fixed upon that unfamiliar height towards which he is leading the men who come after.

IV

Huysmans very exquisitely represents one aspect of the complex modern soul, that aspect which shrinks from the grosser forces of Nature, from the bare simplicity of the naked sky or the naked body, the 'incessant deluge of human foolishness', the eternal oppression of the commonplace, to find a sedative for its exasperated nerves in the contemplation of esoteric beauty and the difficult search for the mystic peace which passes all understanding. 'Needs must I rejoice beyond the age,' runs the motto from the old Flemish mystic Ruysbroeck set on the front of *A Rebours*, 'though the world has horror of my joy and its grossness cannot understand what I would say.' Such is decadence; such, indeed, is religion, in the wide and true sense of the word. Christianity itself, as we know it in the western church, sprang from the baptism of young barbarism into Latin decadence. Pagan art and its clear serenity, science, rationalism, the bright, rough vigour of the sun and the sea, the adorable mystery of common life and commonplace human love, are left to make up the spirit that in any age we call 'classic'.

Thus what we call classic corresponds on the spiritual side of the love of natural things, and what we call decadent to the research for the things which seem to lie beyond Nature. 'Corporea pulchritudo in pelle solummodo constat. Nam si viderent homines hoc quod subtus pellem est, sicut lynces in Beotia cernere interiore dicuntur, mulieres videre nausearent. Iste decor in flegmate et sanguine et humore ac felle constitit.' That is St Odo of Cluny's acute analysis of woman, who for man is ever the symbol of Nature : beauty is skin-deep, drowned in excretions which we should scarcely care to touch with the finger's tip. And for the classic vision of Nature, listen to that fantastic and gigantic Englishman, Sir Kenelm Digby, whose *Memoirs,* whose whole personality, embodied the final efflorescence of the pagan English Renaissance. He has been admitted by her maids to the bed-chamber of Venetia Stanley, the famous beauty who afterwards became his wife; she is still sleeping, and he cannot resist the temptation to undress and lie gently and reverently beside her, as half disturbed in her slumber she rolled on to her side from beneath the clothes; 'and her smock was so twisted about her fair body that all her legs and the best part of her thighs were naked, which lay so one over the other that they made a deep shadow where the never-satisfied eyes wished for the greatest light. A natural ruddiness did shine through the skin, as the sunbeams do through crystal or water, and ascertained him that it was flesh that he gazed upon, which yet he durst not touch for fear of melting it, so like snow it looked. Her belly was covered with her smock, which it raised up with a gentle swelling, and expressed the perfect figure of it through the folds of that discourteous veil. Her paps were like two globes – wherein the glories of the heaven and the earth were designed, and the azure veins seemed to divide constellations and kingdoms – between both which began the milky way which leadeth lovers to their Paradise, somewhat shadowed by the yielding downwards of the uppermost of them as she lay upon her side, and out of that darkness did glisten a few drops of sweat like diamond sparks, and a more fragrant odour than the violets or primroses, whose season was nearly passed, to give way to the warmer sun and the longest days.' They play with the same counters, you observe, these two, Odo and Digby, with skin, sweat, and so forth, each placing upon them his own values. Idealists both of them, the one idealizes along the line of death, the other along the line of life which the whole race has followed, and both on their own grounds are irrefutable, the logic of life and the logic of death, alike solidly founded in the very structure of the world, of which man is the measuring-rod.

The classic party of Nature seems, indeed, the stronger – in seeming only, and one recalls that, of the two witnesses just cited, the abbot of Cluny was the most venerated man of his age, while no one troubled even to publish Digby's *Memoirs* until our own century – but it carries weakness in its very strength, the weakness of a great political party formed by coalition. It has not alone idealists on its side, but for the most part also the blind forces of robust vulgarity. So that the more fine-strung spirits are sometimes driven to a reaction against Nature and rationalism, like that of which Huysmans, from 'L'Extase' onwards, has been the consistent representative. At the present moment such a reaction has attained a certain ascendency.

Christianity once fitted nearly every person born into the European world; there must needs be some to whom, in no modern devitalized form but in its purest essence, it is still the one refuge possible. No doubt conditions have changed; the very world itself is not what it was to the mediæval man. One has to recognize that the modern European differs in this from his mediæval ancestor that now we know how largely the world is of our own making. The sense of interiority, as the psychologists say, is of much later development than the sense of exteriority. For the mediæval man – as still to-day for the child in the darkness – his dreams and his fancies, every organic thrill in eye or ear, seemed to be flashed on him from a world of angels and demons without. In a sense which is scarcely true to-day the average man of those days – not the finer or the coarser natures, it may well be – might be said to be the victim of a species of madness, a paranoia, a systematized persecutional delusion. He could not look serenely in the face of the stars or lie at rest among the fir-cones in the wood, for who knew what ambush of the Enemy might not lurk behind these things? Even in flowers, as St Cyprian said, the Enemy lay hidden.

> Nil jocundum, nil amœnum,
> Nil salubre, nil serenum,
> Nihil dulce, nihil plenum.

There was only one spot where men might huddle together in safety – the church. There the blessed sound of the bells, the contact of holy water, the smell of incense, the sight of the Divine Flesh, wove a spiritual coat of mail over every sensory avenue to the soul. The winds of hell might rave, the birds of night dash themselves against the leaden spires of that fortress whence alone the sky seemed blue with hope.

Huysmans, notwithstanding a very high degree of intellectual subtlety, is by virtue of his special aesthetic and imaginative temperament carried back to the more childlike attitude of this earlier age. The whole universe appears to him as a process of living images; he cannot reason in abstractions, cannot *rationalize*; that indeed is why he is inevitably an artist. Thus he is a born leader in a certain modern emotional movement.

That movement, as we know, is one of a group of movements now peculiarly active. We see them on every hand, occultism, theosophy, spiritualism, all those vague forms on the borderland of the unknown which call to tired men weary of too much living, or never strong enough to live at all, to hide their faces from the sun of nature and grope into cool, delicious darkness, soothing the fever of life. It is foolish to resent this tendency; it has its rightness; it suits some, who may well cling to their private dream if life itself is but a dream. At the worst we may remember that, however repugnant such movements may be, to let fall remains a better way of putting Satan to flight than to cast away. And at the best one should know that this is part of the vital process by which the spiritual world moves on its axis, alternating between darkness and light.

Therefore soak yourself in mysticism, follow every intoxicating path to every impossible Beyond, be drunken with mediævalism, occultism, spiritualism, theosophy, and even, if you will, protestantism – the cup that cheers, possibly, but surely not inebriates – for the satisfaction that comes of all these is good while it lasts. Yet be sure that Nature is your home, and that from the farthest excursions you will return the more certainly to those fundamental instincts which are rooted in the zoological series at the summit of which we stand. For the whole spiritual cosmogony finally rests, not indeed on a tortoise, but on the emotional impulses of the mammal vertebrate which constitute us men.

Meanwhile we will not grieve because in the course of our pilgrimage on earth the sun sets. It has always risen again. We may lighten the darkness of the journey by admiring the beauty of night, plucking back the cowl if needs must we wear it. – *Eia, fratres, pergamus.*

(FROM 'AFFIRMATIONS', 1899)

GEORGE MOORE

1852 - 1933

George Augustus Moore, novelist, autobiographer and critic, was born at Moore Hall, County Mayo, in the West of Ireland, on 24 February 1852. His father was an Irish landowner, of a long-established family which had turned Catholic in the eighteenth century. His father accordingly sent him to Oscott where he had himself been educated, but George reverted to Protestantism, the faith which the family had originally professed.

Perhaps it would be truer to describe his vocal enthusiasm for the Protestant position as an *attitude* rather than a *faith*. Moore was an exceedingly provocative man and reading of his religious disagreements with his Catholic younger brother Maurice in *Salve* (1912), one cannot help recalling Lionel Johnson's statement that he had himself joined the Catholic Church for polemical purposes.

As far as an instinctive commitment is concerned, Moore was more of a pagan than a Catholic or a Protestant. *Confessions of a Young Man* (1888) is full of brash and flashy declarations of paganism which became more muted and decorous by the time he wrote *Memoirs of my Dead Life* (1906). There, in the last pages of that lovely book, he describes how at his mother's funeral, during a Mass for her soul, he plays with the fancy of a burial urn – a Greek vase carried with bacchanals – in which he will have his own ashes preserved. It is surprising how Moore has succeeded in endowing this whim of an aesthete with a rare, grave beauty of expression. The beauty results from the author's increased mastery of the medium of prose rather than from the intrinsic ideas; or, to put the matter another way, one could say that the maturing subtlety of his sensibility never met up with mental concepts of a commensurate delicacy. One of the notions which enters into

Moore's mind in this passage is the odd one of cyclic rebirth or
eternal recurrence, which he may probably have derived from Yeats.
Ideas as such – as philosophic digits – were certainly not Moore's
strong point.

The strength of Moore as a critic results from the intensely
personal nature of his thought. The revelations that came to him
were fuelled always by promptings of impulse. He recalled how,
when at school, 'Neither Latin, nor Greek, nor French, nor History,
nor English composition could I learn, unless, indeed, my curiosity
or personal interest was excited – then I made rapid strides in that
brand of knowledge to which my attention was directed. A mind
hitherto dark seemed suddenly to grow clear, and it remained clear
and bright as long as the passion was in me.'[1] Often such passion
flickered and faded, and Moore's uncertainty as a critic as well as
his genuine sensitiveness is related to this fickleness of temperament.
Wisely, no doubt, Moore did not attempt to impose consistency
upon what were essentially discrete or even contradictory insights.
Even so, Max Beerbohm twitted him delightfully in *A Christmas
Garland* as to his inconstancy of preferences. 'There never was a
writer except Dickens,' Max makes Moore declare in his parody
of him. 'I remember that when I was a young man in Paris, I read
a praise of him in some journal, but in those days I was kneeling
at other altars, I was scrubbing other doorsteps. . . . So has it ever
been since, always a false god, always the wrong doorstep. I am
sick of the smell of incense. I have swung to this and that false
god – Zola, Yeats, *et tous ces autres.* I am angry to have got house-
maids' knees, because I got it on doorsteps that led nowhere. There
is but one doorstep worth scrubbing. The doorstep of Charles
Dickens. . . .'[2]

Most education is a matter of information : Moore's was a matter
of self-discovery. The most valuable part of it he acquired in France.
Confessions of a Young Man and *Memories of My Dead Days*
relate how it meant learning that he was not a poet (even when
writing French !) and that he was not a painter. Positively, however,
it did teach him that he had the making of a good art critic – a
responsiveness towards the efforts of others.

Arthur Symons, who met him first in Paris and was a neighbour

[1] *Confessions of a Young Man*, 1888
[2] 'Dickens by G—rge M—re' (*A Christmas Garland*, 1912)

of his in the Temple, described Moore's weaknesses as a critic when commenting on his volume of essays *Modern Painting* (1893). It contained, stated Symons, 'injustices, brutality, and ignorances'.[3] At the same time, it was full of 'the most discriminating sympathy, and the genuine knowledge of the painter'.[4] 'Here,' wrote Symons, 'you will find some of the secrets of the art of painting, let out . . . by an intelligence all sensation, which has soaked them up without knowing.'[5] 'An intelligence all sensation' – in this phrase, Symons has hit the nail on the head. Equally true is his reference to Moore's sensitive passivity – his intuitive, partly unconscious, manner of acquiring knowledge : an instinctive way of absorbing the facts and details of a cultural environment which happened to intrigue him.

The off-beat and 'unofficial' mode of Moore's education is responsible for the intensely personal nature of his criticism – the unashamed egotism of his judgment. Robert Ross, in one of his bright back-biting dialogues, expresses this amusingly. 'I don't care for his novels,' he makes his speaker say, 'but his essays are delightful. . . . Few people know so little about art; yet how delightfully he writes about it. Everything comes to him as a surprise.'[6]

Moore's first volume of literary essays by its very title, *Impressions and Opinions* (1891), implies the author's individualism. Full of anecdotes and first-hand encounters, of paraded personalities and gossip, it appealed by its easy intimate tone. In a second edition in 1913, Moore related in his preface that 'the author was sinking in a flood of public disfavour caused by *Spring Days* [1888], and the book that followed *Spring Days* [*Mike Fletcher*, 1889] . . . when *Impressions and Opinions*, like a big Newfoundland dog, dived after him and brought him to the shore'. Moore tells us that public response to the book continued, and it seems always to have been one of the author's own favourites.

One reason for this kindly reaction on the part of 'the common reader' was, no doubt, its intimate approach. Moore was one of the first to use the interview or profile-sketch as a means of criticism. So enamoured was he, in fact, of this approach that he invented meetings which had not in fact taken place. Havelock Ellis, whose

[3] 'Confessions and Comments' (*Dramatic Personae*, 1925)
[4] *Ibid*
[5] *Ibid*
[6] 'The Jaded Intellectuals' (*Masques and Phases*, 1909)

acquaintance with him was less a direct relationship than the by-product of Moore's friendship with Olive Schreiner and Arthur Symons, reported how 'when he [Moore] planned to meet Verlaine for the first time, and something prevented the meeting, he was so annoyed (though later a meeting seems to have taken place) that he wrote an account of it, in the manner he felt sure it would have occurred, as an actual occurrence. He here described Verlaine as unbinding and displaying his ulcerated leg, which no one who knew the poet could regard as a likely incident.'[7]

For all Moore's lack of respect for the facts of life as to details, he remains an important and enjoyable critic. His very fallibility was endearingly human, and he was as ready to tell a story against himself as against an enemy or a friend. Along with Arthur Symons, he did a great deal to introduce fresh French writers to this country – both in his critical writings properly so called, and in his autobiographies. His own art of fiction can also be taken as a species of brilliant translation. *Esther Waters* (1894) can justly be taken as the finest French naturalist novel ever written in English, just as *Evelyn Innes* (1898) is perhaps the best Symbolist novel ever to be published over here.

As a writer, Moore responded to those aspects of literature which chiefly distinguish the culture of the 'nineties : a sense of style and a sense of sex. With regard to the latter, Robert Ross remarked that 'Moore is one of the many literary Acteons who have mistaken Diana for Aphrodite',[8] and Max Beerbohm, in his parody of him, teased him unmercifully for his obsession with art and sex and his odd confounding of the two : 'There are moments when one does not think of girls, are there not, dear reader?' he makes Moore declare, 'and I swear to you that such a moment came to me while Dolmetsch mumbled the last two bars of that Mass. The notes were "do, la, sol, fa, do, sol, la", and as he mumbled them I sat upright and stared into space, for it became suddenly plain to me why when people talked of Tintoretto I always found myself thinking of Tourguèneff.'[9]

Yet if Moore did confuse the nature and claims of sex and style, at least he fought for them both as they pertain to the novel. As

[7] 'George Moore' (*My Confessional*, 1934)
[8] 'The Jaded Intellectuals' (*Masques and Phases*)
[9] 'Dickens by G—rge M—re' (*A Christmas Garland*)

early as 1885, he had published his polemical pamphlet *Literature at Nurse, or Circulating Morals* – on the selection of books at Mudie's Library. In three years time, he returned to the theme. 'The villa,' he wrote in *Confessions of a Young Man*, 'made known its want, and art fell on its knees. Pressure was put on the publishers, and books were published at 31s 6d; the dirty, outside public was got rid of, and the villa paid its yearly subscription, and had nice large, handsome books that none but the *élite* could obtain, and with them a sense of being put on a footing of equality with my Lady This and Lady That, and certainly that nothing would come into the hands of dear Kate and Mary and Maggie that they might not read, and all for two guineas a year.' Thinking back to those days, Arthur Symons recalled how there entered into literature 'a new licence in dealing imaginatively with life, almost permitting the Englishman to contend with the writers of other nations on their own ground, permitting him, that is to say, to represent life as it really is'.[10] That this new licence was established was very largely due to Moore, who both by theory and example crashed the Victorian inhibition barrier.

His battle against official morality in literature found its counterpart in his battle against official taste in painting. In his pamphlet[11] on the Summer Show of the R.A. in 1895 he loosed off a salvo against that institution, while in 1897 he wrote, 'The hatred of artistic England for the Academy proceeds from the knowledge that the Academy is no true centre of art, but a mere commercial enterprise protected and subventioned by the Government.'

Moore's devotion and response to style is implicit in the words which Havelock Ellis wrote on the day following his death : 'Certainly Moore's ideal was that of the pure artist. Nor has any writer in English of our time . . . laboured so indefatigably throughout a long life to attain to the summit of that ideal. . . . In the sphere where we usually apply the title, George Moore was by no means a saint. But he will live as a saint of art.'[12]

The standard biography is *The Life of George Moore* by J. Hone (1936). There is a neat all-over cover of his life and work by A. Norman Jeffares in the British Council Writers and their Work

[10] 'Confessions and Comments' (*Dramatis Personae*)
[11] *The Royal Academy, 1895* (1895)
[12] *My Confessional*

Series (1965), while the best brief assessment of him as a critic is Graham Hough's essay 'George Moore and the Nineties' in his book *Edwardians and Late Victorians* (1960).

George Moore died on 21 January 1933 in London, aged eighty. His last years had been spent in revising his work, leaving still unaccomplished *A Communication to My Friends* (1932) – the story of his sufferings in the name of art. Some short while before he died he told his disciple Geraint Goodwin that if he had a tombstone he would like this written on it : 'Here lies George Moore, who looked on corrections as the one morality.'

MY IMPRESSIONS OF ZOLA

Manet had persuaded me to go to the *bal de l'Assommoir* dressed as a Parisian workman, for he enjoyed incongruities, and the blouse and the casquette, with my appearance and my accent, appealed to his imagination. 'There is no Frenchman living in London who occupies the same position as you do in Paris,' he said, and I pondered over his words as I followed him through *tout Paris* assembled at the Elysée Montmartre, for the ball given in honour of the play that was being performed at the Ambigu. 'But I must introduce you to Zola. There he is,' he said pointing to a thickly built, massive man in evening clothes for, as Manet said, a serious writer cannot be expected to put on fancy dress.

Zola bowed and passed on, chilling us a little; Manet would have liked to watch him struggling into a new acquaintanceship, and we walked on together conscious of our failure, myself thinking how pleasant it would have been to have gone with them into a corner, and talked art for half an hour, 'and what a wonderful memory it would have been!' I thought, and begged Manet a few minutes later to come with me in search of Zola. But he was nowhere to be found.

'He must have gone home,' I said, and Manet answered : 'It doesn't matter. You'll find him at home at Mèdan any day you like to go there.'

For one reason or another it was not till some months later that

I summoned courage and took the train at the Gare St Lazare. There is no station at Mèdan, the nearest station is – (the curious are referred to the time table for I have forgotten the name of it) – and Mèdan is a village known only to peasants, about a mile and a half from the station. Some chance had led Zola there, and being in want of a country residence he had purchased a cottage from one of the peasants, which he had just finished building into a sort of castle; an ugly place it seemed to me, a great red brick wall with a small door in it through which I was taken into the house, and left waiting in the billiard room.

It was not Zola that came down to me, but Madame Zola. She had forgotten me, though I had met her at Manet's studio, and it was only after many tedious explanations that she somewhat reluctantly led me through the house, up many staircases of polished oak, narrow and steep. On the wall of the last little flight there were Japanese prints depicting furious fornications; a rather blatant announcement, I thought of naturalism – but they were forgotten quickly, for in a few seconds I should be in the master's presence. She opened a door and left me, and I found myself in a place as large as the studio of an Academician, lighted by a skylight and a huge window. For a moment or two I lost my way among the massive furniture, and it was not until I passed a lectern that I discovered the master on a sofa by a window correcting proofs.

He did not rise to meet me, but contented himself with untucking his fat leg and motioning with his hand to a seat. His manner was terribly aloof and cold, and my embarrassment increased, for suddenly I remembered I had heard that Zola was never long in doubt as to whether he was talking to a fool or a man of wit, and that at the end of minute a fool was dismissed peremptorily. 'And he has discovered me to be a fool though I haven't said a word.' I glanced at the terrible master who lay on the sofa, his glasses on his nose, reading me, divining the commonplace remarks that I was trying to conjure up. 'If Homer and Shakespeare were suddenly introduced they would have to begin with remarks about the weather or the pleasure each had taken in the other's work' I said to myself, 'and if this man would only give me as much rope as he would to Shakespeare or Homer I might think of something more interesting that the compliments that I am gabbling.'

Zola was not then what he is now, a gracious, kindly man in the habit of receiving every one who chooses to call on him, and answering all sorts of questions. He was then the iconoclast, the idol-breaker, a bear that cursed the universe, and bade all comers begone. All the same his writings exhaled a certain large-heartedness and sympathy, and I had always felt while reading his weekly article in *The Voltaire* that we were intended to understand each other. I had imagined that when I went to see him he would come forward, his hands extended in benevolent gesture, taking me at once into his confidence. This Buddha lying on the sofa, fixing his glasses from time to time on his short, strangely square-cut nose, was in such strange conflict with my dream that I could hardly believe that this could be my Zola in those terrible moments during which I tried to improvise compliments. Not one had produced the faintest impression, no more than water flowing over a block of granite, and feverishly I sought for a subject of conversation, something, no matter what, that might interest him.

The power that the circulating libraries exercised on literature occupied my mind a good deal at that time, and I hurried to the subject, seizing the first transitional phrase.

'The position of the novelist in England is that of a slave,' I said, 'for books are not bought in England, but hired.'

'But if a man writes a book that interests the public, the public will find it.'

'The public will find it in time no doubt,' I answered, 'but the man may starve in the interval.'

'Yes, he may; and your difficulty is no small one, a middle-man always between you and your public.'

'Ah, he's beginning to see I'm not such a fool after all,' I said to myself, and as soon as I had explained the power that their monopoly gave to Mudie and Smith I deflected the conversation dexterously from the practical to the moral question, dropping some disparaging remarks about Puritanism as an artistic influence. Zola, who had been waking for some time out of his slumber, was now wholly awake.

'What you say,' the great man said, 'is extremely interesting. I have written an article on the influence of Protestantism on art; it will appear in tomorrow's *Figaro*, and I make this statement, that Protestantism has never produced great art. Milton is the one Protestant writer. The Elizabethans, Shakespeare, and Jonson lived before Protestantism had taken hold of the national spirit, the genius of the nation, and so on.'

The conversation then became friendly and pleasant. Zola asked me about George Eliot; which did I think was her best book? What French writer was she most like? Though I felt I was risking my newly-acquired reputation, I had to admit that I could think of no one to compare her with. The conversation paused a moment, and to my surprise and pleasure Zola began to tell me about the novel he was writing. We must have talked for three-quarters of an hour, and then, fearing to outstay my welcome, I bade the master good-bye. He took me downstairs, vivacious all the time, and asked me to come to see him again. Then I knew I had made a friend. 'I have made a friend,' I repeated to myself as the carriage rolled through the flat, green French country, my eyes noting the mystery of the long low horizon, the poplars pointing to the first stars. A train shrieked across the solitude. 'I have made a friend,' I repeated to myself as I listened to the distant rattle, and as the rattle died away in faint echoes, absorbed one by one in the dusky night of the long low plain I said : 'Yes, he is the very man I had imagined from reading his articles. A clear, well-balanced mind, a sympathetic nature, passionate in his convictions, loyal to his opinions. A little roughness at first; possibly what I mistook for roughness was mere shyness; besides it cannot be amusing to be told to your face that you are a great writer. I shouldn't like it myself.'

Years passed. I had written many books. *A Mummer's Wife* had been translated into French; it had been published in *The Voltaire* and the *Vie Populaire*. Charpentier was about to issue it in book form, and Zola had promised to write a preface. The *Confessions of a Young Man* was appearing in *La Revue Independante*, and the report had gone abroad that the next instalment would contain a scathing attack on *La Terre*. I wrote to Zola saying that this was not true, and proposing to spend Monday with him. 'On Monday morning you will receive the new number of the *Review*, and we shall be able to discuss the matter at breakfast.' I knew that the number contained – well, some frivolous remarks about naturalism; these I hoped to be able to explain away. But I did not feel quite at ease, so I called on my way for the faithful Alexis – bulky Alexis's placid temperament would serve as a buffer when the discussion became strained. However happily it might end there could hardly fail to be moments when. . . . I don't think I finished the sentence at the time; I will not seek to do so now.

Our walk lay by the river shimmering like watered silk between green banks full of the lush of June, and beyond them the green French country seemed to rejoice in the sunshine like a living creature. We sauntered, talking about our books, and I took exquisite pleasure in the poplars growing so tall and straight out of the plain, and the white clouds hanging between the trees. And when remembrances of Zola interrupted my reveries I told Alexis exactly what I had written, and the dear fellow assured me that Zola could not take offence at such light criticism.

'Yes, Alexis, but you always say what is agreeable to hear.'

As before, Zola was lying on the sofa by the window and after a few words of greeting, he said :

'I'm afraid, my dear friend, that I shall not be able to write the preface. You have made it impossible for me to do so.'

The phrases I had used when subjected to a close critical examination proved more difficult of explanation than I had anticipated. The discussion was painful, and the breakfast bell was a welcome relief. 'It's over at last,' I said to myself; but to my horror instead of answering my thought the master said :

'We are going down to breakfast now, but after breakfast we will go into the matter thoroughly; I will read the passages aloud to you.'

'Good Heavens !' I thought, 'I wish I hadn't come.'

After breakfast Zola, Alexis, and myself walked in the garden talking of indifferent things for an hour or more. Then Zola said :

'We will now go upstairs.' He led the way, and I followed, feeling very much as I used to feel at school when ordered a flogging. The master lay on the sofa; I took a small chair; he said : 'You'll be more comfortable in a larger one.'

The passages were already marked, and they were read to me in a low and deliberate voice. I listened, thinking what was the best defence to set up; Zola commented on every fresh sarcasm.

'How can I write your preface after that? I want to, you know, but I ask you how can I? Listen !'

'Don't you see, my dear friend, that that book is not my real opinion about life and things, but rather an attempt to reduce to words the fugitive imaginings of my mind, its intimate workings, its shifting colours? Has it never come to you to think differently about things? To find your mind in a ferment of contradition?'

'No,' he said, 'I do not change my opinions easily. There is Alexis' (he was indeed there, round as a barrel with the inevitable cigar between his teeth); 'I have known Alexis these five and twenty years, and I think of him to-day exactly as I always thought of him. With me an opinion is like a heavy piece of furniture; it is moved with difficulty.'

'But,' I said, 'the passages you have just read are from a chapter entitled "La Synthèse de la Nouvelle Athenes" . . . and must be taken as an expression of the opinions of the various *ratés* who assemble there.'

'I will admit that as a legitimate defence, but you see the opinions expressed in the café coincide exactly with those which you express yourself in an earlier part of the book.'

I had to fall back on the original defence, that a man changes, contradictory thinking should not be taken for the opinions which he holds by and abides by.

'How often do we hear Christians make jokes against Christianity?' I thought the argument specious, but Zola did not notice it. He continued reading:

'After what you have written about Goncourt,' he said, 'you never can go to his house again.'

'I don't want to; he isn't a friend.'

'The disciples, the childish vanity, the *bric-à-brac*, even the accusation of making copy out of his brother's corpse, *tout est là, rien ne manque*. What you say of me is nothing compared with what you say of Goncourt.' I hastened to concur in this opinion, but Zola was not to be wheedled. 'No, my dear friend,' he said gravely and sadly, 'you don't call your book *Memoirs d'un Jeune Anglais* you say *Confessions d'un Jeune Anglais*, and when we use the word Confessions we mean that at last we are going to tell the truth. I have gone through these pages calling attention to the expressions used, not because I am angry, but because I want to convince you that you have made it impossible for me to write the preface to your *Mummer's Wife*. What you think of me does not affect me, no, I won't say that; we are old friends. What you say about me does affect me, I mean that nothing that you can say can affect my position. . . . You admit in your book that you owe your first inspiration to me. I am proud that this is so, and thank you for saying it. I am sorry you have changed your opinions; after all it is the eternal law – children devour their fathers. I make no complaint. Nature has willed it so.'

He spoke these words sadly as he walked across the room. The twilight was gathering, the great furniture loomed up like shadows. There were tears in my eyes. Never did I feel so distinct a sensation of my inferiority; the man was great in his simplicity. 'The man is greater than his books,' I said to myself, 'and that is a great deal, for he has written some very fine books.'

I have told the story of these two meetings with some levity, but I was deeply moved at the time, and I am troubled even now, for is it always right to wear one's heart on one's sleeve, and to publish one's opinions as they come up in one's mind? Or is it better to look upon one's opinions as heavy pieces of furniture that are moved with difficulty. Alexis had devoted months to the correction of the translation that Charpentier was about to issue, and looked to Zola's preface to recoup himself for the labour he had spent upon the book, and a few casual words of mine had wrecked these hopes. He did not reproach me with having cost him some monetary losses; he merely said, '*C'est Charpentier que va boire un bouillon. Mille francs de corrections.*' The grey-green country stretched out before us, flat and dim – a dark mass of trees in front of us, a poplar striking out of the long plain. Alexis lectured me as we walked through the solitary country, but I did not listen. All the while I thought of Zola's last words as he bade me good-bye. 'I hope you understand that our personal relations are the same as they always were, only you have made it impossible for me to write the preface.'

At this time Zola was a fat man; soon after he became a thin one. By abstaining from drink at his meals he reduced his weight thirty-six French pounds in two months. He seems to have accepted Balzac's maxim, that the elegance of life exists mainly in the waist. As his waist narrowed his manner of life became more expansive. No longer is he the recluse of Mèdan; he has added a tower to his country house – with what intention I never fully understood – and he lives in a spacious mansion in the Rue de Bruxelles, which he has furnished with oak carvings, tapestries, portraits of archbishops and wrought-iron railings. A plaster cast of the Venus de Milo stands on the balustrade that encircles the staircase. The house seems to reveal a large coarse mind, a sort of coarsely woven net through whose meshes all live things escape, and that brings to shore only a quantity of *débris*. 'From the *Rue de Lafayette*,' I said. Why should he consider it incumbent upon him to collect these things? Great artists need not be learned in *bric-à-brac*. Manet lived all his life amid red plush furniture; and I am not sure that I should have spoken of Zola's furniture (has it not been described by reporters and reproduced in photography in every illustrated periodical?) if it had not been that with the acquisition of a waist and much general *bric-à-brac* a definite mental change has come upon Zola. I once heard him say he was going to give a ball. I don't think he ever carried the project into execution. However this may be, his house has, for the last three years, been open to visitors, and he has answered the ten thousand heterogeneous questions that the eleven hundred and fifty-seven interviewers have put to him with unfailing urbanity, and I am bound to admit, with extraordinary common-sense.

His mind is not as intense or penetrating as Tourguèneff's, but it looks with admirable lucidity over a wide surface, and he can answer the most foolish questions reasonably. An elderly lady's applecart has been upset in the Place Cliche, and a reporter calls on Zola for his opinion. He says that he has no precise information on the subject of apples, but he believes that apple-growing is a very large industry in the north of France. If the apple sellers of Montmartre are prevented from exposing their wares for sale, the liberty of the individual is called into question, and a very large and important industry is possibly affected. At the same time the streets cannot – and so on. But even these platitudes he will relieve with some touch of rare common-sense. This touch I have left out, it is the incommunicable secret of his genius. But if any reader of this article should desire to hear Zola talk, I will recommend him to a book called *Enquête Litteraire* by Jules Huret. Huret's interview with Zola is an astonishing piece of literature. In this interview we perceive, as we should in a long intercourse with Zola himself, that his genius is but the triumph and apotheosis of common-sense. For his genius is wingless, it never rises towards the stars; it maintains itself at what I may term the level of superior mediocrity, and it is with him always, on small as on great occasions. Take his answer to an interviewer who called on him at the Savoy Hotel. Zola had

arrived late the night before, and had only just got out of bed.
The question was: 'What are your impressions of London?' The
answer was: 'My first impression of London was an excellent
appetite. The train was late, and we didn't dine until nine o'clock,
but we dined excellently well.' Is it possible to answer a foolish
question more sensibly?

I said just now that Zola's vision of life was not so intense,
penetrating, or subtle as Tourguèneff's. It is radically different.
Zola's mind is patriarchal; he is an old-world hero, a patriarch
belated in the nineteenth century. Not Abraham himself encamped
amid his flocks, herds, and a numerous servitude saw or thought
more simply than he does. There are hackney carriages, washerwomen, and *châssepots* in the *Rougon Macquart* series, but these
are merely adventitious attractions which affect in no way the
general character of the work. Hugo is said to be the last of the
old-world poets; but the real difference between Zola and Hugo is
that one can, and the other cannot, write verse. Take from Hugo
his genius of versification and you would get the novelist. He would
have produced a set of novels very similar to the *Rougon Macquart*
series. It would have been in twenty volumes, possibly in more, and
would have sold as largely. Robbed of his versification, Hugo would
have accepted the hackney carriages and the washerwomen. He
could not have done otherwise, and both men saw life from the
outside, and their tendency was to exaggerate the outside. All the
same the hypothetical work would have differed from the *Rougon
Macquart*. Hugo was more naturally an artist than Zola. His
imagination was rarer, but it was not more powerful nor more
fecund. Zola's imagination is one of the most extraordinary that
ever found expression in literature. Think, you who have read the
twenty volumes, of the hundreds of places he has shown you and
familiarized you with, even as you are familiar with the room you
live in. Can you not see incestuous Renée dreaming in her yellow
boudoir, or feverishly flung on the skins under the malign shade of
tropical plants in the great conservatory? Are not the market-places
in your mind – the roofs for ever silhouetting against the pale sky?
The smell of the fish and the hundred colours of the fish; the vaults
where the children roll amid the feathers? And the scene where
they chop the pigeons' heads, disputing how many so-and-so can
bleed in an hour? And how intimately conscious we are of the

great garden of the Paradou and the adorable death of Albine, who dies asphyxiated by the flowers with which she has filled the room; the enumeration of the flowers, the evocation of an orchestra of scents, for every scent recalls the sound of an instrument, and the last phrase – 'Albine dies in a supreme hiccup of flowers' – how wonderful!

And the modes of life, the trees, the various ways in which the human animal gains his livelihood! Do we not all remember the gold chain-makers in *L'Assommoir* and the vestment makers in *Le Rêve*? In *Au Bonheur des Dames* the work of every employé is explained; the phenomena of each passing hour is revealed to us. *Germinal* is full of every detail of miner life, the ropes, the pulleys, the furnaces, the trucks, the horses. But I must stay my pen or this article will degenerate into a mere catalogue.

But has Zola furnished these extraordinary evocations of the externals of human life with human souls? Has he created characters that will not suffer by comparison with Balzac's? Zola's evocation of souls is slight, nearly always fragmentary and shadowy. A soul haunts in Gervaise, and Coupeau, too, has a soul, and through the numberless pages a few shades flit vaguely recognizable as human souls. That is all. In the line of souls Gervaise is his greatest achievement, and that is why I place *L'Assommoir* above all his other books. There are other reasons. When he wrote *L'Assommoir* Zola was more than he ever was before, and certainly more than he ever was since, a pupil of Flaubert. The book is written entirely in Flaubert's manner, the short sentences relieved by the pictorial epithet. The old masters thought that originality was found in individual feeling and seeing rather than in mannerism, and as I share their opinion I think that it is regrettable that Zola did not continue to write in the style in which he produced his finest book. But the style became too laborious for him just as pre-Raphaelism became too laborious for Sir John Millais, and after *L'Assommoir* his style became looser, and with every fresh book he seems more and more inclined to abandon himself to the ease of redundant expression. There are fine pages even in his worst books, but so far as my personal taste and interest are engaged in his work I would choose to have revised editions of his early works rather than the new novels he contemplates writing – *Lourdes, Paris, Rome*, etc.

Revised editions of Zola's works! How easily one drops into

talking nonsense. His method of novel-writing does not admit of
revision. As well might we ask the editor of a daily paper for
concentration of expression in leading articles, dramatic notes, and
reports of boat races. During the last ten or a dozen years a striking
resemblance has grown up between the Zola novel and the popular
newspaper. The novel and the newspaper seem to me to stand on
the same footing; the intention of both is the same, and the means
employed are the same. It is true that Zola's reports on the Franco-
German war are better done than the reports of the war corres-
pondent of the *Daily Telegraph*. It is also true that scenery at the
'Lyceum' is better painted than the scenery at the 'Surrey', but
that is hardly a reason for confusing a set taken from *Much Ado
about Nothing* with the pictures of Turner, Constable, and Wilson,
and we find a like difference between the battle pieces in *War and
Peace* and those in *La Débâcle* – a difference not of degree but a
difference of kind. Zola's novel is practically the daily paper. He
has discovered a formula that suits the average man as well as the
Daily Telegraph or the *Petit Journal*, and he chooses his subjects,
not in obedience to an artistic instinct, but in accordance with
public taste. Three hundred thousand pilgrims go to Lourdes yearly.
Every pilgrim is a certain reader, and the afflicted in all countries
are interested in the question. Between belief and unbelief he will
steer a middle course just as he steered a middle course between
France and Prussia. I heard him boast, without ever perceiving the
enormous artistic significance of what he was saying, that he had
written a French novel on the war without giving Prussia cause
for offence. I take it that the sublime impartiality of the true artist
is very different from the mock impartiality of the journalist who
wants to get up a controversy. The true artist sees life as God sees
it, without prejudice; life is for him – I think the phrase is
Flaubert's – *une hallucination à transporter*.

Zola told me that he had gone into calculation, and allowing
for a fortnight's holidays at Christmas, *Lourdes* would take him
seven months to write. Five hundred pages in seven months!
Tolstoy took six years to write *Anna Karenina*, ten to write *War
and Peace*; Flaubert took seventeen years to write *La Tentation de
St Antoine*, eight or nine to write *L'Education Sentimental*; and
seven or eight translators are already at work on *Lourdes*; it will
appear in the *New York Herald*, and Mr Bennet has paid a thousand

pounds for the serial rights. But adequate information regarding the various forms and languages in which this book will appear would be the subject of an article on bibliography. Suffice it to say here that it will bring Zola something like four thousand pounds before it reaches Charpentier in book form; it will then be read by everybody except men of letters – but their number is so small that the abstention will not materially affect the sale. If the book does not sell three hundred thousand copies it is a failure, and if the book on the Russian Alliance which will follow does not sell half a million it will be a failure. Did any great writer ever see literature from this point of view before?

The idea of conquest seems inherent in Zola. Five and twenty years ago he wrote a book called *Le Conquête de Plassans*. The idea of conquest cropped up again in *L'Oeuvre*, and this time it was Paris that was conquered. And now it seems that Zola meditates the conquest of the world. He came to England at the head of an army of journalists; rockets were let off at the Crystal Palace, and trumpets were blown in his honour at the Mansion House. He will probably proceed on a similar mission to St Petersburg (it has already been spoken of); he may even visit America. Why not? There are sixty millions in the United States, who through the medium of translation, may read the *Rougon Macquart*! The newspapers reported that Madame Zola, astonished at the length of our London suburbs, said: 'This is a town that would suit you, Emile.' Every house represented to her a possible sale of a novel, Charpentier edition, three francs fifty. If Zola were told that a *concierge* had not heard his name he would feel discouraged. An enquiry would be set on foot, and if a *concierge's* guild could be discovered he would arrange to address a meeting. He looks upon all men who do not read his novels as lost. Lost to what? Ah, that I cannot say; not to art, for the quality of his writing does not seem to concern him any more than the quality of the things he buys. The carved woodwork and the iron railings may not be finely wrought, but they photograph all right, and every interviewer is received and every sightseer – Chinese, Peruvians, Esquimaux – all and sundry are granted audience, and the afternoon passes in talking of how books may be best put on the market.

Some translation of his works must appear in every dialect, and to discover one not yet reduced to written characters, and to arrange that the first work printed in it should be a translation of the *Rougon Macquart* series would be fame indeed. M. Bruneau comes in with the score of the music he has just written for one of the novels, and the gentleman from Paraguay jumps up and proposes to do the opera into the language spoken in his country; the Thibetian might do the same. Bruneau and Zola put their heads together. Hurrah! another outlet has been discovered, and the terms of the contract are discussed. Only the other day in an article on the lyrical drama, after coupling Wagner and Bruneau together, Zola explained that he would create a lyrical drama with human characters; and when he has done this 'the colossal Wagner will grow pale on the high pedestal of his symbols'. Zola believes that young French composers have not written great music because their libretti are not sufficiently human. In a word, he imagines himself writing various libretti to which the young French composers will add a little music as cream is added to *méringues*. Well, if a man will talk on all subjects the time will come when he will talk nonsense. I am afraid that time has come for Zola!

The desire of gold for its own sake is comprehensible in a way; but Zola has no love of money, he has squandered all he made on vulgar decoration and absurd architecture. The pleasures of life bore him exceedingly, so he says; but I am afraid that he has not acquainted himself with them. Of the pleasures of Art he is equally ignorant. His youth was beset with difficulties sufficient, be it admitted to his credit, to conquer all but the most resolute. He wrote for four hours every morning at a novel, and every afternoon he wrote an article for a newspaper, and those who have felt the pressure of a weekly article, while engaged on a work of the imagination, will appreciate severity of the ordeal that Zola bore for many years unflinchingly. He had little time for reflection or study, and was only able to catch the few ideas abroad in his day as they passed him. He read his contemporaries, Flaubert, Goncourt, Daudet, and to obtain a platform whence he might preach his doctrine he read Balzac and Hugo; but with the heart of French literature, with Montaigne, St Simon, and La Bruyère it may be doubted if his knowledge is more than rudimentary. The influence of Manet and Flaubert and Goncourt persuaded him that he was interested in the external world, and we hailed *L'Assommoir* as a masterpiece, for we wished to group ourselves round some great writer. We hugged the belief that, set free from pecuniary anxieties, he would read, think, travel, and refrain from constant production, giving three or four years to the composition and the writing of each book. We believed that he would cultivate refinement of thought, and refinement of literary expression. But Zola was not naturally an artist. Instead of the books becoming more and more beautiful, they have become larger, looser, and uglier, and they serve no purpose whatsoever, except to find money for the purchase of cock-eyed saints on gold backgrounds.

Alas! the ridiculous towers of Mèdan! Alas! the arrival of translators from Paraguay! Alas! the blowing of trumpets before the Lord Mayor of London in honour of *La Terre, La Débâcle, L'Argent,* and *Docteur Pascal*!

And, three times, alas, for are we not now menaced by a novel on Lourdes, on Rome, and on Paris? In these novels he will re-write everything that he has written before. His friends will drop away from him; he will be left alone; his excellent cigars will fail to attract us, and smoking bad ones in the café we shall regret his life and his works, and the mistake we made; and when the café closes we shall stand on the edge of the pavement wondering what the end will be. One of us will say, it will probably be Huysmans: 'In *Le Ventre de Paris* there is a pork butcher who, after having worked ten hours a day all his life is found dead sitting before a table *son nez dans le boudin.*'

'And you think,' I shall say, 'that he will just drop from sheer exhaustion over his writing table *son nez dans le boudin?*'

Huysmans will not answer, he will remember that Zola is the friend of his life. The little group will separate, and wending my way to my little flat in the Rue de la Tour des Dames, I shall think of Zola as a striking instance of the insanity of common-sense.

(FROM IMPRESSIONS AND OPINIONS, 1891)

LIONEL PIGOT JOHNSON

1867 - 1902

Lionel Pigot Johnson, poet and critic, was born at Broadstairs, Kent on 15 March 1867.

At Winchester he laid the basis of his considerable scholarship and of what remained, after his submission to Rome, as a probably suppressed homosexuality. New College, Oxford, confirmed these traits and added others : an addiction to alcohol and a tendency to treat life ritualistically. George Santayana's recollection of his room, dating from those days, offers us a significant still-life : a jug of 'Glengarry whiskey between two open books – *Les Fleurs du Mal* and *Leaves of Grass*'.[1] Looking down upon this *nature mort* were portraits of Cardinal Newman and Cardinal Wiseman – the religion of art contemplated and transcended by the art of religion proper.

Constitutional factors were also important. 'Physically,' as Rupert Croft-Cooke relates, 'Lionel Johnson was little more than a dwarf. From glandular or other causes he grew only to five-foot-two and for many years kept the appearance (though not, seen from close at hand, the fresh complexion) of a boy of fifteen. . . . Pictures show an almost triangular face, a broad brow narrowing to a pointy chin, not particularly attractive though the eyes are kind and frank.'[2] To Richard Le Galliene his face bore 'no little resemblance to De Quincey's, though it was finer, keener, more spiritual'.[3] The same

---

[1] *The Middle Span,* 1947
[2] *Feasting with Panthers,* 1967
[3] *The Romantic '90s*

191

observer also commented on Johnson's 'almost diaphanous frame'[4] and noted he was lacking in 'protective phlegm'.[5]

During his years at Winchester, he passed with considerable excitement through most of the higher religions and some of the higher atheisms. But in the letters he wrote, while he was yet at school, one refrain becomes predominant: 'I will be a priest.'[6] Johnson did not become a priest. On St Alban's Day, 22 June 1891, however, he was received into the Latin Church at St Etheldreda's, Holborn.

Johnson lived a scholarly bachelor existence tempered with bibulous deviations, and, in the last stage of his life, certain Fenian plottings at Mooney's in the Strand. 'The police, he said, were after him everywhere.'[7]

During his life-time, Johnson published three books only; two of verse, and one of prose: *Poems*, 1895; *Ireland*, 1897; and *The Art of Thomas Hardy*, 1894. It was this work which established his reputation, and Le Gallienne, reviewing it, declared that 'I do not remember to have read a book of criticism so exalted in its note of almost religious devotion towards all great and good literature'.[8] Apart from this, he executed a valuable body of work, in the form of reviews and articles, contributed to daily and weekly papers. Two posthumous selections from these writings have been made: *Post Limenium*, in 1911, edited by Thomas Whittemore; and *Reviews and Critical Papers*, in 1921, edited by Robert Shafer. An impressive number of prose pieces by him, consisting of stories, essays, and reviews, have still to be published in book form.

Biographically, there is a shortage of organized information about him. Part of his school-day correspondence was printed in 1919 under the title *Some Winchester Letters of Lionel Johnson*. Katherine Tynan's *Memoirs* (1924) contain a hageographical chapter on him, but the best all-round impression of the man is still that conveyed by Dr Ian Fletcher in his introduction to *The Complete Poems of Lionel Johnson*, 1953.

The stature and achievement of this critic is something known to very few readers. General opinion and recognition of him – when

[4] *The Romantic '90s* [5] *Ibid*
[6] *Some Winchester Letters of Lionel Johnson*, 1919
[7] *The Middle Span* by George Santayana, 1947
[8] 'Art of Thomas Hardy' (*Retrospective Reviews*, 1896)

concerned with particulars – is mostly limited to some such trait as his archaic preference for spelling the words 'subtle' and 'enchantment' with an 'i' and a 'u' or his excessive addiction to the colon as a mark of punctuation.

The charge of decadence levelled at Johnson – decadence as referring, not to some defect of constitution, but the elaborate and conscious espousal of a cult of the abnormal in literature – is easily answered from his own writings.

No nineteenth-century critic held in higher honour literary craftmanship than did Johnson; but artistry, as he understood it (the consummate means to the worthy end), and verbal virtuosity as the aesthetes pursued it (a self-regarding preciousness) were quite antithetical notions. 'Style,' he wrote, in an essay on Kipling, 'the perfection of workmanship, we cannot do without that; but still less can we endure the dexterous and polished imitation of that.'[9]

Of the literary psychology behind the 'decadence', Johnson had much that was pertinent to say. 'There are plenty of reasons,' he declared, 'why literature should be in a somewhat unsatisfactory state : but the chief reason is surely too much ignorance of the past, an unreflecting concentration upon the present, and a morbid haste to anticipate the future. Able men commit follies of taste in style and idea which are incompatible with a willing study of the old masters, and of the old writers who came worthily after them. Many a dull book written a hundred years ago, is better reading than many a popular book of our time : for its faults are faults on the right side. There are living today [1891] men capable of the finest work, but lacking humility, patience, reverence, three forms of one inestimable spirit.'[10]

In the same essay he speaks of the young 'decadent' poet who refuses to refuel himself from the wells of tradition as 'my friend of self-sustaining and self-devouring genius' – a statement pre-dating T. S. Eliot's counsel concerning the 'nearly indispensable nature of "the historical sense" for anyone who would continue to be a poet beyond his twenty-fifth year'.[11]

To the 'decadent contention of the essential amorality of the masterpiece', Johnson replied that 'So long as art proceeds from, and

[9] *Reviews and Critical Papers*, 1921
[10] 'Friends that Fail Not' (*Post Liminium*, 1911)
[11] 'Tradition and the Individual Talent' (*The Sacred Wood*, 1920)

appeals to, men of a whole and harmonious nature, art must express that wholeness and that harmony : an artist is forbidden by the facts of his natural structure to dissociate his ethics from his aesthetics : as well might he try to live by bread alone, without exercising reason, or by reason alone, not eating bread.'[12]

It was, no doubt, these elements of traditionalism, of intellectual moralism and formal discipline, which led Paul Elmer More, one year after Johnson's death, to speak of him as 'the one writer' among 'the little band of Gaelic enthusiasts . . . who held his genius in perfect control.'[13]

But though the elaboration of Johnson's principles as a critic (best seen in the first chapter of his book on Thomas Hardy), show him as far removed from the chief artistic concerns of the Decadents and the Symbolists, by friendship and by background influence he was near enough to them for his judgment not to spring from misunderstanding. There was, for example, Johnson's great and abiding admiration for Pater whose *Marius the Epicurean* he described as 'a book to love and worship'.[14] 'It is Johnson's opinion,' writes Barbara Charlesworth, 'that Pater's scholarship, taste and prose style made him the final authority and arbiter of critical taste for his time.'[15]

But if Johnson was aware of Pater's points of strength, he must have registered likewise his near scepticism and the melancholy fascination which he felt for philosophies of flux. As it was, Johnson possessed an antidote to the dark side of Pater in another author – *an author of belief.* 'Certainly, to the present writer,' he confessed, 'the thirty-six volumes of Newman, from the most splendid and familiar passages down to their slightest and most occasional note, are better known than anything else in any literature and language.'[16]

'This is an age,' wrote Johnson, 'of greater sensibility, more governed by the emotions and desires, than any other; literature abounds with sick and morbid beauty; everywhere men are drifting from one philosophy of doubt to another, aware of their own

---

[12] 'Two Poets of the Irish Movement' (*Shelburne Essays*, First Series, 1904)
[13] *Ibid*
[14] *Some Winchester Letters of Lionel Johnson*
[15] *Dark Passages*, 1965
[16] 'Cardinal Newman' (*Post Liminium*)

futility, and tired of all thought and action. . . . To such an age comes Newman, and sets forth a solution and a cure. Not, as some have said, an anodyne or opiate; because Newman's method has a logical consistency, though it may not be the logic of the sciences.'[17]

It was Pater, one may say, who provided Johnson with the key to an understanding of his contemporaries; but it was Newman who imparted to him the means of rightly assessing them. That Johnson knew what it was like either side of the moral fence can be seen in his response to Wilde. Their relationship began in the February of 1890 when the latter came to visit Pater at Oxford. Here is the account which Johnson gave his friend Arthur Galton of their meeting: 'On Saturday at mid-day, lying half asleep in bed, reading Green, I was roused by a pathetic and unexpected note from Oscar: he plaintively besought me to get up and see him. Which I did: and I found him as delightful as Green is not. He discoursed, with infinite flippancy, of everyone: lauded the *Dial*: laughed at Pater: and consumed all my cigarettes. I am in love with him.'[18] When Johnson's friend 'Bosie' – Lord Alfred Douglas – came under Wilde's influence, however, he addressed to him a severe poem entitled *The Destroyer of a Soul*. 'A cold, corrupting fate,' as he held Wilde to be, it did not prevent him from writing his hymn of praise to Oscar on the appearance of *Dorian Gray* in 1891. The poem is Latin and contains the following lines, given here in Ian Fletcher's translation: 'Behold the Man! Behold the God! . . . The more his soul is darkened, His face displays its brightness more. . . . Here are apples of Sodom; here the hearts of vices and sweet sins.'[19]

There is no better brief assessment of Lionel Johnson's colleagues and contemporaries than the notes which he sent in 1895 to Katherine Tynan for a talk she was to give in Ireland on the younger British poets. (These notes are reprinted here.) If he is severe on Arthur Symons – whose amoral impressionism he disliked and whose verse declarations of free-love he parodied in *A Decadent's Lyric*[20] – he is equally critical of William Watson's pseudo-traditionalism, which one might think would have met with

---

[17] 'Cardinal Newman' (*Post Liminium*)
[18] *Feasting with Panthers* by Rupert Croft-Cooke
[19] *The Complete Poems of Lionel Johnson*, 1953
[20] *Ibid*

his approval : 'An almost unfailing dignity of *external* manners; and always an attempt at *internal* gravity and greatness. . . . An understudy, as actors say, of the great man . . . capable of deceiving you for a time by his air of being the true master instead of a very serious and accomplished substitute. . . . Read Wordsworth's *Ode to Duty*, and Watson vanishes.'[21]

Johnson's significance as a critic might be considered under three heads : historical, theological, and intrinsic. For literary history, his importance resides largely in his opposing the currents of relaxed thought and style in the verse and prose of the 'nineties, and in resisting the fashionable 'decadent' flux. Because of his more intellectual cast of mind he saw the connection between a fluid phenomenalism (' "the flowing philosophers" to whom life is a drifting and a change') and sensationalism, and firmly repudiated them both.

The value and importance of Johnson for a Christian criticism of literature is that he pre-eminently possessed the gift of imaginative charity to supplement and, at times, temper the hardcutting-edges of dogma. In this light, he has a good claim to be considered as the first Catholic critic of the nineteenth century writing in England.

Thirdly, his value lies in the potentially perennial pleasure which his writings open to us : their felicity of composition, their genial and courteous reflectiveness, the relish in literary good manners which they so readily attest. 'To have committed regularly to paper a criticism of literature so eminently literative in itself, is to have fulfilled, in a way quite other than its author intended, what Oscar Wilde campaigned for in his phrase "the critic as artist".'[22]

FRIENDS THAT FAIL NOT

The glowing of my companionable fire upon the backs of my companionable books; and then the familiar difficulty of choice ! Compassed about with old friends whose virtues and vices I know better than my own, I will be loyal to loves that are not of yester-

[21] *The Complete Poems of Lionel Johnson*
[22] 'Lionel Johnson as Critic' by Derek Stanford (*The Month*, August 1954)

day. New poems, new essays, new stories, new lives, are not my company at Christmastide, but the never-ageing old. 'My days among the dead are passed.' Veracious Southey, how cruel a lie! *My* sole days among the dead are the days passed among stillborn or moribund moderns, not the white days and shining nights free for the strong voices of the ancients in fame. A classic has a permanence of pleasurability : that is the meaning of his estate and the title. It is the vexing habit of many, whose loving intimacy with the old immortals is undoubted, to assume and say that no one now reads the *Religio Medici*, or the *Pickwick Papers*, or Ben Jonson's Masques, or the *Waverley Novels*, or Pope's 'Essay on Man', or Dr Johnson's *Rambler* and *Idler*. Themselves accepted, there are no votaries, no willing bond-slaves, of such works. It is not credible. I believe that in numbers we are a goodly company who joy in the fresh humanities of the old literature, and are not without a portion of Lamb's spirit. The eight volumes of *Clarissa Harlowe* – does the world contain volumes more passionately pulsing than these, 'my midnight darlings', which tell me of white Clarissa in her sorrows, of the brilliant villainies of Lovelace? How can that tragedy, that comedy, grow old; and who in his right mind wishes one word away from its voluminous unfolding? Or the evening choice may fall upon the dazzling cruelties of the 'Dunciad', and its brutal brilliancy people the room with ghosts in tattered raiment, under their fleshless arms piles of 'Proposals' for a new version of Horace, and in the pallor of their grotesque countenances the signs of an habitual starvation : it is reality, a gaunt, historic truth.

Presently comes a voice of majestic vastness from the chambers of the incalculable dead, plangent, triumphant, mystically sweet : the voice of him who in life was 'a king among death and the dead'. Has our world to-day outworn the wisdom, wearied of the music, processionally flowing from the Knight of Norwich? As little as it has outgrown the poignant thinking of Pascal, the sad, the haughty, the proudly prostrate before God; or the lacerated heart of Swift the lacerating. But at this cordial period of the calendar Swift may appear too grim. Let Fielding, Homer of novelists, lead in Parson Adams with his *Æschylus*, or escort Slipslop, the fair and frail. It were stupid and mendacious to aver that we have spoken of friends too antiquated for ease of converse with them, that the books of yesterday must claim our preference, that we are affected

and ineffective else, and aliens in the air we breathe. 'Peace, for
I loved him, and love him for ever! The dead are not dead, but
alive,' cries Tennyson. What is true of loved humanity is true also
of loved humanities, the high expressions of man's mind. As
Augustine said of the Christian faith, here is a beauty both old
and new; only a starveling imagination is so hampered by the
accidents of any ancient excellence that it cannot discern the essence
which is dateless. Quaint, old-fashioned, say some when they read
the writings of their forefathers; and it is said with a confused
and confounding foolishness. Language, manners, circumstances –
these may not be ours; but have we different passions and human
relationships, another interest in life and death? Stripped of our
'lendings', our ancestors and we are the same, and their writings
are contemporary with our own. Smiles can be kindly : but there
is something painful in the smiling indulgence with which we are
wont to regard the works of old which were once in the very forefront of modernity. We live in time, and the past must always be
the most momentous part of it. It will be all past when time, that
accident of God, is over. 'I will remember the days of old!'
'Whatever else we read, Gibbon must always be read too.' The spirit
of Freeman's verdict applies to all mastership of any Muse. To
ignore, to treat with impatience, to be soon weary of an ancient
excellence and fame, is like blindness to the natural humanities of
the world, to sea and wind and stars, to the forests and mountains.
If only we had more of that spirit of tremulous delight, of awe in
ecstasy, with which the men of the Renaissance read the recaptured,
the resurgent classics of Greece and Rome! Few of us would dare
to write at all, had we always before the eyes of our minds
remembrance of the mighty. Are *we* of the Apostolic Succession?
are *our* reforms legitimate? do *we* consult the general consent of
the forefathers? Milton smiles austerely at the thought, and
Shakespeare smiles compassion; Virgil says gently : 'I, dying, wished
my *Æneids* to be burnt.' But the torrent of trash runs gaily on, and
the struggling critic longs for a breath of the 'diviner air' : he
remembers Bacon's saying, that some books may be read 'by deputy',
and wishes that he could so read the futilities upon his table. And
yet all is repaid by those happy rarities of time, the days on which
there comes his unexpectant way occasion for 'the noble pleasure
of praising' : when he can say : 'This is the right thing, here is

the true touch; my shelves welcome their new companion.' There is little fear of excellence escaping him; he fears that fear too much. We do not envy the fate and fame of him who said of Wordsworth: 'This will never do!' nor of him who bade Keats 'back to his gallipots'. We desire no experience of the feelings with which publisher or editor remembers that he 'declined with thanks' what the general judgment of the judicious came afterwards to applaud. But, to employ the impressive imagery of Mr Chadband, I will not go into the city, and, having seen an eel, return to bid the literary world 'rejoice with me, for I have seen an elephant!' In the words of that eloquent divine: 'Would that be te-rewth?' But when I encounter living genius which may grow to noble proportions, it were a churlish folly to belittle it, to bestow an elegant and timid mediocrity of praise. 'All Horace *then*, all Claudian *now*,' is as rash a wail as when Byron uttered it, though the voices of Wordsworth and Coleridge were heard in his land. But the classics have attained; they are at rest. Complete, immutable, they have for us no surprises, save the permanent surprise of genius, that 'strangeness' without a strain of which 'there is no excellent beauty', and which keeps its virginal first freshness from the 'valley of perpetual dream'. We are so sure of the classics 'strongly stationed in eternity'.

> There exist moments in the life of man
> When he is nearer the Great Soul of the World
> Than is man's custom,

says Coleridge, translating Schiller. The readers share with the writers of masterpieces the exaltation of such moments, but they come chiefly at sound of 'ancestral voices'. About contemporary voices there is an element of uncertainty not undelightful, yet forbidding the perfection of faith. We prophesy and wait. And, if the noble ancients are more comforting to us than even the worthiest-seeming moderns, how much more tolerable and pardonable are the mediocrities of the past than of the present! They are historically interesting. I would rather laugh over the poems of a Cibber or a Pye, than over the poems of their living likes! It is better to be amused than exasperated, and kindly time lets me laugh at that past incompetence which would annoy me were it present. A monody upon the Death of the Princess Charlotte, totally devoid of merit, does not rouse the wrath aroused by similar performances upon the death of Prince Christian Victor. The insanities of a Lodowick Muggleton or a Joanna Southcott provoke me to more patient an anger than the diatribes of a Dr Dowie. The blunders of the dead are over and done, harming no one; the blunders of the living are a danger and a nuisance. It is a pity than anyone, however uncritical, should enjoy the Martin Tuppers or Robert Montgomerys of the day; it implies an inability to enjoy Milton. No man can serve two masters : you cannot be Fielding's friend, and also accept the colossal ineptitudes of our most popular novelists, artless, humourless, most brazen. Bad novels of the last century have never failed to give me a certain pleasure. I thrust that posterity may be able to extract pleasure from the bad novels of last year, for I am not. They fill me with the sourest sadness, which is an unwholesome state of mind.

. . . Perhaps there is no country where literary knowledge more abounds than England; and none where so many men, capable of acquiring it, are content to go without it. Never was a country where men of ability, and sometimes of genius, were less anxious to strengthen and to nourish their minds with learning, its discipline or its delight. There are some twenty great writers of English literature, from Chaucer down to our day, of whom every intelligent man knows something; but there are hundreds of writers, worth reading daily, to whom professed men of letters are indifferent or blind.

The fact was illustrated for me by meeting in one month with three men of letters, each of recognized capacity, and each young, who each remarked in the course of conversation : 'Oh, I don't read anything' : and it was clear they did not. Voluntary paupers ! starving their souls, impoverishing their brains, and trying to live upon the vital heat of their personal genius. It may be remarked among nearly all classes of literary men : a deliberate indifference to the great riches of literature stored up from old times. No doubt the men of self-sustaining genius read something sometimes in the department of letters. They must have looked into the correspondence of Pope, of Gray, of Cowper, of Lamb. But how many hours have they spent over the letters of Sir Henry Wotton, of Sir John Suckling, of Farquhar? Oh, the grave courtesy, the merry wit, the brilliant good humour, of these three ! Yet if a simple reader of pleasant books make a remark about them to some flourishing impressionist or scientific comedian, he will be met with something like blank ignorance. Or look at lyric poetry : our friends of genius have read their Herrick and Herbert, and a few more. But what of Vaughan, most solemn and beautiful of mystics? Of Crashaw, most polite of devout poets? Of Cotton, that charming poet of genial enjoyment and dainty passion? Or Habington's *Castara,* or Donne's 'Anniversaries', or Marvell's perfect work? One might go on to a dozen names : Cleveland, Denham, Flatman, Campion, Wither, Lovelace, Carew, and all the inspired company. Are you so intent upon the latest eccentricity of Paris, that you have no ears for these singers? Or go to biography : Boswell, of course, and Lamb and Gray. But there is a long, long list of good biographies : begin by reading through a few thousand pages of Anthony à Wood, to get the true savour of those lives of the ancient worthies. Or travels : when Mr Stanley and Lord Randolph Churchill cease to fascinate, Sandys and Addison, Ralegh and Smollet, Ray and Coryat, might prove their powers. If the monthly magazines grow monotonous, there are all the immortal *Spectators* and *Tatlers,* or even the less lively *Ramblers,* ready to tempt us. Perhaps we are a little tired of the wrangles of science and metaphysics : even those eminent men, Mr Spencer, Mr Harrison, Mr Huxley, are not perennially delightful. Then we might try the taste of some older controversies : Dr Henry More on the Nullibists and Holenmerians, Locke and Bishop Stillingfleet, Berkeley and the Minute Philosophers. Even Beattie on Truth can be read in fine weather. You refuse to talk of Ibsen for a month? Well, you can read all Webster, Ford, and Marlowe, in less than that time. You have not seen a novel worth reading for six months? Perhaps you may get through *Clarissa Harlowe* and *Sir Charles Grandison* during the next six. Or perhaps a diet of contemporary sonnets leaves you hungry; let me prescribe Drayton's *Polyolbion.* It is true that Mr. Bohn's translations from the Greek and Latin lack the graces of style, besides creating a false impression that the classic writers of prose or poetry were all prose poets. But go, search the bookstalls : between 1500 and 1700 the translations from the classics are to be counted by hundreds.

It is of no use : the starving modern man of letters, like the typical philosopher of Germany, 'shuts his eyes, and looks into his stomach, and calls it introspection.' So it is : but the process 'by any other name' would be no less foolish. Tired of himself, of other people, of his four walls, and of the street outside, what can he do? Clearly, not read something both old and new, but rather compose a 'lyrical note' upon 'world-weariness', and an 'aquarelle' or 'pastel' upon 'Pimlico at twilight'. That adds to the stock of beauty and wisdom and wit in the world. It is done with a light touch, a penetrating vision, and yet, how it brings the tears to our eyes!

> The sickness of the weeping wind
>   And dusty tears of Pimlico!
>   And emerald stars begin to glow;
> O sickness of the weeping wind
>   In twilit Pimlico!
>
> Yet was it thus, in Pimlico,
>   Ere sickness seize the weeping wind?
>   Surely the music was not blind,
> Chaunting of love in Pimlico!
>   O sick and weeping wind!

If I call upon my friend of self-sustaining and self-devouring genius with a newly-bought folio under my arm, will he not smile sadly at my dull pedantic care for the old and outworn masters? I have but grubbed in the dust of ages, but he has caught the gray and vanishing soul of a tragic impression. If my friend is not of this pallid school, he will probably belong to the school of fresh and vigorous Blood. He is an emphatic person, not unlike the Muscular Christian of forty years ago, but with the Christianity changed into Paganism. Mind you, he is not an Athenian pagan, an Alcibiades, but something brawnier and burlier, with Yankee smartness instead of Attic quickness. He has all the virtues, but he hates squeamishness: his metaphors are hot and red. No sick and weeping winds for him. He will write you a short story, or tell you a long one, and wind up with the brief words: 'Currie's conscience just then was like a butcher's shop on a hot summer's day.' We know, whatever the story may have been about, that it wasn't, but, hang it all! you must show that you don't shirk nasty things, like a girl. 'Give me a man!' (That you may turn him, my dear friend, into a savage?)

A great deal is said nowadays about the various follies of modern literature, and various theories are given to account for them.

Lionel Pigot Johnson

There are plenty of reasons why literature should be in a somewhat unsatisfactory state : but the chief reason is surely too much ignorance of the past, an unreflecting concentration upon the present, and a morbid haste to anticipate the future. Able men commit follies of taste in style and in idea which are incompatible with a willing study of the old great masters, and of the old writers who come worthily after them. Many a dull book written a hundred years ago, is better reading than many a popular book of our time : for its faults are faults on the right side. There are living to-day men capable of the finest work, but lacking humility, patience, reverence, three forms of one inestimable spirit.

. . . Perish, cried Newman, the whole tribe of Hookers and Jewels, so Athanasius and the majestic Leo may be mine! We cannot afford to let go the Shining Ones upon the heights. It does not matter that the heights are so high, that our intelligences climb up so poor a portion of the way. He would be a liar full of impudence who should dare to say that he felt wholly at ease with the awful Milton or Dante, with the solemn meditations of Browne, with the dread death-march over death of dread Lucretius. There are times when the high things of art seem almost incredible; magnificent delusions, golden dreams : their creators' pains must surely have been too vast for bearing. We, with our little lamps of intelligence in our hands, go tremblingly through the sacred dimness, hoping to comprehend at last a little more. Our reverence is a religion; genius, like love and beauty, is a pledge of divinity and the everlasting; a light perfected lyric lures us heavenward; and from of old come the proudest and the clearest voices. The voices of the day must wait for their consecrate authority and confirmed applause till Time, the just, shall please. Take me with you in spirit, Ancients of Art, the crowned, the sceptred, whose voices this night chaunt a *gloria in excelsis,* flooding the soul with a passion of joy and awe.

(FROM 'POST LIMININIUM')

RICHARD
LE GALLIENNE

1866 - 1947

Richard Le Gallienne – *bellettrist* and legendary 'Golden Boy' of
the 'nineties – was born in Liverpool on 20 January 1866. He was
the eldest son of a brewery manager, said to come of sea-faring
folks from Brittany via the Channel Islands. Another statement
respecting his origins declares that his family hailed from Ireland,
bearing the surname of Gullien. His long, wandering and amorous
life is carefully chronicled by R. Whittington-Egan and G. Smerdon
in their loving but unlaboured study, *The Quest of the Golden
Boy* (1960). His own reminiscences of the Beardsley era – *The
Romantic '90s* (1926) – offer entertaining vistas on the past and
some details of his own early life.

About Le Gallienne's appearance, there was something histrionic,
a little 'ham'. He had probably himself in mind when in his novel
Young Lives (1898) he wrote of a 'tall young man with a long thin
face, curtained on each side with enormous masses of black hair –
like a slip of the young moon glimmering through a pine wood'.
Comely, if conspicuous good-looks must certainly be attributed to
him. 'Who's that beautiful woman?'[1] a stranger had once asked
staring at him in the theatre; while Max Beerbohm, for whom these
attractions and their adjuncts were a matter for mirth, wrote to his
friend Reggie Turner : 'I send you a page from the *Sketch* which
I think you would not like to miss,'[2] – the reference being to a

---

[1] *My Life and Times* by Jerome K. Jerome, 1926
[2] *Max Beerbohm: Letters to Reggie Turner*, 1964

full-page photograph of 'Mr Richard Le Gallienne in his Cycling Costume' (25 August 1897).

There is plenty in Le Gallienne to make us wince. Even his most unbending contemporaries found occasion for wit in the publicized exposure of his thought and feelings. Solemn Arthur Symons himself made him the butt of one small witticism, in seeking to pay back an old score. Le Gallienne had attacked him as precious and affected (both of which things he undoubtedly was), as well as sniping at the Decadent poets whose fugleman Symons was popularly thought to be. Referring to one of his opponent's ventures into religious discourse, he remarked that Le Gallienne had 'forsaken the domesticity of the muse, to officiate, in *The Religion of a Literary Man*, as the Canon Farrar of the younger generation'.[3] Other more polemically attuned critics did better. Of this same 'Religio Scriptoris' Lionel Johnson wrote with more urbane censure : 'It is as though triolets and villanelles were interpolated into Euclid and the Thirty-nine Articles . . . the hinting method of poetry will not do for prose, if the prose is to state a plain argument',[4] while the militant Henley attacked the work, not in any role of 'Defender of the Faith', but because he could not stand the man or his Bodley Head – Yellow Book associations. 'As a conjunction of pretentiousness and cheapness, affectation and simplicity, shallowness and foppery, it is all that the Heart of Woman could desire.'[5]

Much as these shafts make for interesting reading, one should be careful not to take them for the whole truth about Le Gallienne, Katherine Lyon-Mix's summary is both a juster and kinder affair. 'His appreciation of poetry,' she writes, 'outstripped his talent, but his enthusiasm was pleasant. As a critic and historian of his age he should be heeded; he saw most of its foibles and failings, including his own, clearly and with a twinkle in his eye.'[6] Being John Lane's reader at the Bodley Head and a regular reviewer on *The Star*, he was not without supporters, and used his position in the main for the benefit of brightly aspirant writers. And if he was something of

---

[3] 'Confessions and Comments' (*Dramatis Personae*, 1921)
[4] *Reviews and Critical Papers* edited by Robert Shafer, 1925
[5] *National Observer*, 2 December 1893
[6] *A Study in Yellow: The Yellow Book and its Contributors*, 1960

a go-between – a persuasive reconciler of Bohemian and Philistine – at least he was not without courage.

On the whole, Le Gallienne proves himself a gentle and generous critic, but he was not afraid to denounce a rising reputation when his principles were in question. Thus, his book *Kipling: A Criticism* (1900) is untypically harsh. In it he describes his subject as one of 'the true end-of-the-century decadents', whose aim it was 'to begin the twentieth century by throwing behind them all that the nineteenth century has won [democracy, female emancipation and the education of the masses]'. 'As a writer,' Le Gallienne declared, 'Kipling is a delight; as an influence he is a danger.'

Le Gallienne was also the author of another monograph, *George Meredith: Some Characteristics* (1890). The best of his critical writing, however, is to be found in the short-sprint notices making up the two volumes of *Retrospective Reviews: A Literary Log* (1891–5).

Le Gallienne is essentially *the critic as reviewer* – 'secretary to the public', as Saint-Beuve once put it. With limited space at his command, the reviewer will hardly find his page or his column the place for elaborating literary theory. A catholic taste and vivid sensibility will assist him and his readers more than any systematic blue-print of values. Not over-logically inclined by nature, Le Gallienne could claim a clear and 'charming' style, which assisted him in his role of *apostle to the middle-brow* more than any neat four-square metaphysic. Even so, he had his 'points of departure', which he set forth in a kind of prose prologue to the first volume of *Retrospective Reviews*. Broadly entitled 'Some First and Second Principles of Criticism', it comprises twenty-five numbered aphorisms, with a further three under the heading of 'Postscript'. These suggest both the liveliness and limitation of Le Gallienne's approach. For example, he esserts that 'Literature is the art of writing – not the art of telling stories or of creating character'. This statement places a premium on style and elevates the compositional virtues above the attractions of human interest. It is all part of the reference to the miniature, flawless within the scanty plot, rather than the work of capacious proportions. A leaning towards the condensed, the distilled leads him to write that 'the perfection of prose is the essay, of poetry the lyric', – a valid choice, temperamentally speaking; but when he completes his sentence by saying 'and the most beautiful book is that which contains the most beautiful words', one sees the critic's aestheticism operating vapidly in a vacuum. Elsewhere the belief of the early Yeats that 'words alone were certain good',[7] draws him into error causing him to see merits of a large kind in terms of a smaller. 'Shakespeare is the greatest English poet, not because he created Hamlet and Lear, but because he could write about Perdita's flowers and Claudio's speech on death in *Measure for Measure*.'

If Le Gallienne's style as a reviewer is allowed to be 'charming', it must be added it is *charming pastiche*. Here, as in the volume of *Prose Fancies* (1895–6), he takes the *mannered naturalness* of Lamb, popularizing it to the level of the daily newspaper. If this style lacks purity, so does the medium for which it was written : the daily press. Le Gallienne's prose in *Retrospective Reviews* is a rare triumph of compromise between the avant-garde's essay and the man-in-the-street's book-review page. Such triumphs, if un-inspiring, are rare.

After 1898, Le Gallienne settled in America. With the conclusion of the First World War, he returned to Europe, settling in Paris with his third wife, and dying at the age of eighty-one, on 15 September 1947 at Mentone.

SOME FIRST AND SECOND PRINCIPLES OF CRITICISM

1. Criticism is the Art of Praise.

2. A critic is a man whom God created to praise greater men than himself, but who, by a curious blindness, has never been able to find them.

3. A critic is one of those candles by which we behold the sun.

4. A critic is one who makes odious comparisons, and invidious distinctions. He is a writer of prey, the shark that gobbles up young writers, or the wasp that stings to pathetic irritation the old ones,

[7] 'The Song of the Happy Shepherd' (*Crossways*, 1889)

and generally he is the cur that snaps and snarls at the heels of success. He is the goal-keeper of literature, the guardian of its vested interests, and it is his business to keep young genius as long as possible from its birthright.

5.   There are three schools of criticism : the school that praises, the school that blames, and the school that judges. The school that praises is the most important.

6.   Praise is more important than judgment. It is only at agricultural societies that men dare sit in judgment upon the rose.

7.   There is Epical Criticism and Lyrical Criticism. Sainte-Beuve, the Balzac of criticism, may be taken as the type of the one, Charles Lamb of the other.

8.   The first thing for a critic to do – is to be thankful that there is anything to criticize.

9.   The greatest critic is he who can appreciate the greatest number of beautiful things.

10.   A necessary gift for the critic of poetry is – the love of it.

11.   Literature is the World in Words.

12.   Literary Criticism is man's sulky complaint that he was not invited to the creation.

13.   The world is great, and strong, and beautiful : so must be the words. The world is little, and weak, and ugly – but so must never be the words.

14.   Literature is the art of writing – not the art of telling stories or of creating character.

15.   Many of the great novelists, and all the lesser ones, belong rather to drama than to literature : for as the novel sprang originally from the drama, it still remains a drama – with extended stage directions.

16.   Shakespeare is the greatest English poet, not because he created Hamlet and Lear, but because he could write that speech about Perdita's flowers, and Claudio's speech on death in *Measure for Measure*.

17.   Keats is the greatest English poet since Shakespeare.

18.   The perfection of prose is the essay, of poetry the lyric, and the most beautiful book is that which contains the most beautiful words.

19.   Anything that is not beautiful, or that cannot be *made beautiful*, has no place in literature.

20.   It is not sufficient criticism of a writer that he does not suit your taste – though it will be sufficient that he suits it.

21.   In criticism you cannot be too positive. Negative criticism dies with what it slays. One critic may 'make' a good book, but fifty cannot kill it.

22.   You may point out the spots on the sun, or you may foul with mud the silver face of the moon, but they will each go on shining for all that.

23.   'Personalities' are poor missiles against a Personality.

24.   You may deny everything to Greatness, and spit in his face to make it sure : but that will not prevent his going to your funeral.

25.   Life, they say, is more important than literature, yet, without literature – what were life?

Postscript

1.   A critic is any undergraduate of Oxford or Cambridge.

2.   William Watson, John Davidson, Francis Thompson, and W. B. Yeats, are the greatest poets since Algernon Charles Swinburne, Dante Gabriel Rossetti, William Morris, George Meredith, and Coventry Patmore, long since classic – a classic, by the way, being an old book which continues to be read by young men.

3.   A gentleman is always a gentleman – even when he writes anonymous criticism.

(FROM 'RETROSPECTIVE REVIEWS 1893–5', 1896)

MAX BEERBOHM

1872 - 1956

Henry Maximilian Beerbohm – essayist, caricaturist and critic – was
born on 24 August 1872 at 57, Palace Gardens Terrace, Kensington.
Lord David Cecil, who has written the standard biography of Max,
describes the Beerbohms as belonging to 'the cream of Memel's
upper bourgeoisie'. The family on the father's side were of mixed
blood – Dutch, Lithuanian, and German – as are the people of that
region. The suggestion of Jewish blood in the family was denied by
Max, though he found the notion attractive and married a Jewish-
American actress, Florence Kahn. His half-brother was the actor-
manager Sir Herbert Beerbohm-Tree – a tall imposing figure
depicted by Max in all his Regency hauteur.

Max was educated at Charterhouse, and has left a recollection
of his old school in a late collection of broadcast essays *Mainly on
the Air* (1946). It was Oxford which set its hall-mark upon him,
encouraging all his precocious propensities for irony, wit, and
affectation. 'I was a modest good-humoured boy,' he wrote
mischievously in 1899, five years after coming down. 'It is Oxford
which has made me insufferable.'[1]

While still an undergraduate at Merton, he contributed to the
egregious *Yellow Book* published by John Lane, 'that poor fly in
the amber of modernity',[2] as Max described him, shrewdly
unimpressed. He had, however, already contributed to other
magazines and journals, his first appearance being in the *Anglo-
American Times* for 25 March 1893. Masquerading under the

[1] 'Going Back to School' (*More*, 1899)
[2] *Max Beerbohm: Letters to Reggie Turner* (17 September 1893) edited
by Rupert Hart-Davis, 1964

signature 'An American' he proceeded to give his impression of young Oxford's idol, Oscar Wilde. Perspicaciously, and unexpectedly, perhaps, he criticizes the cult of Wilde, lightly but carefully distinguishing between the pose of the disciples and the gifts of the Master. ('Sitting eternally at the feet of Gamaliel,' he wrote, 'they have learned nothing but the taste of boot polish.'[3])

Max's *Yellow Book* contributions together with his other essays published in *The Works of Max Beerbohm* and *More* are quizzically ironical contributions to the culture of the artificial. Aligning the lesser with the greater, it is not difficult to relate Baudelaire's chapter 'In Praise of Cosmetics'[4] with Arthur Symons's poem 'Maquillage',[5] and Max's essay 'The Pervasion of Rouge'.[6] All three spring from that way of thinking which associates perfection with artifice.

The elaborately fabricated sentiments and fastidious sentences of *The Works of Max Beerbohm* and *More* have concealed, for many readers, the sense lurking in many of these pieces. Yet, it is here, in his essay on Ouida, that Max offers his happy definition of the good critic as 'a cultured man with brains and a temperament'.[7] Elsewhere he has declared 'A definite self – that is what one most needs in a critic' :[8] a definite *self* not a definite system.

Max possessed two properties as an author which numerous critics must do without : a good self-knowledge and sense of limitation, and a feeling for the relativity of ideas. 'For my own part,' he wrote in his essay on Ouida, 'I am a dilettante, a *petit maître*. I love best in literature delicate and elaborate ingenuities of form and style.' Secondly, concerning that pluralistic universe of individual readers and writers – a reality which certain critics gainsay – Max writes that ' "It takes all kinds to make a world". Every quality has its defects, and it is only by eclectic reading that we can behold that monster, the perfect critic.'[9]

Despite these signposts of discursive common-sense, the conven-

[3] 'Oscar Wilde', 1893
[4] *The Painter of Modern Life*, 1863
[5] *Silhouettes*, 1892
[6] *The Works of Max Beerbohm*, 1896
[7] 'Ouida' (*More*, 1899)
[8] 'An Aesthetic Book' (*Around Theatres*, 1924)
[9] *Ibid*

tional view of Max is that which sees him as an adjunct to the
'nineties – a being belonging to 'the Beardsley Period'[10] as he
ironically described himself. Such a view is well represented by
G. S. Fraser's statement that 'Sir Max is a writer who is all
"manner" and nothing but manner; his style like his personality
is artificial, a conscious construction.'[11]

This view – held alike by detractors or praisers, though, of course,
with a different stress in either case – has been challenged by Lord
David Cecil, both in his biography of Max and in a television
broadcast on *The Yellow Book*.[12] In the latter, Lord David
distinguished between the decadence of *fin-de-siècle* authors in love
with the morbid and the tragic, and the 'anti-decadence' of Max
who, for all his fripperies and affectations, expressed himself in
terms of the comic. In later life Max said of one of his favourite
novelists that 'Trollope reminds us that sanity need not be
philistine';[13] and the quality of sanity, all unlooked for here, is the
preservative element, concealed but present, in Max's airy talent.
Lord David argues that he must be exempted from the charge of
decadence, preferred against other men of the 'nineties. He had, he
said, too much good sense, a feeling for proportion, and far too
much humour. More and more we see now that is the true assessment. Max was in the 'nineties without being ultimately of them.
The most famous of his sketches in *Seven Men* (1919) is a proof
of his resistance to the *fin-de-siècle* cult. As Lord David Cecil
remarks, ' "Enoch Soames" is the product of Max's *Yellow Book*
days. . . . Soames himself and his works are a composite picture of
the more absurd features of the typical *Yellow Book* writer.'[14] It is
Max's less stereotyped personality which makes him of the 'Beardsley
generation',[15] 'the most convincing in tone and opinion. Wilde was
weighed down by his "chrysoberyls", Lionel Johnson by his antique
erudition, Symons by his excitement over "sin". All of these authors
found it difficult to extricate themselves from their original
premises, from the hardened shell of their own self-ritual. Max,

---

[10] 'Diminuendo' (*The Works of Max Beerbohm*, 1896)
[11] *The Modern Writer and His World*, 1953
[12] 'More Best Sellers: *The Yellow Book*' 15 January 1968
[13] *Max: A Biography* by Lord David Cecil
[14] *Ibid*
[15] 'Diminuendo' (*The Works of Max Beerbohm*)

Max Beerbohm

alone of these, had the temerity of each new impression and pre-judice.'[16]

Until 1898, when Max took over from Bernard Shaw as dramatic critic of the *Saturday Review*, his directly critical writings had been few in number. For those who recognize the critical spirit at work outside the precincts of formal criticism, it was clear that here was a critic, however. In an essay entitled 'The Spirit of Caricature' (1901), he defined his subject as 'the delicious art of exaggerating, without fear or favour, the peculiarities of this or that human body, for the mere sake of exaggeration.'[17] Four collected volumes of drawings – *Caricatures of Twenty-five Gentlemen* (1896), *Poets' Corner* (1904), *Rossetti and His Circle* (1922), and *Heroes and Heroines of Bitter-Sweet* demonstrate the critical spirit informing this art of deft distortion.

The literary counterpart of caricature is parody: and in his introductory note to *A Christmas Garland* (1912), Max tells us that 'I acquired the habit of apeing, now and again . . . this and that live writer – sometimes, it must be admitted, in the hope of learning rather what to avoid.' The highest form of flattery may be imitation, but parody is the one empirical and verifiable procedure in criticism. Such a procedure is engaged in by Max in his sheaf of parodies *A Christmas Garland* – one of the most valuable documents of criticism on certain modern writers : Kipling, George Moore, Henry James, Meredith, Bennet, Bernard Shaw, H. G. Wells and others.

Upon his marriage in 1910, Max gave up his dramatic post, and retired with his wife to Rapallo on the Italian Riviera. On the death of Florence in 1951, he was cared for by Elizabeth Jungman whom he married on his death bed in 1956. He died on 20 May, and after cremation his ashes were sent to England where on 29 June they received the honour of burial in St Paul's Cathedral.

Max's dramatic writings are gathered together in three volumes, edited, introduced and published by Rupert Hart-Davis : *Around Theatres* (1953) – first published in 1924; *More Theatres* (1969); *Last Theatres* (1970).

Two further books on him which may be referred to are : *Sir*

[16] 'The Writings of Sir Max Beerbohm' by Derek Stanford (*The Month*, June 1955)
[17] *A Variety of Things*, 1928

Max Beerbohm: Man and Writer by J. G. Riewald (1953, The Hague), and *Conversations with Max* by S. N. Behrman (1960).

OUIDA

The Democracy of Letters will exasperate or divert you, according to your temperament. Me it diverts merely. It does no harm to literature. Good books are still written, good critics still criticize, in the old, quiet way; and, if the good books are criticized chiefly by innumerable fools hired to review an imponderable amount of trash, I do not really see that it matters at all. The trash itself is studied, now and again, by good critics and so becomes a springboard for good criticism, and it were unfair as it were useless, therefore, to shield good books from the consideration of ordinary reviewers. You may call it monstrous that a good writer should be at the mercy of such persons, but I doubt whether the good writer is himself aggrieved. He needs no mercy. And, as a matter of fact, the menaces hurled by the ordinary reviewers, whenever something new or strange confronts them, are very vain words indeed, and may at any moment be merged in clumsy compliments. A good critic – and by that term I mean a cultured man with brains and a temperament – may at any moment come by, and, if he praise, the ordinary reviewers, most receptive of all creatures, will praise also. I was glancing lately through a little book of essays, written by a lady. At the end of the book were printed press-notices about a volume of this lady's book of verse. Among these gems, and coruscating beyond the rest, was one graven with the name of Mr William Sharp : 'In its class I know no nobler or more beautiful sonnet than "Renouncement"; and I have so considered it ever since the day when Rossetti (who knew it by heart), repeating it to me, added that it was one of the three finest sonnets ever written by women.' Such a confession as Mr William Sharp's is not to be found in the ordinary press-notice, but that is merely because the ordinary reviewer is of a less simple and sunny disposition than our friend, and speaks not save as one having his own authority. Nevertheless, he is in no wise more clever than Mr Sharp (or Captain Sumph), and very likely he did not even know Rossetti. Whether Mr Sharp liked this sonnet before he met it under high auspices, is a point which may never be made clear, but there can be no doubt that the method of the ordinary reviewer is to curse what he does not understand, until it be explained to him. The element of comedy becomes yet stronger if the reviewers be subsequently assured that the explanation was all wrong. Who shall forget the chorus of adulation that rent the welkin for the essays of this very lady whose sonnet Mr Sharp 'so considered'? Two great writers had greatly praised her. I, humble person, mildly suggested that their praise had been excessive, and gave some good reasons for my opinion. Since then, the chorus has been palpably less loud, marred even by discordant voices. I do not pride myself particularly on this effect; I record it only because it gives a little instance of a great law.

Simpler, more striking, and more important, as an instance of reviewers' emptiness, is the position of Ouida, the latest of whose long novels, *The Massarenes*, had what is technically termed 'a cordial reception' – a reception strangely different from that accorded to her novels thitherto. Ouida's novels have always, I believe, sold well. They contain qualities which have gained for them some measure of Corellian success. Probably that is why, for so many years, no good critic took the trouble to praise them. The good critic, with a fastidiousness which is perhaps a fault, often neglects those who can look after themselves; the very fact of popularity – he is not infallible – often repels him; he prefers to champion the deserving weak. And so, for many years, the critics, unreproved, were ridiculing a writer who had many qualities obvious to ridicule, many gifts that lifted her beyond their reach. At length it occurred to a critic of distinction, Mr G. S. Street, to write an 'Appreciation of Ouida', which appeared in the *Yellow Book*. It was a shy, self-conscious essay, written somewhat in the tone of a young man defending the moral character of a barmaid who has bewitched him, but, for all its blushing diffidence, it was a very gentlemanly piece of work, and it was full of true and delicate criticism. I myself wrote, later, in praise of Ouida, and I believe that, at about the same time, Mr Stephen Crane wrote an appreciation of his own in an American magazine. In a word, three intelligent persons had cracked their whips – enough to have called the hounds off. Nay more, the furious pack had been turned suddenly into a flock of nice sheep. It was pretty to see them gambolling and frisking and bleating around *The Massarenes*.

Ouida is not, and never was, an artist. That, strangely enough, is one reason why she had been so little appreciated by the reviewers. The artist presents his ideas in the finest, strictest form, paring, whittling, polishing. In reading his finished work, none but a few persons note his artistic skill, or take pleasure in it for its own sake. Yet it is this very skill of his which enables the reviewers to read his work with pleasure. To a few persons, artistic skill is in itself delightful, insomuch that they tend to overrate its importance, neglecting the matter for the form. Art, in a writer, is not everything. Indeed, it implies a certain limitation. If a list of consciously artistic writers were drawn up, one would find that most of them were lacking in great force of intellect or of emotion; that their intellects were restricted, their emotions not very strong. Writers of enormous vitality never are artistic : they cannot pause, they must always be moving swiftly forward. Mr Meredith, the only living novelist in England who rivals Ouida in sheer vitality, packs tight all his pages with wit, philosophy, poetry, and psychological analysis. His obscurity, like that of Carlyle and Browning, is due less to extreme subtlety than to the plethoric abundance of his ideas. He cannot stop to express himself. If he could, he might be more popular. The rhapsodies of Mr Swinburne, again, are so overwhelmingly exuberant in their expression that no ordinary reader can cope with them; the ordinary reader is stunned by them before he is impressed. When he lays down the book and regains consciousness, he has forgotten entirely what it was all about. On the other hand, reticence, economy, selection, and all the artistic means may be carried too far. Too much art is, of course, as great an obstacle as too little art; and Pater, in his excessive care for words, is as obscure to most people as are Carlyle and Browning, in their carelessness. It is to him who takes the mean of these two extremes, to that author who expresses himself simply, without unnecessary expansion or congestion, that appreciation is most readily and spontaneously granted.

Well! For my own part, I am a dilettante, a *petit maître*. I love best in literature delicate and elaborate ingenuities of form and style. But my preference does not keep me from paying due homage to Titanic force, and delighting, now and again, in its manifestation. I wonder at Ouida's novels, and I wonder still more at Ouida. I am staggered when I think of that lurid sequence of books and short stories and essays which she has poured forth so swiftly, with such irresistible *élan*. What manner of woman can Ouida be? A woman who writes well never writes much. Even Sappho spent her whole life in writing and rewriting some exquisite, isolated verses, which, with feminine tact, she handed down to posterity as mere fragments of her work. In our own day, there are some ladies who write a large number of long books, but I am sure that the 'sexual novel' or the 'political novel', as wrought by them, must be as easy to write as it is hard to read. Ouida is essentially feminine, as much *une femme des femmes* as Jane Austen or 'John Oliver Hobbes', and it is indeed remarkable that she should yet be endowed with force and energy so exuberant and indefatigable. All her books are amazing in their sustained vitality. Vitality is, indeed, the most patent, potent factor in her work. Her pen is more inexhaustibly prolific than the pen of any other writer; it gathers new strength of its every dip into the ink-pot. Ouida need not, and could not, husband her unique endowments, and a man might as well shake his head over the daily rising of the indefatigable sun, or preach Malthusianism in a rabbit-warren, as counsel Ouida to write less. Her every page is a riot of unpolished epigrams and unpolished poetry of vision, with a hundred discursions and redundancies. She cannot say a thing once; she must repeat it again and again, and, with every repetition, so it seems to me, she says it with greater force and charm. Her style is a veritable cascade, in comparison with which the waters come down at Lodore as tamely as they come down at Shanklin. And, all the while, I never lose interest in her story, constructed with that sound professional knowledge, which the romancers of this later generation, with their vague and halting modes, would probably regard as old-fashioned. Ouida grips me with her every plot, and – since she herself so strenuously believes in them – I can believe even in her characters. True, they are not real, when I think of them in cold blood. They are abstractions, like the figures in early Greek tragedies and epics before psychology was thought of – things of black or white, or colourless things to illustrate the working of destiny, elemental puppets for pity or awe. Ouida does not pretend to the finer shades of civilized psychology.

Her men and women of Mayfair are shadows, as I see when I am not under the direct spell of her writing, and she reproduces real life only when she is dealing with childish or half-savage natures – Cigarette the *vivandière*, Redempta the gipsy, Italian peasants, dogs and horses. She cares for the romance and beauty and terror of life, not for its delicate shades and inner secrets. Her books are, in the true sense of the word, romances, though they are not written in Wardour Street. The picturesqueness of modern life, transfigured by imagination, embellished by fancy, that is her *forte*. She involves her stock-figures – the pure girl, the wicked woman, the adorable hero and the rest – in a series of splendid adventures. She makes her protagonist a guardsman that she may describe, as she alone can, steeplechases and fox-hunts and horses running away with phaetons. Or she makes him a diplomat, like Strathmore, or a great tenor, like Corèze, or a Queen's messenger, like Erceldoune, or something else – anything so that it be lurid and susceptible of romance. She ranges hither and thither over all countries, snatching at all languages, realizing all scenes. Her information is as wide as Macaulay's, and her slips in local colour are but the result of a careless omniscience. That she should have referred to 'the pointing of the *digito monstrari*', and headed one of her chapters with the words 'Thalassis! Thalassis!' and made the Queen present at a Levée, and thrown one or two false side-lights on the Oxford Eights Week, may seem very terrible to the dullards who think that criticism consists in spotting mistakes. But the fact remains that Ouida uses her great information with extrordinary effect. Her delight in beautiful things has been accounted to her for vulgarity by those who think that a writer 'should take material luxury for granted'. But such people forget, or are unable to appreciate, the difference between the perfunctory faking of description, as practised by the average novelist – as who should say 'soft carpets', 'choice wines', 'priceless Tintorettos' – and description which is the result of true vision. No writer was ever more finely endowed than Ouida with the love and knowledge of all kinds of beauty in art and nature. There is nothing vulgar in having a sense of beauty – so long as you have it. Ouida's descriptions of boudoirs in palaces are no more vulgar nor less beautiful than her descriptions of lakes and mountains.

With their fair, silken moustachios and their glengarries and their velvet jackets, Ouida's guardsmen, pegs for luxury and romance, are vastly stimulating. I should like to have peered through the cloud of 'Turkish' that did always involve them, and have seen Lord Vaulerois tossing aside a pile of millefleurs-scented notes and quaffing curaçoa, as he pondered the chances of Peach-Bloom for the Guards' Steeplechase, or the last mad caprice of Léla Liette! Too languid, as he lay there on his divan, to raise the vinaigrette to his nostrils, he was one who had served his country through more than one campaign on the boiling plains of the Sahara; he who, in the palace of a *nouveau riche*, had refused the bedchamber assigned to him, on the plea that he could not sleep under a false Fragonard, had often camped *à la belle étoile* in the waste places of Central Asia; thrice he had passed through the D.C. as calmly as he would swim the Hellespont or toss off a beaker of rosy Comet-Wine; with his girlish hands that Duchesses envied he had grappled lions in the jungle, and would think nothing of waiting for hours, heedless of frost and rain, to bring down some rocketer he had marked in a warm corner at Crichel or Longleat. Familiar with Cairene Bazaars as with the matchless deer-forests of Dunrobin, with the brown fens round Melton Mowbray as with the incomparable grace and brilliance of the Court of Hapsburg; *bienvenu* in the Vatican as in the Quirinal; deferred to by Dips and Décorés in all the *salons* of Europe, and before whom even Queens turned to coquettes and Kings to comrades; careless, caressed, *insouciant*; of all men the beloved or envied; inimitable alike in his grace of person and in the perfection of his taste; passing from the bow-windows of St James's to the faded and fetid alleys of Stamboul, from the Quartier Bréda to the Newski Prospect, from the citron-groves of Cashmere, the gay fuchsia-gardens of Simla, to the hideous chaos of Illinois, a region scorched by the sirocco, swept by inextinguishable prairie-fires, sepultured in the white shrouds of remorseless blizzards, and – as though that were not enough – befouled with the fumes and crushed with the weight of a thousand loathsome cities, which are swift as the mushroom in their growth, far more deadly than the *fungus fatalis* of the Midi – it was here, passing with easy non-chalance as the foal passes from one pasture to another, with a flight swifter than the falcon's, luxurious in its appurtenance as a Shah's seraglio; it was here, in these whirling circles of intrigue and pleasure and romance, and in this span of an illimitable nomady, that flew the nights and days of Philip, nineteenth Marquis of Vaulerois, as the world knew him – 'Fifi' of the First Life.

I am glad that in her later books Ouida has not deserted 'the First Life'. She is still the same Ouida, has lost none of her romance, none of her wit and poetry, her ebullitions of pity and indignation. The old 'naughtiness' and irresponsibility which were so strange a portent in the Medio-Victorian days, and kept her books away from the drawing-room table, seem to have almost disappeared; and, in compliment of her love of luxury for its own sake, there is some social philosophy, diatribes against society for its vulgar usage of luxury. But, though she has become a mentor, she is still Ouida, still that unique, flamboyant lady, one of the miracles of modern literature. After all these years, she is still young and swift and strong, towering head and shoulders over all the other women (and all but one or two of the men) who are writing English novels. That the reviewers have tardily trumpeted her is amusing, but no cause for congratulation. I have watched their attitude rather closely. They have the idiot's cunning and seek to explain their behaviour by saying that Ouida has entirely changed. Save in the slight respect I have noted, Ouida has not changed at all. She is still Ouida. That is the high compliment I would pay her.

(FROM 'MORE', 1899)

W. E. HENLEY

1849 - 1903

William Ernest Henley, poet, critic and editor, was born in the city of Gloucester on 23 August 1849. His father was a bookseller of more convivial habit than business acumen, and his son, accordingly, did not receive the happiest start in life. He was always a bookish boy, however, and at the Crypt Grammar School he benefited greatly from the influence of the new headmaster, the Manx poet T. E. Brown – a former Fellow of Oriel College, Oxford – who generously befriended him.

A scarcity of means was not Henley's only cross. From childhood he was the victim of tuberculosis, which caused the amputation of one foot, after which he spent many months between 1873 and 1875 in the Royal Infirmary, Edinburgh, having the other saved from the same fate. It was here that he wrote his *Hospital Verses* published first in the *Cornhill* and issued in book form in 1887. 'And so,' wrote Arthur Symons, with approval, 'instead of prattling about Phyllis, Henley has set himself to the task of rendering the more difficult poetry of the disagreeable.'[1] English verse was well on its way to the *Wasteland*.

It was at Edinburgh that Henley encountered Stevenson, and largely through him was launched on his career of journalist and editor. Though they collaborated in the writing of four plays, they quarrelled grievously in 1885 and were never truly reconciled. Each, none the less, was haunted by the memory of this friendship and its break.

The three indispensable documents for understanding Henley's life and thought are : the brief eight-page account of him in Yeats' *Autobiographies* (1926); Jerome Hamilton Buckley's *William Ernest*

---

[1] 'W. E. Henley' (*Studies in Two Literatures*, 1897)

Henley: A Study in the 'Counter-Decadence' of the 'Nineties (1945), and John Cornell's fine biography *W. E. Henley* (1949).

Henley edited many papers – *London*, a weekly; the *Magazine for Art*, a monthly; and, more consequentially, the weekly *Scots Observer*, later to be known as the *National Observer*. It was as the editor of this last – a hard-hitting Tory paper – that Yeats encountered him. 'I wrote my first good lyrics and tolerable essays for the *National Observer*,'[2] recollected Yeats in 1922, recalling also that 'I disagreed with him about everything, but I admired him beyond words'.[3]

Henley's politics (those of a 'violent unionist and imperialist'[4]) were much disliked by Yeats; nor were the former's critical principles (anti-Pre-Raphaelite and pro-Realist) any the more congenial. Even so, to Yeats and other young men – Charles Whibley, G. S. Street and George Wyndham – 'Henley was our leader and our confidant.'[5] As an editor he stimulated, corrected, and praised. 'If he had changed every "has" into "hath" I would have let him, reminisced Yeats, 'for had we not sunned ourselves in his generosity. "My young men outdo me and they write better than I do," he wrote, in some letter praising Charles Whibley's work, and to another friend with a copy of my own *Man Who Dreamed of Fairyland* : "See what a fine thing has been written by one of my lads." '[6]

The essence of Yeats's portraits, however, is an image of Henley as a sort of daemonic war-smith armourer : 'When I think of him ... I see his crippled legs as though he were some Vulcan perpetually forging swords for other men to use.'[7]

This notion is elaborated further in J. H. Buckley's thoughtful study, where it is interpreted in terms of modern psychology. According to Dr Adler, physical debility will always be a determining influence in mental health. One way, then, in which a cripple, say, can react is by raising a defensive 'masculine protest'[8] against uncertainty, insecurity, indecision, in short against every token of effeminacy. J. H. Buckley believes that Henley, physically

[2] 'Four Years: 1887–1891' (*The Trembling of the Veil*, 1922)
[3] *Ibid*
[4] *Ibid*
[5] *Ibid*
[6] *Ibid*
[7] *Ibid*
[8] *The Neurotic Constitution* by Alfred Adler (1917)

crippled as he was, reacted in just such a manner. He feels that his writings are thick with the symptoms of this compensating protest: from the strident and assertive poem 'Invictus' to his activist programme in politics and letters. Nor was this a diagnosis reached only in retrospect. Reviewing Henley's volume *The Song of the Sword* in May 1892, Richard Le Gallienne described the book as 'this sword-evangel begot of Jingoism by a Berserker', and 'not so much a gospel as a pose'.[9]

Real, as distinct from paraded, manliness is the salient note of the man as expounded by John Connell in his vivid book on Henley. 'He was,' writes Connell, 'big, noisy, corpulent and untidy; he was zestful and hearty – and he ought to have been hale. Yet by determination and courage he kept his ailment in its place; menacing as it was, it remained always a disease of his body. No man was less obviously a cripple in mind or spirit. That was no small triumph; and it was due to his own conscious and disciplined effort.'[10]

Henley's position as a critic of the 'nineties is interesting and distinct. 'He hated,' Yeats tells us, 'all that Ruskin praised . . . pre-Raphaelitism affected him as some people are affected by a cat in the room.'[11] Aestheticism was anathema to him, and he reconciled the initial attraction he felt for Wilde's personality by declaring that Wilde was no aesthete – 'one soon finds that he is a scholar and a gentleman'.[12] Yeats reports Wilde as saying, on his first meeting with Henley, that 'the basis of literary friendship is mixing the poisoned bowl',[13] and Henley was soon mixing the poisoned bowl for Wilde. On 5 July 1890, the *Scots Observer* reviewed *The Picture of Dorian Gray* which had appeared in *Lippincott's Magazine*. The writer of the notice, which was unsigned, was not Henley himself but his first lieutenant Charles Whibley. Whilst allowing the story to be 'ingenious, interesting, full of cleverness', Whibley made open innuendoes as to the scandals surrounding its author's life. He censored Wilde for 'grubbing in muck-heaps', for presenting a drama whose interest was 'medico-

---

[9] *Retrospective Reviews: A Literary Log*, vol. I 1891–3 (1896)
[10] *W. E. Henley*, 1949
[11] 'Four Years: 1887–1891' (*The Trembling of the Veil*, 1922)
[12] *Ibid*
[13] *Ibid*

legal' and only 'fitted for the Criminal Investigation Department or a hearing *in camera*'. The controversy, which raged for weeks, characterized the *Observer* as the chief opponent of the *fin-de-siècle* movement.

Henley's principles as a critic both aligned him with, and divided him from, the *Yellow Book-Savoy* nexus of writers. As with these men, he championed 'the way of realism',[14] but whereas they derived their theory and practice from Flaubert, Maupassant and the French, Henley returned to the fictional roots of English realism in the eighteenth century, being, in fact, engaged upon a long essay on Henry Fielding, whose works[15] he edited, at the time of his death.

Even so, Henley engages in the 'nineties' scrupulous religion of style. 'A king of the feuilleton' (his phrase for Berlioz as critic), Henley composed with methodic care and 'an honest regard for letters'. He sets forth his own ideal of good writing in a piece on 'Essays and Essayists', contained in the two volumes of *Views and Reviews* (1890). These essays in appreciation on literature and art are Henley's chief critical claim to be enjoyably remembered. His longer, more considered pieces were first collected in volume two (*Essays*, 1920) of his *Collected Works*.

In retrospect, Henley's life and career is a chequer of triumph, sadness and defeat. His six-year-old and only daughter – idolized by her father and nicknamed 'the Emperor' by him – died in 1894 of cerebral meningitis. The same year his *National Observer* ended its vivid and polemical existence. In 1895 – the year of Wilde's trial – he hoped to receive the Chair of Rhetoric at Edinburgh then vacant, but found George Saintsbury preferred in his place. Once more, he hoped for public office, believing the Laureateship might be his. This also was not to be, the prime minister choosing to honour Alfred Austin in his stead.

In 1898 he was awarded a Civil List pension, but in that same year he was seriously ill and underwent an operation necessitating prolonged convalescence. Sick as he was, he worked on to the end, dying on 12 July 1903 at Woking.

[14] 'Robert Burns' (A Terminal Essay to the Centenary Edition of the Poet, 1896)
[15] *Complete Works of Henry Fielding*, 16 vols., with essay, 1903

W. E. Henley

ARABIAN NIGHTS ENTERTAINMENTS

Its Romance

He that has the book of the *Thousand Nights and a Night* has Hachisch-made-words for life. Gallant, subtle, refined, intense, humourous, obscene, here is the Arab intelligence drunk with conception. It is a vast extravaganza of passion in action and picarooning farce and material splendour run mad. The amorous instinct and the instinct of enjoyment, not tempered but heightened greatly by the strict ordinances of dogma, have leave to riot uncontrolled. It is the old immortal story of Youth and Beauty and their coming together, but it is coloured with the hard and brilliant hues of an imagination as sensuous in type and as gorgeous in ambition as humanity has known. The lovers must suffer, for suffering intensifies the joy of fruition; so they are subjected to all such modes of travail and estrangement as a fancy careless of pain and indifferent to life can devise. But it is known that happy they are to be; and if by the annihilation of time and space then are space and time annihilated. Adventures are to the adventurous all the world over; but they are so with a difference in the East. It is only Sindbad that confesses himself devoured with the lust of travel. The grip of a humourous and fantastic fate is tight on all the other heroes of this epic-in-bits. They do not go questing for accidents : their hour comes, and the finger of God urges them forth, and thrusts them on in the way of destiny. The air is horrible with the gross and passionate figments of Islamite mythology. Afrits watch over or molest them; they are made captive of malignant Ghouls; the Jinns take bodily form and woo them to their embraces. The sea-horse ramps at them from the ocean floor; the great roc darkens earth about them with the shadow of his wings; wise and goodly apes come forth and minister unto them; enchanted camels bear them over evil deserts with the swiftness of the wind, or the magic horse outspreads his sail-broad vannes, and soars with them; or they are borne aloft by some servant of the Spell till the earth is as a bowl beneath them, and they hear the angels quiring at the foot of the Throne. So they fare to strange and dismal places : through cities of brass whose millions have perished by divine decree; cities guilty of the cult of the Fire and the Light wherein all life has been stricken to stone; or on to the magnetic mountain by whose horrible attraction the bolts are drawn from the ship, and they alone survive the inevitable wreck. And the end comes. Comes the Castle of Burnished Copper, and its gates fly open before them : the forty damsels, each one fairer than the rest, troop out at their approach; they are bathed in odours, clothed in glittering apparel, fed with enchanted meats, plunged fathoms deep in the delights of the flesh. There is contrived for them a private paradise of luxury and splendour, a practical Infinite of gold and silver stuffs and jewels and all things gorgeous and rare and costly; and therein do they abide for evermore. You would say of their poets that they contract immensity to the limits of desire; they exhaust the inexhaustible in their enormous effort; they stoop the universe to the slavery of a talisman, and bind the visible and invisible worlds within the compass of a ring.

Its Comedy

But there is another side to their imaginings. When the Magian has done beating his copper drum – (how its mysterious murmur still haunts the echoes of memory!) – when Queen Lab has finished her tremendous conjurations, wonder gives place to laughter, the apotheosis of the flesh to the spirit of comedy. The enchanter turns harlequin; and what the lovers ask is not the annihilation of time and space but only that the father be at his prayers, or the husband gone on a fool's errand, while they have leave to kiss each other's mouths, 'as a pigeon feedeth her young', to touch the lute, strip language naked, and 'repeat the following verses' to a ring of laughing girls and amid all such comfits and delicates as a hungry audience may rejoice to hear enumerated. And the intrigue begins, and therewith the presentment of character, the portraiture of manners. Merry ladies make love to their gallants with flowers, or scorn them with the huckle-bones of shame; the Mother Coles of Araby pursue the unwary stranger for their mistress' pleasure; damsels resembling the full moon carouse with genial merchants or inquiring calenders. The beast of burden, even the porter, has his hour : he goes the round at the heels of a veiled but beautiful

lady, and lays her in the materials of as liberal and sumptuous a
carouse as is recorded in history. Happy lady, and O thrice-fortunate
porter! enviable even to the term of time! It is a voluptuous farce,
a masque and anti-masque of wantonness and stratagem, of wine-
cups and jewels and fine raiment, of gaudy nights and amorous
days, of careless husbands and adventurous wives, of innocent
fathers and rebel daughters and lovers happy or befooled. And high
over all, his heart contracted with the spleen of the East, the tedium
of supremacy, towers the great Caliph Haroun, the buxom and
bloody tyrant, a Muslim Lord of Misrule. With Giafar, the finest
gentleman and goodliest gallant of Eastern story, and Mesrour,
the well-beloved, the immortal Eunuch, he goes forth upon his
round in the enchanted streets of Baghdàd, like François Premier
in the maze of old-time Paris. The night is musical with happy
laughter and the sound of lutes and voices; it is seductive with the
clink of goblets and the odour of perfumes : not a shadow but has
its secret, or jovial or amorous or terrible : here falls a head, and
there you may note the contrapuntal effect of the bastinado. But
the blood is quickly hidden with flowers, the bruises are tired over
with cloth-of-gold, and the jolly pageant sweeps on. Truly the
comic essence is imperishable. What was fun to them in Baghdàd
is fun to us in London after a thousand years.

Sacer Vates

The prose of Mr Payne's translation is always readable and often
elegant; Sir Richard Burton's notes and 'terminal essays' are a
mine of curious and diverting information; but for me the real
author of *The Arabian Nights* is called not Burton nor Payne but
Antoine Galland. He it was, in truth, who gave the world as much
exactly as it needed of his preposterous original : who eliminated
its tediousness, purged it of its barbarous and sickening, immorality,
wiped it clean of cruelty and unnaturalness, selected its essentials of
comedy and romance, and set them clear and sharp against a light
that western eyes can bear and in an atmosphere that western lungs
can breathe. Of course the new translations are interesting –
especially to ethnologists and the critic with a theory that translated
verse is inevitably abominable. But they are not for the general nor

the artist. They include too many pages revolting by reason of unutterable brutality of incident and point of view – as also for the vileness of those lewd and dreadful puritans whose excesses against humanity and whose devotion to Islam they record – to be acceptable as literature or tolerable as reading. Now, in Galland I get the best of them. He gave me whatever is worth remembering of Bedreddin and Camaralzaman and that enchanting Fairy Peri-Banou; he is the true poet alike of Abou Hassan and the Young King of the Black Islands, of Ali Baba and the Barber of the Brothers; to him I owe that memory – of Zobeide alone in the accursed city whose monstrous silence is broken by the voice of the one man spared by the wrath of God as he repeats his solitary prayer – which ranks with Crusoe's discovery of the footprint in the thrilling moments of my life; it was he who, by refraining from the use of pepper in his cream tarts, contrived to kitchen those confections with the very essence of romance; it was he that clove asunder the Sultan's kitchen-wall for me, and took me to the pan, and bade me ask a certain question of the fish that fried therein, and made them answer me in terms mysterious and tremendous yet. Nay, that animating and delectable feeling I cherish ever for such enchanted commodities as gold-dust and sandal-wood and sesame and cloth of gold and black slaves with scimitars – to whom do I owe it but this rare and delightful artist? 'O mes chers *Mille et une Nuits!*' says Fantasio, and he speaks in the name of all them that have lived the life that Galland alone made possible. The damsels of the new style may 'laugh till they fall backwards', etc., through forty volumes instead of ten, and I shall still go back to my Galland. I shall go back to him because his masterpiece is – not a book of reference, nor a curiosity of literature, nor an achievement in pedantry, nor even a demonstration of the absolute failure of Islamism as an influence that makes for righteousness, but – an excellent piece of art.

(FROM 'VIEWS AND REVIEWS : ESSAYS IN APPRECIATION –
LITERATURE', 1890)

FREDERICK
WEDMORE

1844 - 1921

Frederick Wedmore – short-storyist and critic of three arts (painting, drama, and literature) – was born at Richmond Hill, Clifton, Bristol in 1844. Coming of an old Quaker family, he was educated at a Quaker private school before proceeding to study in Lausanne and Paris.

A note of reserve pervades all he wrote, whether in the realm of fiction or criticism; and although he left a volume of reminiscences, its first sentence tells us that 'The title of this book itself implies that there is here no Autobiography.'[1] 'He seldom, I think, made confidences,' wrote Sir George Douglas, who knew him well, 'and excepting in relation to his work, he seldom sought for sympathy.'[2] The same authority also adds that 'his nature, though by no means cold, was sober, chaste, restrained though these attributes must be thought of along with a 'Gallic gaiety and charm ... good looks ... [and] fine courtesy.'[3]

For nearly thirty years he was an art critic for the *Standard* and wrote steadily for the *Academy*, of which he was a dramatic critic, and various other papers. Eleven of his books deal with painting and etching, and only three with literature: *Balzac* (1889) which appeared in the popular 'Great Writer Series', *On Books and Art* (1899), and the posthumous volume of short reviews published in 1925.

Wedmore was an older man than most of the animators of the

[1] *Memories*, 1912
[2, 3] *Certain Comments* by Sir Frederick Wedmore, with Introductory Essays by Sir George Douglas, Bart. and George C. Williamson, D.Litt., 1925

'nineties. Even so, he belongs to the culture of those years by reason of three affinities : his predeliction for things French, a batch of finely-shaped short stories, executed with the economy and polish prized and cultivated by that decade, and perhaps the first important mini-treatise on that genre of fiction in English. This twenty-four page essay entitled *The Short Story*[4] was published in a magazine[5] in 1898 and in book form,[6] with other pieces, in the following year. *On Books and Arts* (1899) contains only four literary pieces. In addition to the essay on the short story, there is one on Balzac, one on George Eliot, and one on Zola's *Thérèse Raquin*. This last is of importance because it records Wedmore's dissatisfaction with the standard realism of the day. 'On Saturday night,' he writes, 'I went to *Thérèse Raquin* at the Royalty Theatre, and while I found the piece itself . . . far less of a melodrama than certain of its critics had said, I discovered that the performance, though good and creditable, was not quite so noteworthy as had been pronounced. . . . The intelligent unprejudiced person who goes to see *Thérèse Raquin* comes away with the knowledge that he has witnessed an exposition of certain bitter truths – an exposition made by M. Zola with power and singleness of aim, but here and there accompanied by a purposeless, or at least an unsuccessful diffuseness, which is one of the many characteristics and abiding defects of this important writer's method.

'This diffuseness, this fulness of detail which is not actually illustrative and exploratory, Balzac, who was Zola's master, had in a measure; but he had it far less than Zola. A profuse enjoyment of the commonplace, in order that one may be "natural" – this avoidance of selection and rejection, when selection and rejection are of the very essence of Art, commends itself, as I understand, to a little school of criticism, or of dogmatism, which has now found voice among us; and that it does so is an entertaining evidence of the capacity of its professors for critical preachment.'

Wedmore, here, expresses his discontent on aesthetic grounds. Elsewhere, it is the moral aspect of the new realism which troubles him. In the prefatory note to *Orgeas and Miradou*, with other

---

[4] There is a full discussion on this essay in the introduction to *Short Stories of the '90s*

[5] *Nineteenth Century*, March 1898

[6] *On Books and Arts* (1899)

pieces (1896), he speaks of 'a literary "realism" so far from reality that it is ignorantly proud to be bereft of tenderness'. In the *fin-de-siècle* context of his day, Wedmore was a square and an 'oldie'. The formal demands of realism, in the short story and the novel, seemed to have called for what can be referred to as an ethical Darwinianism – a vision of society, as of animal nature, gloatingly red in tooth and claw. Wedmore accepted the aesthetic discipline of the new realism while repudiating its moral associations, seeking to preserve in his own stories the values of a gentlemanly liberalism. (Politically speaking, he was a Tory.)

Pastorals of France (1877) – his first volume of short stories – was regarded appreciatively by Pater. A second volume *Renunciations* (1893) was saluted by a reviewer in the *Athenaeum* as constituting 'studies in polite realism', while the realism of a third collection, *English Episodes* (1894) was spoken of as poetic.

Wedmore, and all he stood for, was a lost cause by the middle of the 'nineties. He represents *the critic as gentleman* and the merely genteel and 'decent' values derived from social conventions unbacked by stronger supporting conceptions, were rapidly loosing a grip on art and letters as these latter became more increasingly 'way out'. Gentleman he was, but not man-of-the-world – a kind of *rentier Puritanism* constantly blinkering his imagination. In addition, he lacked intellectual courage, returning only the mildest of fire when Whistler – that impossible peacock – attacked him, while reserving his censorious sallies for the 'lower orders' and the under-privileged. One imagines he found *Punch* amusing (which Yeats and his friends most certainly did not).

Wedmore's name, in this bevy of critics, is entered under the rubric of 'style'. George C. Williamson, a friend of his, once distinguished Wedmore's style most aptly. 'His literary work,' he wrote, 'was exquisite, but not precious, the two words having very different meanings. . . . His style was always good, but it improved enormously as years went on; one had more and more the feeling of the deliberate care he had taken with his sentences and yet how different they were from the highly polished ones of Walter Pater, a writer whom he greatly admired while feeling his limitations. Wedmore's sentences never smelled of the lamp.'[7]

[7] *Certain Comments* by Sir Frederic Wedmore, with Introductory Essays by Sir George Douglas, Bart. and George C. Williamson, D.Litt.

THE SHORT STORY

One of the most engaging of the wits of our day wrote lately in a weekly newspaper that it is, for the most part, only those who are not good enough actors to act successfully in Life, who are compelled to act at the Theatre. Under the influence of such an amiable paradox it is possible that we may ask ourselves, in regard to story-writing, whether the people singled out to practice it are those, chiefly, to whose personal history Romance has been denied : so that the greatest qualification even for the production of a lady's love-tale, is – that the lady shall never have experienced a love-affair. Eminent precedents might be cited in support of the contention. A great editor once comfortably declared that the ideal journalist was a writer who did not know too much about his subject. The public did not want much knowledge, he said. The literary criticism in your paper would be perfect if you handed it over to the critic of Music; and the musical criticism would want for nothing if you assigned it to an expert in Art. And Mr Thackeray, speaking of love-tales, said something that pointed the same way. He protested, no one should write a love-story after he was fifty. And why? Because he knew too much about it.

But it was a personal application I was going to have given to the statement with which this paper begins. If the actor we see upon the boards be only there because more capable comedians are busy on the stage of the world, I am presumably invited by the Editor of *The Nineteenth Century* to hold forth on the Short Story because I am not a popular writer. The Editor, in the gentle exercise of his humour, bids me to fill the place which should be filled by the man of countless editions. It is true that in the matter of short stories, such a writer is not easy to find; and this too at a time when, if one is correctly informed, full many a lady, not of necessity of any remarkable gifts, maintains an honourable independence by the annual production of an improper novel. Small as my personal claims might be, were they based only on my books – *Renunciations*, for example, or *Pastorals of France* – I may say my say as one who, with production obviously scanty, has for twenty years been profoundly interested in the artistic treatment of the Short Story; who believes in the short story, not as a ready means of hitting the big public, but as a medium for the exercise of the finer art – as a medium, moreover, adapted peculiarly to that alert intelligence, on the part of the reader, which rebels sometimes at the *longueurs* of the conventional novel : the old three volumes or the new fat book. Nothing is so mysterious, for nothing is so instinctive, as the method of a writer. I cannot communicate the incommunicable. But at all events I will not express opinions aimed at the approval of the moment : convictions based on the necessity for epigram.

In the first place, then, what is, and what is *not*, a short story? Many things a short story may be. It may be an episode, like Miss Ella Hepworth Dixon's or like Miss Bertha Thomas'; a fairy tale, like Miss Evelyn Sharp's : the presentation of a single character with the stage to himself (Mr George Gissing); a tale of the uncanny (Mr Rudyard Kipling); a dialogue of comedy (Mr Pett Ridge); a panorama of selected landscape, a vision of the sordid street, a record of heroism, a remote tradition or an old belief vitalized by its bearing on our lives to-day, an analysis of an obscure calling, a glimpse at a forgotten quarter. A short story – I mean a short imaginative work in the difficult medium of prose; for plot, or story proper, is no essential part of it, though in work like Conan Doyle's or Rudyard Kipling's it may be a very delightful part – a short story may be any one of the things that have been named, or it may be something besides; but one thing it can never be – it can never be 'a novel in a nutshell'. That is a favourite definition, but not a definition that holds. It is a definition for the kind of public that asks for a convenient inexactness, and resents the subtlety which is inseparable from precise truth. Writers and serious readers know that a good short story cannot possibly be a *précis*, a synopsis, a *scenario*, as it were, of a novel. It is a separate thing – as separate, almost, as the Sonnet is from the Epic – it involves the exercise almost of a different art.

That, perhaps, is one reason why it is generally – in spite of temporary vogue as pleasant pastime – a little underrated as an intellectual performance. That is why great novelists succeed in it so seldom – or at all events fail in it sometimes – even a novelist like Mr Hardy, the stretch of whose canvas has never led him into carelessness of detail. Yet with *him*, even, in his short stories, the inequality is greater than befits the work of such an artist, and greater than is to be accounted for wholly by his mood; so that by the side of *The Three Strangers*, or, yet better, that delightful thing, *Interlopers at the Knap*, you have short tales tossed off with momentary indifference – as you can imagine Sheridan, with his braced language of comedy, stooping once to a charade. And if a *master* nods sometimes – a master like Hardy – does it not almost follow that, by the public at least, the conditions of the short story are not understood, and so, in the estimate of the criticism of the dinner-table, and by the criticism of the academic, the tale is made to suffer by its brevity? But if it is well done, it has done this amazing thing: it has become quintessence; it has eliminated the superfluous; and it has taken *time* to be brief. Then – amongst readers whose judgments are perfunctory – who have not thought the thing out – it is rewarded by being spoken of as an 'agreeable sketch', 'a promising little effort', and 'earnest of better things'. In this wise – not to talk of any other instance – one imagines the big public rewarding the completed charm of *The Author of Beltraffio* and of *A Day of Days*, though pregnant *brevity* is not often Mr James's strength. And then Mr James works away at the long novel, and, of course, is clever in it, because with him, *not* to be clever might require a passiveness more than American. Very good; but I go back from the record of all that 'Maisie' ought not to have known, to *The Author of Beltraffio* and to *A Day of Days* – 'promising little efforts', 'earnests of better things'.

Well, then, the short story is wont to be estimated, not by its quality, but by its size; a mode of appraisement under which the passion of Schumann, with his wistful questionings – in *Warum*, say, or in *Der Dichter spricht* – would be esteemed less seriously than the amiable score of *Maritana*! And a dry-point by Mr Whistler, two dozen lines laid with the last refinement of charm, would be held inferior to a panorama by Philippoteau, or to the backgrounds of the contemporary theatre. One would have thought that this was obvious. But in our latest stage of civilization it is sometimes only the obvious that requires to be pointed out.

While we are upon the subject of the hindrances to the apprecia-tion of a particular form of imaginative work, we may remind ourselves of one drawback in regard to which the short story must make common cause with the voluminous novel: I mean the inability of the mass of readers to do justice to the seriousness of any artistic, as opposed to any moral, or political, or pretentiously regenerative fiction. For the man in the street, for the inhabitant of Peckham Rye, for many prosperous people on the north side of the Park, perhaps even for the very cream of up-to-date persons whose duty it is to abide somewhere where Knightsbridge melts invisibly into Chelsea, Fiction is but a *délassement,* and the artists who practise it, in its higher forms, are a little apt to be estimated as contributors to public entertainment – like the Carangeot Troupe, and Alexia, at the Palace Theatre. The view is something of *this* nature – I read it so expressed only the other day: 'The tired clergyman, after a day's work; what book shall he take up? Fiction, perhaps, would seem too trivial; history, too solid.'

The serious writer of novel or short story brings no balm for the 'tired clergyman' – other than such balm as is afforded by the delight of serious Art. At high tension he has delivered himself of his performance, and if his work is to be properly enjoyed, it must be met by those only who are ready to receive it; it must be met by the alert, not the fatigued, reader; and with the short story in particular, with its omissions, with the brevity of its allusiveness, it must be met half way. Do not let us expect it to be 'solid', like Mill, or Lightfoot, or Westcott – or even like an A B C Railway Guide. You must condone the 'triviality' which puts its finger on the pulse of life and says 'Thou ailest *here* and *here'* – which exposes, not a political movement, like the historian of the outward fact, but the secrets of the heart, rather, and human weakness, and the courage which in strait places comes somehow to the sons of men, and the beauty and the strength of affection – and which does this by intuition as much as by science.

But to go back to considerations not common in some degree to all Fiction, but proper more absolutely to the short story. I have suggested briefly what the short story may be; we have seen briefly the one thing it *cannot* be – which is, a novel told within restricted space. Let us ask what methods it may adopt – what are some of the varieties of its form.

The short story admits of greater variety of form than does the long novel, and the number of these forms will be found to be increasing – and we must not reject conventionally (as we are terribly apt to do) the new form because we are unfamiliar with it. The forms that are open to the novel are open to the short imaginative piece, and, to boot, very many besides. Common to both, of course, is the most customary form of all – that in which the writer narrates as from outside the drama, yet with internal knowledge of it – what is called the 'narrative form', which includes within its compass, in a single work, narrative proper and a moderate share of dialogue. Common again to both short and long stories, evidently, is a form which, in skilled hands, and used only for those subjects to which it is most appropriate, may give strange reality to the matter presented – the form, I mean, in which the story is told in the first person, as the experience and the sentiment of one character who runs throughout the whole. The short story, though it should use this form very charily, adopts it more conveniently than does the long novel; for the novel has many more characters than the short story, and for the impartial presentation of many characters this form is a fetter. It gives of a large group a prejudiced and partial view. It commended itself once or twice only to Dickens. *David Copperfield* is the conspicuous example. Never once, I think, did it commend itself to Balzac. It is better adapted, no doubt, to adventure than to analysis, and better to the expression of humour than to the realization of tragedy. As far as the presentation of *character* is concerned, what it is usual for it to achieve – in hands, I mean, much smaller than those of the great Dickens – is this: a life size, full length, generally too flattering portrait of the hero of the story – a personage who has the lime-light all to himself – on whom no inconvenient shadows are ever thrown – the hero as beheld by Sant, shall I say? rather than as beheld by Sargent – and then, a further graceful idealization, an attractive pastel, you may call it, of the lady he most frequently admired; and, of the remainder, two or three Kit-Cat portraits, a head and shoulders here, and there a stray face.

The third and only other form that I remember as common to both novel and short story, though indeed not equally *convenient* to both, is the rare form of Letters. That again, like any other that will not bear a prolonged strain, is oftener available for short story than for big romance. The most consummate instance of its employment, in very lengthy work, is one in which with infinitely slow progression it serves above all things the purpose of minute and searching analysis – I have named the book in this line of description of it: I have named *Clarissa*. For the short story it is used very happily by Balzac – who, though not at first a master of sentences, is an instinctive master of methods – it is used by him in the *Mémoires de Deux Jeunes Mariées*. And in a much lighter way, of bright portraiture, of neat characterization, it is used by an ingenious, sometimes seductive, writer of our period, Marcel Prévost, in *Lettres de Femmes*. It is possible, of course, to *mix* these different forms; but for such mixture we shall conclude, I fancy, that prolonged fiction offers the best opportunity. Such mixture has its dangers for the short story; you risk, perhaps, unity of effect. But there are short stories in which monotony is avoided, and the force of the narrative in reality emphasized, by some telling lines from a letter, whose end or whose beginning may be otherwise imparted to us.

I devote a few lines to but two or three of the forms which by common consent are for the short story only. One of them is simple dialogue. For our generation, that has had the fascination of an experiment – an experiment made perhaps with best success after all in the candid and brilliant fragments of that genuine humorist, Mr Pett Ridge. The method in most hands has the appearance of a difficult feat. It *is* one, often – and so is walking on the slack-wire, and the back-spring in acrobatic dance. Of course a writer must enjoy grappling with difficulties. We understand that. But the more serious artist reflects, after a while, that the unnecessary difficulty is an inartistic encumbrance. 'Why,' he will ask, 'should the story-teller put on himself the fetters of the drama, to be denied the drama's opportunities?' Pure dialogue, we may be sure, is apt to be an inefficient means of telling a story; of presenting a character. There may be cited one great English Classic who has employed the method – the author of *Pericles and Aspasia*, of that little gem of conversation between Henry the Eighth and Anne Boleyn. But then, with Walter Savage Landor, austere and perfect, the character existed already, and there was no story to tell. Mere dialogue, under the conditions of the modern writer, leaves almost necessarily the problem unsolved, the work a fragment. It can scarcely be a means to an end; though it may, if we like, be a permissible little end in itself, a little social chatter, pitched in a high key, in which one has known tartness to be mistaken for wit. Thus does 'Gyp' skim airily over the deep, great sea of life. All are shallows to her vision. And as she skims you feel her lightness. I prefer the adventure of the diver, who knows what the depths *are* : who plunges, and who rescues the pearl.

Then, again, possible, though not often desirable for the short story, is the diary form – extracts from a diary, rather. Applied to work on an extensive scale, your result – since you would necessarily lack concentrated theme – your result would be a chronicle, not a story. Applied to the shorter fiction, it must be used charily, and may then, I should suppose, be used well. But I, who used the form in 'The New Marienbad Elegy' in *English Episodes*, what right have I to say that the form, in the hands of a master, allows a subtle presentation of the character of the diarist – allows, in self-revelation, an irony, along with earnestness, a wayward and involved humour, not excluding sympathy? It is a form not easily received, not suffered gladly. It is for the industrious, who read a good thing twice, and for the enlightened, who read it three times.

I throw out these things only as hints; we may apply them where we will, as we think about stories. But something has yet to be said. Of the two forms already named as generally unfitted for the long novel, and fitted only now and then for the short story, one, it will be noticed, is all dialogue; the other, necessarily, a form in which there is no dialogue at all. And I think we find, upon reflection, the lighter work leans oftenest to the one form; the graver work leans oftenest to the other.

Indeed, from this we might go on to notice that as far as the short story is concerned, most of the finer and more lasting work, though cast in forms which quite *permit* of the dialogue, has, as a matter of fact, but little dialogue in it. Balzac's *La Grenadière* – it is years since I read it; but has it any dialogue at all? Balzac's *L'Interdiction* – an extraordinary presentation af a quaint functionary, fossiliferous and secluded, suddenly brought into contact with people of the world, and with the utmost ability baffling their financial intrigue – this is certainly the most remarkable short story ever written about money – *L'Interdiction* has not much dialogue. In the *Atheist's Mass*, again – the short story of such a nameless pathos – the piece which, more even than *Eugénie Grandet* itself, should be everybody's introduction, and especially every woman's introduction, to the genius of Balzac : *La Messe de l'Athée* has no dialogue. Coming to our actual contemporaries in France, of whom Zola and Daudet must still, it is possible, be accounted the foremost, it is natural that the more finished and minute worker – the worker lately lamented – should be the one who has made the most of the short story. And in this order of his work – thus leaving out his larger and most brilliant canvas, *Froment Jeune et Risler Aîné* – what do we more lastingly remember than the brief and sombre narrative of *Les Deux Auberges*? – a little piece that has no story at all; but a 'situation' depicted, and when depicted, *left*. There is an open country; leagues of Provence; a long stretching road; and, on the roadside, opposite each other, two inns. The older one is silent, melancholy; the other, noisy and prosperous. And the land-lord of the older inn spends all his time in the newer; taking his pleasure there with guests who were once his own, and with a handsome landlady, who makes amends for his departed business. And in his own inn, opposite, a deserted woman sits solitary. That is all – but the art of the master !

Now this particular instance of a pregnant brevity reminds me that in descriptions of landscape the very obligations of the short story are an advantage to its art. Nature, in Fiction, requires to be seen, not in endless detail, as a botanical or geographical study, but, as in Classic Landscape Composition, a noble glimpse of it, over a man's shoulder, under a man's arm. I know, of course, that is not the popular view. Blameless novels have owed their popularity to landscape written by the ream. Coaches have been named after them; steamboats have been named after them. I am not sure that, in their honour, inaccessible heights have not been scaled and virgin forests broken in upon, so that somewhere in picturesque districts the front of a gigantic hotel might have inscribed on it the title of a diffuse novel.

But that is not the great way. The great way, from Virgil's to Browning's, is the way of pregnant brevity. And where dialogue *is* employed in the finer short story, every line of it is bound to be significant. The short story has no room for the reply that is only *near* to being appropriate, and it deserves no pardon for the word that would not have been certainly employed. It is believed, generally, and one can well suppose that it is true, that the average dialogue of the diffuse novel is written quickly. That is in part because so little of it is really dramatic – is really at all the inevitable word. But the limited sentences in which, when the narrator must narrate no more, the persons who have been described in the short story express themselves on their restricted stage, need, if I dare assert it, to be written slowly, or, what is better, re-read a score of times, and pruned, and looked at from without, and surveyed on every side.

But, indeed, of the long story, as well as of the short, may it not be agreed that on the whole the dialogue is apt to be the least successful thing? The ordinary reader, of course, will not be dramatic enough to notice its deficiencies. In humorous dialogue, these are seen least. Humorous dialogue has a legitimate licence. You do not ask from it exactitude; you do not nail it down to its statement. But in the dialogue of the critical moment, when the fire of a little word will kindle how great a matter, how needful then, and how rare, that the word be the true one! We do not want laxity, inappropriateness, on the one hand; nor, on the other, the tortured phraseology of a too resolute cleverness. And those of us who have a preference – derived, it may be, from the simpler generation of Dickens – for an unbending when it is a question of *little* matters, and, when it is a question of great ones, for 'a sincere large accent, nobly plain' – well! there is much of modern finessing we are hardly privileged to understand. Yet if one wants an instance, in a long novel, in which the sentence now said at a white heat is the result, inevitable, burningly true to life, of the sentence that was said just before, one condones the obscurity that has had its imitators, and pays one's tribute of admiration to the insight of *Diana of the Crossways*.

One of the difficulties of the short story, the short story shares with the acted drama, and that is the indispensableness of compression – the need that every sentence shall tell – the difference being, that in the acted drama it must tell for the moment, it must tell till it is found out, and in the short story it must tell for at least a *modest* eternity, and something more, if that be possible – for if a 'Fortnight is eternity' upon the Stock Exchange, a literary eternity is, perhaps, forty years.

Of course the short story, like all other fiction to be read, does not share the other difficulties of the acted drama – above all, the disadvantage which drags the acted drama down – the disadvantage of appealing to, at all events of having to give sops to, at one and the same moment, gallery and stalls: an audience so incongruous that it lies outside the power of Literature to weld it really together.

Frederick Wedmore

In the contemporary theatre, in some of the very cleverest of our acted dramas, the characters are frequently doing, not what the man of intuition, and the man who remembers life, *knows* that they would do, but that which they must do to conciliate the dress circle, to entertain the pit, to defer not too long the gentle chuckle with which the 'average sensual man' receives the assurance that it is a delusion to suppose our world contains any soul, even a woman's soul, that is higher and purer than his. To such temptations the writer of the short story is not even exposed, if he be willing to conceive of his art upon exalted lines, to offer carefully the best of his reflection, in a form of durable and chosen grace, or, by a less conscious, perhaps, but not less fruitful, husbanding of his resources, to give us, sooner or later some first-hand study of human emotion, 'gotten,' as William Watson says, 'of the immediate soul.' But again, contrasting his fortunes with those of his brother, the dramatist, the writer of short stories must, even at the best, know himself denied the dramatist's crowning advantage – which is the thrill of actual human presence.

I have not presumed, except incidentally and by way of illustration, to sit in rapid judgment, and award impertinently blame or praise to the most or the least prominent of those who are writing short stories to-day. Even an occasional grappler with the difficulties of a task is not generally its best critic. He will criticize from the inside, now and then, and so, although you ought to have from him, now and again, at least – what I know, nevertheless, that *I* may not have given – illuminating commentary – you cannot have final judgment. Of the art of Painting, where skill of hand and sense of colour count for much more than intellect, this is especially true. It is true, more or less, of Music – in spite of exceptions as notable as Schumann and Berlioz : almost perfect critics of the very art that they produced. It is true – though in a less degree – of creative Literature. We leave this point, to write down, before stopping, one word about *tendencies*.

Among the better writers, one tendency of the day is to devote a greater care to the art of expression – to an unbroken continuity of excellent style. The short story, much more than the long one, makes this thing possible to men who may not claim to be geniuses, but who, if we are to respect them at all, must claim to be artists. And yet, in face of the indifference of so much of our public here

241

to anything we can call Style – in face, actually, of a strange insensibility to it – the attempt, wherever made, is a courageous one. This insensibility – how does it come about?

It comes about, in honest truth, partly because that instrument of Art, our English tongue, in which the verse of Gray was written, and the prose of Landor and Sterne, is likewise the necessary vehicle in which, every morning of our lives, we ask for something at breakfast. If we all of us had to demand breakfast by making a rude drawing of a coffee-pot, we should understand, before long – the quickness of the French intelligence on that matter being unfortunately denied us – the man in the street would understand that Writing, as much as Painting, is an art to be acquired, and an art in whose technical processes one is bound to take pleasure. And, perhaps, another reason is the immense diffusion nowadays of superficial education; so that the election of a book to the honours of quick popularity is decided by those, precisely, whose minds are least trained for the exercise of that suffrage. What *is* elected is too often the work which presents at a first reading everything that it presents at all. I remember Mr Browning once saying, *àpropos* of such a matter, 'What has a cow to do with nutmegs?' He explained, it was a German proverb. Is it? Or is it German only in the way of 'Sonnets from the Portuguese'? Anyhow, things being as they are, all the more honour to those younger people who, in the face of indifference, remember that their instrument of English language is a quite unequalled instrument of Art.

Against this happy tendency, one has to set – in regard at least to some of them – tendencies less admirable. For, whilst the only kind of work that has a chance of engaging the attention of Sainte-Beuve's 'severe To-morrow' is work that is original, individual, sincere, is it not a pity, because of another's sudden success, to be unremittingly occupied with the exploitation of one particular world – to paint for ever, say, in violent and garish hue, or in deep shades through which no light can struggle, the life of the gutter? to paint it, too, with that distorted 'realism' which witnesses upon the part of its practitioners to *one thing only*, a profound conviction of the ugly! I talk, of course, not of the short stories of the penetrating observer, but of those of the dyspeptic pessimist, whose pessimism, where it is not the *pose* of the contortionist – adopted with an eye to a sensational success of journalism, to a commercial effect – is hysteria, an imitative malady, a malady of the mind. The profession of the literary pessimist is already overcrowded; and if I name two writers who, though in different degrees, have avoided the temptation to join it – if I name one who knows familiarly the cheery as well as the more sombre side of Cockney character and life, Mr Henry Nevinson, the author of the remarkable short stories, *Neighbours of Ours*, and then again a more accepted student of a sordid existence – Mr George Gissing, in *Human Odds and Ends* especially – I name them but as such instances as I am privileged to know, of observant and unbiassed treatment of the subjects with which they have elected to deal.

In France, in the short story, we may easily notice, the uglier forms of 'Realism' are wearing themselves out. 'Le soleil de France,' said Gluck to Marie Antoinette, 'le soleil de France donne du génie.' And the genius that it gives cannot long be hopeless and sombre. It leaves the obscure wood and tangled bypath; it makes for the open road : 'la route claire et droite' – the phrase belongs to M. Leygues – 'la route claire et droite où marche le génie français.' Straight and clear was the road followed – nay, sometimes actually cut – by the unresting talent of Guy de Maupassant, the writer of a hundred short stories, which, for the world of his day at least, went far beyond Charles Nodier's earlier delicacy and Champfleury's wit. But, somehow, upon De Maupassant's nature and temperament the curse of pessimism lay. To deviate into cheeriness he must deal with the virtues of the *déclassées* – undoubtedly an interesting theme – he must deal with them as in the famous *Maison Tellier*, an ebullition of scarcely cynical comedy, fuller much of real humanity than De Goncourt's sordid document, *La Fille Elisa*. But that was an exception. De Maupassant was pessimist generally, because, master of an amazing talent, he refreshed himself never in any rarefied air. The vista of the Spirit was denied him. His reputation he may keep; but his school – the school in which a few even of our own imitative writers prattle the accents of a hopeless materialism – his school, I fancy, will be crowded no more. For, with an observation keen and judicial, M. René Bazin treats to-day themes, we need not say more 'legitimate' – since much may be legitimate – but at least more acceptable. And then again, with a style of which De Maupassant, direct as was his own, must have envied even the clarity and the subtler charm, a master draughtsman of ecclesiastic and bookworm, of the neglected genius of the provincial town (some poor devil of a small professor), and of the soldier, and the shopkeeper, and the Sous-Préfet's wife – I hope I am describing M. Anatole France – looks out on the contemporary world with a vision humane and genial, sane and wide. Pessimism, it seems to me, can only be excusable in those who are still bowed down by the immense responsibility of youth. It was a great poet, who, writing of one of his peers – a man of mature life – declared of him, *not* 'he mopes picturesquely', but 'he knows the world, firm, quiet, and gay'. To such a writer – only to such a writer – is possible a happy comedy; and possible, besides, a true and an august vision of profounder things! And *that* is the spirit to which the Short Story, at its best, will certainly return.

(FROM 'ON BOOKS AND ARTS', 1899)

On the 6th of March